$10

And
They
All Sang

ALSO BY STUDS TERKEL

And They All Sang

THE GREAT MUSICIANS OF THE 20TH CENTURY

TALK ABOUT THEIR MUSIC

Studs Terkel

Granta Books
London

Granta Publications, 2/3 Hanover Yard, Noel Road, London N1 8BE

First published in Great Britain by Granta Books 2006
Published by arrangement with The New Press, New York

The section on Mahalia Jackson appeared, in slightly different form, in the
paperback edition of *Talking to Myself: A Memoir of My Times*,
published by The New Press in 1995.

The section on Big Bill Broonzy appeared, in slightly different form,
in *Jazz: A Quarterly of American Music*, No.1, October 1958.

The section on Woody Guthrie appeared, in slightly different form,
as the foreword to Ed Cray's *Ramblin' Man: The Life and Times of Woody Guthrie*,
published by W. W. Norton in 2004.

A CIP catalogue record for this book is available
from the British Library.

1 3 5 7 9 10 8 6 4 2

ISBN-13: 978-1-86207-989-7
ISBN-10: 1-86207-898-X

Printed and bound in Great Britain by
William Clowes Limited, Beccles, Suffolk

For Garry and Natalie Wills

Many say that life entered the human body by the help of music
but the truth is that life itself is music.

—Hafiz, Fourteenth-century Persian poet

In the olden days, everybody sang. You were
expected to sing as well as talk. It was the mark of a
cultured man to sing, to know music.

—Leonard Bernstein

∾ Contents ∾

CONTENTS

PART II

CONTENTS

PART III

PART IV

∾ **Acknowledgments** ∾

I wish to recognize those who in one manner or another helped in the shaping of this book. First of all, thanks to the Chicago Historical Society, where I hang my hat, for their indulgence, especially Lonnie Bunch, its president, Russell Lewis, and Usama Alshaibi.

There are those for whom I worked for so many years at WFMT and who still contribute so much to the catalogue that offered the basis for the portraits in the book: Lois Baum, Steve Jones, Tony Judge, Andy Karzas, Andrea Lamoreaux, Matt McDonnell, Steve Robinson, Dennis Moore, Norm Pellegrini, Ray Nordstrand, and especially Jim Unrath.

I also want to thank my freelance scouts who uncovered areas that would not have occurred to me: Danny Newman (known by the old-time phrase "press agent"), Magda Krance, and music critics Leonard Feather, Gary Giddens, Nat Hentoff, Howard Reich, John von Rhein, Joe Segal, and the late Claudia Cassidy.

One last note of thanks to The New Press—to André Schiffrin, of course, who has been my publisher for the last forty years, as well as to his assistant, Joel Ariaratnam, copy editor Sue Warga, and the rest of the New Press staff.

ACKNOWLEDGMENTS

Thanks also to Sydney Lewis, who is more than a transcriber—she's an interpreter and translator as well, as much of my writing is more or less hieroglyphic in nature—and to Jonathan Cott; I had the inspired idea of including him as editor of this book because of his remarkable track record while roving correspondent for *Rolling Stone*. That was one of my better moves.

As usual, my son Dan came through as a go-between in keeping things moving.

∾ Introduction ∾

Nineteen forty-five, early autumn. A month before, World War II had ended with a flash and a bang. Four Sundays later, I began as host of a one-hour weekly radio program of recorded music called *The Wax Museum.* The phrase "disc jockey" had not yet entered our working vocabulary. In effect, though, that is what I was.

The program was eclectic in nature. A Caruso aria, *Ombra mai fu* from Handel's *Xerxes,* might have been followed by Louis Armstrong and his Hot Seven's "West End Blues." In turn, there came forth a Woody Guthrie Dust Bowl ballad. Whatever piece of music caught my fancy, I offered it to the listener, no matter what the genre.

In the ensuing months, it captured an audience, limited but fervent. What surprised me was the nature of the listeners. I had expected a teacher or two, a social worker, somebody living alone and sitting in the second balcony of a play on a Saturday matinee, or anyone of the "educated class"—the usual suspects. But—out of nowhere, it seemed—there were more than a few fan letters from a truck driver, a shipping clerk, a waitress, a housewife. It is a phenomenon that Ronald Blythe captured so movingly in *Akenfield,* his portrait of an English village. In the words of David Collyer, a twenty-nine-year-old workingman:

A town boy can drift into an art gallery—if only to get warm—and then see a picture, and then feel and think about art. Or he might go to a concert, just to see what it was like, or hang around in a big public library. From the minute he does these things, he begins to be a different person, even though he doesn't realize it. He has started to be fulfilled. For an ordinary village boy everything to do with these things is somehow unnatural. I was over 20 before I realized that classical music was just "music," and therefore all one had to do was listen to it. I listened and began to enjoy it if I stopped worrying. Everything I do begins with doubt and insecurity. It is as though I am using a language which I haven't a right to use.

Ed Sadlowski, an American steelworker, reflects: "Give a guy the opportunity to have time to read a book and he'll read it. Give him an opportunity to hear music and he'll listen. Human nature is more than punching a time clock. Did you ever watch a guy grow when he is exposed to a new experience? He wants more. He starts reading a book, hearing good music, he starts doing this, doing that. Before you know it—boom!—it's like a flower, just opening up one night." John Donahue, son of a Chicago fireman, remembers the night before his old man died: "I asked him, 'Are there any regrets you have?' He said, 'I wish I could have told the firemen in the firehouse that I loved opera.'" As though it were something not to talk about.

Of all the work in which I have ever been engaged, it was that one-hour weekly radio program that was the most revelatory to me. (The name of the program was something of a pun; the recordings, 78 RPM, were wax-based and highly breakable. God knows how many I, with my slovenly ways, cracked. The long-playing ones were beginning to appear. It was an ancient time, before the era of cassettes and CDs.) Some eight years later, after a roller-coaster experience with jobs—what with "Tail Gunner Joe" McCarthy, and Edgar Hoover being sainted as well as feared, and me occasionally uttering unfashionable thoughts—I astonishingly latched on to a classical music FM radio station, WFMT. The station's owner made me an offer I could under no circumstances refuse. It was a one-hour daily program, during which I could do any damn thing I pleased. I began, naturally, as the eclectic disc jockey I had been. From then on the program, in the manner of Topsy, "growed" into something else. I read short stories I liked, whether they were by Flannery O'Connor, Ring Lardner, Chekhov, you name it. Guests somehow came about. Authors, musicians of course—classical, opera, jazz, and folk of all cultures—and certain neighborhood people that I found of interest. It was the latter assemblage, the "ordinary people," that attracted the attention of a New York publisher, André Schiffrin. From that moment on, the matter of putting forth interviews described as "oral history" occupied most of my working days. Nonetheless, during my forty-five years on WFMT, although there was considerable conversation, a piece of music was invariably included, if merely to italicize what the guests had to say. It could be a pop trifle, a show tune, a folk song, or any art song. It could be a passage from a symphony or concerto. It wasn't as though I was seeking music in the words of my visitors; it was simply my talisman—a fetish, some would say.

As an asthmatic child of eight, hearing came to me with much more ease than breathing. Bound to the hearth, I heard music I might otherwise have missed. The boy next door was sourly fiddling away; if it wasn't "Indian Lament," it was "Flight of the Bumble Bee." Mischa Elman and Jascha Heifetz were the names his parents wistfully called upon. But the kid's ambition was to become a certified public accountant. From the apartment below, a girl was sulkily pounding away at the battered keys of the family Wurlitzer: "Für Elise." Beethoven wept. She hadn't the slightest intention of becoming Myra Hess; she dreamed of being a gym teacher. My mother, several pins in her mouth as she fitted gowns for the neighborhood women, mumbled her complaint of the constant disturbance: noise. Her critique was not favorable. My father, however, wasn't much bothered. He arrived from his tailoring at the factory long after the prospective accountant and gym teacher had ended their aesthetic flights. On a few occasions, he brought home a Victor record and ever so gingerly placed it on the phonograph. It was twelve inches in circumference and easily breakable. One side was blank. "How much did it cost?" My mother was curious. He held up two fingers. "Dollars?" He nodded. She was furious. My father wasn't much for words. He simply said, "Caruso."

John Ciardi, in calling on a childhood memory, explained:

> When I was a kid my uncle used to have a tremendous collection of the
> scratchy old orthophonic Caruso recordings—and especially on rainy days,

but all the time, I had a passion for Caruso. I heard him a couple of times "live," but I remember him best on scratchy recordings because my memory of that is longest. . . . But when you heard this voice you not only heard the song being sung, you suffered an expansion of your imagination—you discovered how well it was possible to sing these songs. Your very imagination was enlarged. You had a large sense of expectation. You couldn't have anticipated that these songs could have been sung so well. On two levels: the first place, you'd think, just in the animal quality of the singing. Caruso would hit a high note and you'd say this is as much as the human voice can do. You couldn't ask more of the human voice. And then he'd be beyond that. He'd exceed the expectation. But there's another thing. It took centuries to form the kind of consciousness that would sing these songs in this way. The kind of musical intelligence that touched the songs perfectly at every moment. We're enlarged by it. We have to hear those best voices. You have to open your imagination to Job asking his question, and when you've really heard that question ringing you know the difference between a great question and a lesser one. Then you know the size of a human decision.

So it was then that I first heard that voice: *Celeste Aïda*. On another occasion, it was Canio's *La commedia è finita* from *Pagliacci*. As I listened to that voice, my breathing came more easily. Caruso had succeeded where the doctors had failed. Even my mother was silenced. Enrico Caruso had become my first personal hero. And liberator.

It was the morning of January 27, 1972, at WFMT, Mozart's birthday—his 216th. I had planned an all-Mozart program. We were going to celebrate Wolfgang Amadeus Mozart by italicizing his singular understanding of women through the recordings of various singers in his serious operas. Schwarzkopf, of course, and Irmgard Seefried. And then a young announcer gently opened the door, handed me a sheet of newswire fresh off the machine, and said, "Mahalia Jackson died this morning." And that's how the day began. Now, I was thinking, *My audience knows Mahalia Jackson as well as they know the singers I had in mind. Do I play one of her songs, pay tribute to her now, or continue with Mozart?* I decided to stick with Amadeus and played Mahalia the next day. That was the sort of program it was.

∾

There was nothing formal about my musical influence. It was higgledy-piggeldy, music heard by a sickly child. Even Balaban & Katz played a role as my operatic mentors. The Chicago Theatre was the flagship house of the Balaban & Katz chain, a 3,600-seat house, with Jesse Crawford and his wife playing the twin organ. It was a tremendous place. They had wanted to make Sunday morning a key event, so in addition to the regular program—a movie plus a vaudeville skit or two—they'd have an opera star come in. I remember Martinelli and José Mojica (the tenor who became a priest) singing the opera arias. I remember the house only half full. I think Tito Schipa sang there as well. I remember this with some wistfulness—I was about fourteen. My first hearing of Dvořák's *New World Symphony* was on a Saturday night at Orchestra Hall. It was pop night, an adjunct to the "serious" works of Thursday nights. It may have been a long walk from the men's hotel where I lived to Orchestra Hall; it seemed but a moment home, as I was humming all the way the symphony's second movement, the largo, which I later discovered to be the old spiritual "Deep River." (It was the Bohemian's discovery as well as a tribute to America's black people.) I, the boy who had never taken part in anything musical at school, no choral work or Christmas show, had suddenly astonished himself by singing out loud. I would never qualify for the Vienna Boys' Choir, but it was good enough for me. Leonard Bernstein once observed that in the olden days everybody sang. You were expected to sing, as you were to talk. It was the mark of a cultured man to sing, to know music. (Even for old roosters. Casey Jones, an old, old black man, was a known Chicago character. He had a rooster, whom he referred to as Baby. Every Sunday at Maxwell Street, the open market, he had Baby sing a song. That tired old rooster, head drooping, and Casey Jones saying, "Sing the blues, oh yeah, sing the blues. Hey, Baby, sing that," and Casey, of course, was humming the song under his breath. He didn't have the rooster talk—he always said, "*Sing* the song, Baby.")

Another thing, before I forget: When Garrick Ohlsson, the pianist, won the Warsaw Chopin Competition, a middle-aged chambermaid in the hotel where he was staying offered her critique of the nationally broadcast program. She told Ohlsson what moved her and what didn't, how she felt about what he'd played. Ohlsson described it as one of the memorable moments of his life.

Opera, of course, had caught my imagination perhaps more than any other form for a time. I heard recordings from one source or another, radio a prime example. I think of memorable scenes. During the early days of the Lyric Opera Company of Chicago, it was Maria Callas whom people remember best for her Lucia, her *Casta diva* from *Norma,* and her Violetta. Which is the Callas performance remembered best? Mine is one that happened backstage. It was Callas and her adversary, who in this case was not her brother in *Lucia* but a gentle, diffident process server named Stanley Pringle, with his fedora top down on his head looking like an elderly Li'l Abner. Callas had just finished performing Cio-Cio-San in *Madama Butterfly*. Here the one so powerful as Norma was suddenly this gentle, sweet Japanese aristocrat. After the show, Callas was seated in her kimono and guests were greeting her. Among them was the uninvited Stanley Pringle, who simply proffered her a paper, a subpoena. She was being sued for breach of contract by some small-time producer. And here's when the cameras started flashing. Callas set forth in her kimono, furious, teeth bared. God knows what words she was saying to poor Stanley Pringle. That scene made the front page of all the papers. That to me is the most memorable of all the Callas scenes. For one thing, it was so impromptu, so jazz, so life.

Another is a story told by Cornell MacNeil, the American baritone, in Parma, the home of Toscanini. In Parma, the people by nature are so involved with music that when a new opera appears they attend *en masse*. Even the henpecked husband, who happens to be a butcher, is there, king of the hill up in the balcony, and regards the singer with thumbs up or thumbs down. If it's thumbs down, have pity, have mercy on the singer. After all, in Parma, opera is regarded as though it were a sport like football or baseball. In this case, the American baritone was there doing *Rigoletto*. MacNeil was furious at what was happening to a young tenor who was being humiliated, with things thrown at him, hoots and hollering. He called out to the audience, *"Cretini!"* and rushed into his dressing room and barred the door. Then came a hammering, a banging, a knocking at the door, and a swarm of penguins appeared, all in tuxedos, the mayor at the head: "How dare you insult us in this way?" MacNeil said, "I wasn't. What were you doing to this young tenor?" "That is nothing! That happens all the time. That's our way of showing that we want him to be *better,* that's all." That perhaps may have been Cornell MacNeil's most memorable scene.

Chicago firefighter John Donahue might have been a long way from Parma, yet he would have understood, because opera was what most delighted him. As for jazz, I don't know Donahue's attitude toward it, but I suspect he would have liked Louis Armstrong—he would have liked jazz if it was played well. As far as my knowledge of jazz, it happened accidentally, because of my love for my middle brother, who was five years older than I, a shipping clerk who loved to dance. Friday nights at Harmon's Dreamland Ballroom he would go dancing in the hope of meeting secretaries and file clerks and being a precocious Don Giovanni, if lucky, meeting a nurse. It was on those nights I accompanied him because I admired him so much. He didn't like the idea of my being an appendage, a burden to him, so in general he sent me home with the promise of a chocolate malted and gingersnaps. But there he was, dancing, and I was sitting outside, waiting on a summer night when the windows were open. The band was a black band, Lottie Hightower and Her Eudora Night Hawks, and Charlie Cook and his band. The musicians were always black and the patrons, the dancers, were all white, working-class. I would hear that music, the blues, especially when it came toward the latter part of the evening, when the couples danced on a dime, which meant, of course, they were belly to belly. It was that slow blues that got me.

But more important is what I learned at the University of Chicago as a law student. It wasn't contracts, corporations, or real property; I flunked them all. What I did learn was accidental but memorable. I was a streetcar student. That is, I transferred a couple of times from the hotel where I lived on the near North Side to the South Side and the university. One of the stops was the black belt, Bronzeville, and it was there, as soon as I got off, that I heard that music: records, some scratched, some otherwise, coming from any number of stores. And not just music stores—they could be clothing stores, gallimaufry stores selling everything. These were nickel-and-dime records, but that's when I first heard, while waiting to go to the university: Big Bill Broonzy; Tampa Red; Memphis Minnie; Roosevelt Sykes; and Peatie Wheatstraw, the Devil's Son-in-Law. It was then that I caught on to the blues, and the blues, as Big Bill would say, "Ain't nuthin' but a good man feeling bad."

And you'd realize the blues was not just a black man's lament, though it was the black man who understood it, the black man and the black woman who invented it. But the blues to me was all the things I wanted to be and never got around to being. That's the blues. The blues is the landlord knocking at the gate. The blues is anything you want to feel. A man chased a rabbit, chased him about a mile, and the rabbit lay down and cried like a baby. Even the rabbit had the blues.

On that corner, while waiting for the streetcar, I'm sure memories of early Caruso recordings I'd heard floated through my head, and memories of Armstrong and those who were his disciples. This love of all strains of music is what I suppose impelled me to do the program *The Wax Museum*. In a way, I was thinking of a similar compote of music in doing this book. The contents are eccentric in nature. There was no rule by which I chose, and many names will be unknown to younger readers. Those included are not necessarily my favorite artists; they are simply the ones who at the moment of writing attracted me the most. I'm reminded at this moment of the Italian plumber who one day, while at work on a defunct pipe, was listening to a record playing in the background. It wasn't an Italian folk song, it wasn't Caruso; it was Duke Ellington. Music is as eclectic as life itself. And the plumber, paraphrasing the fourteenth-century Persian poet Hafiz, said: "Music is my life. Without music, where would we be?"

And
They
All Sang

∾ Prelude ∾

An American Original

JOHN JACOB NILES

1957

I wonder as I wander out under the sky
How Jesus our Savior did come for to die
For poor ornery people like you and like I . . .

As I first listened to his haunting falsetto on an old Victor 78, I was hear-
ing, it seemed, an Elizabethan minstrel offering a medieval carol. It was,
in fact, something John Jacob Niles wrote in the 1930s. He is a writer,
singer, and collector of folk songs. His style of speech is that of an old-
time schoolmaster lecturing a group of enraptured though at times unruly
students. In moments of fervor, his mode may be that of W.C. Fields, a
circuit-riding evangelist, or an old-time medicine man. His ebullience
overwhelms. I initially encountered him at the first annual Newport Folk
Festival of 1959. As master of ceremonies, I introduced him to the assem-
bled young, who at the moment were discovering Bob Dylan. As he held

1

the dulcimer in his arms, close to his breast, he murmured into the microphone, "She is my love, my dear companion." There were audible snickers in the audience. Unperturbed, he sang out the tragic ballad. When someone in the crowd flashed his Kodak camera, Niles stopped midsong to lecture him: "Young sir, would you impinge upon the privacy of a man and a maid making love?" Without missing a beat, he resumed the song. It was, as I recall, a Child ballad, "The Gypsy Laddie." Francis Child was the nineteenth-century Harvard philologist who traveled through the British Isles gathering olden ballads. He accumulated about five hundred. A generation or so later, Cecil Sharp, a British musicologist, traveled through Appalachia gathering mountain variations on the Child ballads. During our conversation at the radio station, Niles' dulcimer lay on the table. He ever so tenderly, gently, touched the strings.

You must court it, sir, as you do a girl. I take her in my arms. [He does so.] It's made out of half a cello, curved in the right places. She falls right into your arms. . . . It is shaped like a teardrop. The sides are made of walnut, the back is walnut, and the top is Carpathian spruce. I got this spruce out of an old piano, destroyed in the Louisville flood of '36. I mean to say, sir, this present dulcimer, which I made, doesn't exist anywhere in the world except right on this table. My great-grandfather was a piano manufacturer and it got into the family. My mother used to say, "Look, little boy, you want some special kind of an instrument, go on and make it." My father gave me lumber, all the tools in the world. He gave me the shop. I'm afraid I was indulged, sir. I believe it has made a strange character out of me.

I got ahold of the dulcimer as a little boy. It had what they called a noting stick—you could run up and down that first string and get a tune. I never needed to do that. You see, sir, the equipment I had to begin with was a voice and musicology taught me by my mother at a very early age. So I didn't need to play the tune. I could *sing* the blooming tunes. Therefore, I supported the tunes with harmonic structure. But that wasn't enough. I very soon realized that I needed that extra tonic. I said, "Father, I want to put four strings on the dulcimer." He said, "Well, don't argue with me, go and put them on." Suddenly, I found myself in business with a four-string dulcimer.

My father took me to hear the Chicago Symphony Orchestra under the direction of Theodore Thomas [founding conductor of the CSO], a great man. He was a friend of my grandfather's. They were Germans together. I'm sure

Thomas was a German because I remember him drinking beer with my grandfather. They came to Louisville and I sang in their chorus. I was a tiny little boy, about seven. I sat near the percussionist and I saw those magnificent drums. At home, I said, "Father, I want to put the drums on the dulcimer." He said, "Boy, I've said you can do anything you like, but I don't see how you can possibly put a *drum on a* dulcimer." I said, "I think I can get it with strings." He says, "If you can do that, you're a genius." Six months later, I had this, sir. [Strums] Bum-bum-bam-bum! I had my drums. I had the percussion effect.

My father, who sang in public, always began the program with "My Little Mohee." I have done exactly the same thing.

The one about the Indian maiden in love with the white guy . . . ?

You have heard the cleaned-up, shall I say expurgated, version of a song sung by British sailors. If you go to the trouble, sir, next time you're in Cambridge, Massachusetts, they have a little school up there called Harvard College and they have a magnificent rare book library. They have a broadside collection. If you convince them you're an adult and broad-minded, that you're not going to carry it out in your inside pocket, you can see the original text of "Mohee." And I tell you, sir, it is something *to behold*. Not for juveniles. It's the same tune as "On Top of Old Smoky." The tune is an American invention. Our tunes are all our own. American, not English. The "Mohee" is the variation of a Scottish story. It's a universal theme. Denmark, Norway, Finland, all the way into the Baltic states, into Hungary, Turkey, and finally into India. But the tunes are ours! Don't be deceived.

Lo, the poor Indian maid. Did her sweetheart leave her forever?

I think he returned to her. It's one of those extraordinary happy endings. [Solemnly] We don't have many of them, you know. The American girl double-crossed this poor lad and he went back to this Indian. I don't know how it worked out, the crossing of bloods. I wonder what happened. He may have produced Nehru.

Since we're dealing with love, what about "Lass from the Low Country"?

3

I did not find it in the Child collection. It came from a strange little man in North Carolina, who'd never been out of the county. This poor girl who loves this man of high degree. How many times, sir, has it happened in the history of the world? A case of one human being yearning for another of higher status. "She smiled as she spoke. And he walked right on by." Possibly going to the hunt, or going off to the Crusades, and he never even raised his eyes. "No one knows she loved him but herself and God." Oh, my goodness, what heartbreak. The swine.

Isn't there the case of the girl who rebuffs the guy . . . ?

"Go Away from my Window." Of course. I wrote it, yes sir, words and music. There was this colored man named Old Draw Jacket. He got that name because he came to my mother and said, "Miss Lou, I want to get me fifty cents to buy me an old draw jacket. I ain't got no more clothes." He was making maybe a dollar and ten cents a day. In those days, a good deal of money. He got food and privileges. Also protection from my father, who was sheriff. *That* was important. Father could get him out of jail just like that [snaps fingers]. He got him out of jail every Saturday night. Old Draw was a wonderful boy, powerful, strong ditchdigger. I often worked beside him. He was a philosopher of a kind. He would sing, "Go 'way from my winda, go 'way from my doah," over and over and over. Just those lines. This went on fourteen hours a day. We worked long hours in those days. This was 1900 and 8.

I saw this girl and went head over heels in love. A female, blond, blue eyes, intriguing figure. Oh, my goodness. I was sixteen, she was sixteen. I didn't get anywhere with this girl because I was just a Boone Creek boy and she had important suitors. I thought I could beat the field by writing a song. So I took Old Draw's few words and two notes and I expanded it into a song. [Sings] "Go away from my window / Go away from my door / Go away from my window / And bother me no more . . ." [Into W.C. Fields mode] And, my dear Mr. Studs—if the ceiling falls in and hits me, it's the *truth*—may I tell you, she never bothered my bedside, nor, I can make a general confession [an evil growl], I never bothered her bedside. I sent her the song and she wrote back, "You're not a very good composer, are you? You better stick to the plow." [With evangelical fervor] She went on and married the other fellow. It was the greatest blessing that ever happened. I mean, God was my co-pilot. If I had married that female, I would have been an ordinary poor little guy *grinding* out my soul, supporting an *unimportant family* of little people *running* around all those hills. As it is, she married a rich man and the two of them *fell* off a mountainside and they *buried* them. The song was put away and no one paid any attention to it. Everyone thought it was rather silly. I went off to Germany in 1900 and 31 and sang in Berlin, Cologne, Hamburg. It was before Mr. Hitler devastated the country. Mary Wigman, the modern dancer, befriended me. I gave my performance in her studio. The nice, sweet conservative Germans got *out* of their seats and said, "This is it." In one magic moment, I hit the jackpot. The next morning, the papers came out and said, "Herr Niles, the American composer, has written something of importance." I saw the [name] "Johannes Brahms" in the same column. I thought this was fabulous. I came back to America and the publisher said, "You naive thing, no one will listen." The American soprano Eleanor Steber got ahold of it and she said, "Johnny, this is a real song." She sang it and the houses fell on their faces. The publishers ran in, hat in hand, published the thing, and now it is public property.

How I came to write "Black Is the Color of My True Love's Hair"? I went with my father in the mountains on a political junket. Papa was making speeches trying to get somebody elected. We went to a little place called Ary, Kentucky. We visited the Johnson family. They were people who made alcoholic beverages without the benefit of the government's stamps. That is to say, they were bootleggers. With every change of the moon, one of them would be taken in by some swine of an Internal Revenue Department fellow. Terrible people. They'd carry off these good Johnsons and stick 'em in Atlantic—they didn't call it Atlanta. [Delicately] They sent 'em to Atlantic. Then Papa would start out this process, this slow grinding business of writing letters to Chicago and ultimately getting them shorter terms. And if he had saved them one day, yeah verily one hour, he was their man, he was their prophet, and they literally brushed the ground before him as he walked. They'd say, "It's awful pretty to see you people." And food was put on the table. As indigestible a bunch of food as you ever saw. I suffered. After dinner, we danced and we sang and I did music for them and they did music for me.

I took down a piece of their music and when we got home, I timidly said, "Papa, I've got something I want to play you." I sang, "Black is the color. . . ." My father had hysteria. "This is awful. I've often referred to you as a wunderkind. Here you're coming to me with a [roars] *dull* tune. Don't sing it to me again. *Go,* write me a better one." He never heard that tune again.

World War I came along, officers' training camp came. I went to the wars. I went through all the business of the hospitals. I walked on a cane and a crutch. I was working on this song all the time. I tried it out on the officers. They were stupid. They didn't know what it was all about. Frenchmen understood it. Belgians understood. German prisoners of war understood it still better. I came back to Kentucky and said, "Father, I've got this song straight for you." I sang it and he said, "You've got the jackpot, boy. And don't let anybody argue you out of that conclusion." It ends in a strange modal way, not the way tunes usually end.

No one paid any attention to it. It just wasn't worth the paper it was written on. No publisher would take it. My teachers at the Conservatory of Music thought I was a lunatic, worrying about it. Why didn't I worry about *L'enfant prodigue* of Mr. Claude Debussy, why didn't I study Sibelius? I was studying these things, but I was also studying things like "Black Is the Color." Finally, after years passed, I put it on record. The whole world found out about it. Immediately, my imitators began to discover it out in Brooklyn, at Canarsie, at the intersection of Atlantic Avenue and the subway stations. They found it at Fifth Avenue and Forty-second Street, of course, in the library. Of course they found it at the White Top Mountain. They found it at all the little summer camps. [Sings softly] "Black is the color of my true love's hair / Her lips are something rosy fair / The perfect face and the daintiest hands / I love the grass whereon she stands . . ."

Father used to say that the advantage of the folk tune is it ends at the end. It never goes on to any artificial conclusions. It stops short. Just exactly like the Gregorian chant, like the music in the Jewish church. You go there, you sing the Shema Yisrael, Adonai Eloheinu, Adonai Ehad—and you're at the end. It doesn't sound like the average ballad, nothing theatrical. You end when you come to the end of the prayer. Papa said, "Don't let us have any foolishness. End at the end, boy." You'll be wearied by my continually quoting him, but he was a great man who colored all my thinking. My mother, too, profoundly. And my grandfather and great-grandfather, who was an officer in the kaiser's army and ultimately an officer in the Confederacy. My father's mother was Nancy Randolph, yes, John Randolph's people. And her mother was Betty Tolliver. The Tollivers were the greatest singing and fighting family in the business. There were four brothers. Johnny Tolliver, the great one, came out of the Battle of Chickamaugwa—that's what we called it, Chickamaugwa—*unscathed*. He was a great, great, boisterous, noisy, whiskey-drinking, lusty *swine* of a guy who *sang magnificently* and banged the tables and kicked things out of his way in the most wonderful fashion.

When I was a little boy, I was singing "The Seven Joys of Mary" and it was awful. It fell like pieces of wood on the floor. It wasn't getting anywhere. My father said, "You're not singing a carol, you're saying words. What's the carol about, boy?" I said, "It's about our Lord and Master, Jesus Christ." He said, "Okay, but there's not much about the birth of Christ, is there? I'll give you references in Matthew, Mark, Luke, and John where you can study what happened." And then we went back to the Old Testament, where the prophecies were made, and I studied that. And then I caught the spirit of the thing. The reason people fail with songs is they're saying words and singing notes. They're not singing ideas. [Half rises from his chair] *Ideas,* sir! That's what you've got to have. Something simple, clear, that a child could understand.

My song "The Seven Joys of Mary" started out in life as "The Five Joys" in the fifteenth century. The fact was that Mary realized her son was the Son of God, that he could bring off miracles and raise people from the dead, that he could give people sight, and that he could chase away devils. The other two were added as years passed. Once in my lifetime, I encountered a young Holiness minister who sang "Forty-Seven Joys"! Sir, I can tell you and quote my great bishop, there were *too many.* Once upon a time, a young priest came to our bishop and said, "What in heaven's name will I preach about Sunday?" The bishop said, "About twenty minutes. *Not longer.*" [Explodes] Even the joys of the Blessed Mother *cannot be carried to forty-seven verses!*

"I Wonder as I Wander," the song most associated with me, came to me in Murphy, North Carolina, from the singing of a little girl named Annie Morgan. She was unwashed. Her clothes were absolutely falling off her. She looked like she had been made up by a Hollywood expert to look like a Southern mountain girl. She was standing on the fantail of a broken-down 1914 Ford automobile. They had been carrying on a religious meeting, evangelical hoopla. Her father was named Preacher Martin and he was a swine. The police gave him so many hours to get out of town and never darken the soil of North Carolina again. Her mother had been singing [sings high, even above his own falsetto], "Let the church roll on, oh my Lord." And never find Christ in a gambling house or shooting pool or playing craps. They were trying to collect twenty-five cents to buy a gallon of gasoline, they were that broke. Nobody contributed anything. Finally, this little girl got up and sang [sings thinly, drifts off into humming], "I wonder as I wander . . ." I said, "All right, honey, come on, sing the rest of it. It's worth a quarter to me." I threw a quarter up on that fantail and her father raked it in, just like those croupiers in gambling houses. [Sings] All one note that time. I threw up another quarter. Eight times. Everything she said, I wrote down. I can take down music as fast as anyone can sing. I've got that talent. Well, I never did get more than one and a half measures and those few garbled words and it cost me three dollars. They got in the car, went away, and I never saw them again. About two months later, one of those Georgia state policemen, dressed like someone out of a comic opera, came up to me at the Regal Hotel in Murphy—regal in name only. He said, "We have a note concerning your consorting with the Morgan family. Did you ever talk to them? Supply them with funds? Do you know their automobile number?" I said, "I'm not answering any of your questions. You've got nothing on me." He told me the whole story. Their license plate was stolen from a pickup truck that had been burned in a little patch outside of Atlanta. So, you see, it got pretty complicated. And out of these circumstances came one of the greatest carols in the business. I took Annie's three lines and carried them up to New York. My publisher, a very dear man, an Orthodox Jew, Carl Engel, who was president of G. Schirmer's, said to me, "Johnny, I'm not supposed to be a student of Christ. You're the one to do that. These three lines won't do. We can't publish three lines." So I went away and came back about once every two, three weeks. Carl still said, "Johnny, it won't do." About a year later, I came back with two verses. Carl read them. He was a very emotional man. He had tears in his eyes. He said, "Johnny, I'm almost persuaded." He was quoting the New Testament. [He leans over the table, enunciates softly.] "I'm almost persuaded." He says, "We're gonna publish it." So we published it in a little version and sold it for a nickel. The rest is, as they say, history.

It's marginal people, outsiders, from whom you've learned some of these songs: the small daughter of an itinerant preacher, the Negro workman, bootleggers—

Absolutely. I never dealt with the respectable people. I consorted with roughnecks and drunks. Did I ever tell about the blind drunken miner who taught me "Gypsy Laddie"? I know it's a Child ballad, but I didn't learn it from any professor. It was in Louisa, Kentucky. He was playing the fiddle as best he could. He'd lost his eyesight in a mine accident, and in those days nobody paid any attention to a miner who got hurt. This fellow spent his time on the streets and drinking up his earnings as fast as he got 'em. The police said, "You're consorting with this fellow and you're gonna cause trouble." I was feeding him, giving him a great big lunch or dinner to encourage him to *sing*. The cop said, "They ain't got nothin' in their head to sing." Well, those police were mistaken. How he learned this old ballad I never found out. The police didn't give me the [spells it out] t-i-m-e to investigate. Three weeks later, I came through Louisa again. The poor guy had been buried. Fell drunk in the gutter and an automobile run over his head. Oh, a mural could be constructed by the right painter of all my characters. Can't you see 'em?

And you, sir, as one of them.

Absolutely. Here I am, seventy-two. I was born in 1892 by the clock. Time eats me up, you know. Look at my hair, the broken-down Boone Creek boy. The years have fallen down and *mashed* me *flat*!

Head bloody but unbowed . . .

Oh, that's it, boy! Unbowed. And still on the job.

∾ Part One ∾

✌ Vox Humana ✌

TITO GOBBI: GOOD AND EVIL
1959, 1971, 1973

*For fourteen years, he was a guest baritone at the Lyric Opera of Chicago.
His two favorite roles were Scarpia in Puccini's* Tosca *(which, on several
occasions, he directed) and the title role in Verdi's* Simon Boccanegra.
*He passionately defined the one as evil, the police chief "before whom
Rome trembled," and the other, the doge of fourteenth-century Genoa, as
the beloved man of peace. He first performed Germont in* La Traviata *in
1937 at the Royal Opera House in Rome.*

I studied in Rome with Giulio Crimi, the great tenor who sang many times
in Chicago. A wonderful teacher. I was twenty-four years old when I played
Alfredo's father in *La Traviata*. Only twenty years younger than my son the
tenor. [Laughs] I had very funny makeup. I tried to draw age on my face but
the skin was too young. What a crazy debut! Successful, would you believe it?
Do you know how it happened? I wasn't supposed to sing this performance,

13

but the baritone got sick. I was also suffering from a high fever, sneezing all the time. The only thing that could stop me sneezing was a little drop of cognac. They phoned and said, "Tito Gobbi, are you ready to sing Germont in *Traviata*?" "Oh, yes." "Did you ever sing it before?" "Oh, *yes!*" Never. [Laughs] I come in sneezing. "Are you ready to sing tonight?" "Tonight? Oh, sure." I was waiting two years for somebody to let me sing, so I didn't say no. We must risk. I hope I can start in a good way and my career can begin. So I'm in my dressing room, sneezing and drinking drop by drop of cognac, until I finish the bottle. Very good. By the end of the act, when Violetta takes my hand and comes out of the duetto and the aria to take the bow, the audience was making a lot of noise. "Bravo! Bravo! Bravo!" They knew I was a young boy taking the place of the baritone. I couldn't stand. I was absolutely drunk. [Laughs] All the alcohol leads to my victory. So that's how I began.

I'm in opera for no special reason. I was studying first-year law at the University of Padua. One day, I played tennis with an old friend, a musician, and I was singing a famous song [he sings a brief passage from a folk tune] while I go bong, bong, bong with the tennis ball. He said, "Nobody told you you have a good singing voice, baritone?" He said to my father, "Send your son to study music and voice." My father wanted me to be a lawyer. My father had an office in Rome and there I met Giulio Crimi, who sang with Caruso. He took me like his son. He was training me hard, studying voice. One day, I felt I was ready. I sang a basso aria. It was easier to sing basso than baritone. He was against my singing just yet, but he listened. He left the theater without saying a word. Oh my God, I must have been terrible. He waited for me in a big limousine, my maestro, with his head in his two folded hands on the walking stick. I said, trembling, "Commandatore?" He said, "I want you at my home tomorrow. Here is my card. Be there." That's how my career began.

I have always been attracted to a role in which it is possible to be an interpreter of character, an actor as well as a singer. In all my personages, I am putting in a drop of humanity. Even the strong villains, rude and evil, must have a sense of humanity. But not Iago [in Verdi's *Otello*]. He is not susceptible to any kind of good. He's the only character in whom I was not able to find a drop of humanity. His evil is dangerous, devilish. I am against all these people, musicologists, who try to find a reason for the hate of Iago against humanity. If you find a reason for Iago's behavior, you minimize the character. He's just like this because he is Iago. There is no reason. What reason? He suspects that Otello had affair with his wife? You minimize the man. You make him a staid, jealous husband. Right then and there, he becomes a small man. Not Iago. He destroys because he likes to destroy. Rigoletto, in trying to destroy the Duke, has a reason: to avenge the loss of the purity of his daughter. Iago, this man has Otello, the representative of the beauty of love, under his feet. He is not climbing the throne. He doesn't want to be elected. He's not like Macbeth. In the end when Otello says, *"Ah, discolpati,"* what it means in English is: "Confess yourself, tell me you are guilty." Iago says no. He's evil because he believes all men are evil. [Gobbi speaks the lyrics in rich, mellifluous Italian. I repeat the speech in English at his insistence] "I believe a cruel God has created me in his image and whom I hate, from some vile germ or atom. Base am I born. I'm evil because I am a man and I feel the primeval slime." Just the contrary of what I believe. I believe all children are good. Verdi is true to Shakespeare in the case of Iago. "From the germ of the cradle to the worm of the grave": heaven, he is saying, is an old wives' tale. It's a fake.

Verdi's Falstaff is not a comic figure really, he's a tragic figure who drops himself in comic situations. It doesn't matter what he does, he does it with conviction, convinced that he does something good. To be respected is very important to him. He's a man who believes in himself. It doesn't matter if they throw him in the water and they make a lot of mockeries of him, he re-stands up and he comes back. He has a strong sense of survival. The situation is sometimes comic. But he is also pathetic. He is a man that you must love, and then you will also cry for him, suffer for him. Especially when he comes out of the water of the Thames, where they threw him in a basket. He's furious. He goes back to the innkeeper, "Hey, *taverniere* . . . [in Italian]. He asks for a glass of hot wine. While he waits for his drink, he thinks about the sadness of the world and life. [He recites, beautifully, in Italian.] Now you read it in English. "Thieving world, rascal world, evil world. Host! A glass of mulled wine. I, then, having lived so long as a brave and skillful knight, end up carried in a clothes basket, tossed in the river with the stinking wash like a kitten, or a still-blind pup. Without this buoyant paunch, I'd surely have drowned. Mix a bit of wine with the water of the Thames. Ah, good. To loosen one's vest in the sun and drink sweet wine, O sweet thing. Good wine chases away the gloomy thoughts of sorrow, lights up the eye in one's thoughts. A thrilling madness drunkens the happy globe. The trill quivers through the entire world. How good the wine is."

Falstaff is an *immense* character. That is *important*. It happens sometimes that onstage they build the décor and the scenery bigger than Falstaff. If the door is a very big door, you can put heels on my shoes, you can put belly on my stomach, you can make me as big as you want, the door makes me smaller. If you go in all the very old parts of England, in the country, you have to bend to go in. There is a beam which is so low that to pass from this side to the next side of the same room, you have nearly to kneel, because the houses were smaller and I think the people also were small. That's why Falstaff can be so big. If he is big like me, I will do it bigger. As it happened to me once. The innkeeper was so big he was twice the size of Falstaff. [Chuckles] So I protest and say, "No, either you choose between the two of us. You send him home." It is always a question of balance. Everything. If you have a beautiful diamond and you put it between other diamonds, big as it is, the beauty disappears. It's a question of balance and proportion. Verdi, when he finished *Falstaff,* was eighty. When you have a good brain, good health, age means nothing. If the brain is still young, the genius is always there. And he was genius until the last second of his life.

Scarpia [in Puccini's *Tosca*] is one of my favorite roles. I have done more than eight hundred performances of Scarpia, the most in my career. There is a lot of history in this opera, but also fantasy. A good interpreter, to perform this strong character, must believe that everything about him is historical. So fiction and truth must get together. At first, I thought there really was no Scarpia. Now I've discovered that he and Tosca really existed. I try to find somebody who was supposed to be Scarpia at that time. I found in the Archivio di Stato di Roma a chief of police from that time. He was a Sicilian baron named Scarpia, and he was found killed inside of his door by a knife. He was forty-two years old. In Italian dialect, the nickname "Scarpia" is the net of the spider where the flies have to fall prisoner. That's why I don't run anymore following Tosca to capture her. I don't move. She will be out of her mind, she will be so desperate that she will fall in my open arms. And I say, *"Mia, mia,"* because she can't escape because I'm Scarpia. Even though I was starving for so many years in my career, I was always trying to reach the *truth* in my character. Especially when I became a producer (director) of these operas.

Floria Tosca was a girl born near Verona, the country of Romeo and Juliet. Ill and penniless, she recovered in a convent. The nuns took care of her. One day, a great Napoli musician was passing through and listened to the singing of this novitiate. He was impressed by the beautiful voice of this girl. He asked the mother superior to release her, to take her to Rome to study. So she went to Rome, where she studied with Cimarosa, who was a revolutionary. In 1799, Napoli was proclaimed the first republic. Yes, with twenty-five supporters [a small laugh]. So the republic was over, finished, and Angelotti escaped to Rome. A fugitive. King Ferdinand liberated Cimarosa in respect of the great musician on condition that he never came back to Napoli. That's why Cimarosa came to Rome and how Floria Tosca studied with him. Cavaradossi was in Paris first, studying with David, the famous painter. Napoleon and the horse, you remember? A glorious painting. His father was a friend of Diderot, and consequently a Voltairean, a friend of Voltaire. That's why the sacristan in *Tosca* says they are against the church. Cavaradossi decided to come to Rome. It was chic for a painter to come to Italy. At the theater, Tosca was performing. He fell in love with her. Now comes Scarpia. A super-elegant, refined monster. He became the totalitarian chief of the Rome police. He was protected and favorite of Queen Carolina, wife of King Ferdinand, sister of Marie Antoinette. She took Scarpia to Napoli with her and when the revolution broke out took him to Rome. Angelotti, the revolutionary, was a fugitive in Rome, a friend of Cavaradossi. Scarpia in one year was torturing, killing, confiscating property of forty thousand Roman families because they were sympathetic to the revolution.

Scarpia builds up his own character as a super SS image. The pure race. He was very handsome, elegant, fine, knew how to behave. The Church named him Baron Scarpia. But this time, the simple Sicilian origin in him exploded. That's why I have him shouting sometimes, like fury. He cannot control himself 100 percent. I call him a monster because of his self-idolatry. He is sure everything will fall in his arms, even Tosca. The meaning of the word *Tosca* is *il buon falco*. Tosca is a very good little falcon. Scarpia is a hunter. If I follow the falcon, I will find the prey. Because if I put jealousy in her heart, she is going out to the villa of Cavaradossi, and if Angelotti is there, my spy, Spoletta, follows her. It's mostly my fantasy. I try to build this kind of interpretation, to believe in this. This helps bring out the fuller truth. You must, especially, remember the history of the epoch.

When Scarpia sends Cavaradossi to the torture chamber, smiling, he invites Tosca to sit down: "Darling, let's talk as good friends . . ." So he tries to be a gentleman, to be diplomatic, to charm her. Because he has terrific power of self-control. But sometimes his fury is so strong. He's a man of Sicily, he's a man of blood, he's a man of the country where they grow eggplants, oranges, and the sun is hot. His reaction is also wild sometimes. He's always the hunter, suspicious of everything. Inside the church in the first act, he looks around and sees a little dust there, a little thing that can be a trace of an escaped prisoner.

Can you find any redeeming feature in Scarpia?

Yes, even though Scarpia is a monster, he's human. There is one moment in the opera when I like to think that Scarpia can also be human and have a heart, have a human feeling. It is in the end, when he promises to release Cavaradossi. Alone with Tosca, he sings, "I have kept my promise." And she says, "No, I want first to leave the country." And there Puccini wrote, *dolce* [sings gently], "Do you really want to leave . . . now?" And that is very human. He is a man who, for an instant, thinks that his presence, his important position can convince her to make love with him, eh? And when she says, "Okay, I will be your victim, but you give me permission to leave immediately after," this is a terrible disillusion for a man of passion because he's really attracted by the beauty of Tosca. It's a moment in which he opens his arms, his true feeling. He's a man who can really also love, for a second. That's where he is different from Iago. I never attended the opera *Tosca* in my life. I don't like going to the opera. I have been in the audience only twenty times in my life. I have heard about Antonio Scotti as Scarpia, he sang with Caruso. I have a nice picture of him, he had an aquiline nose. I never heard another Iago, never heard a Simon Boccanegra. [A deep sigh]

Ah, Simon Boccanegra. Maybe my very favorite Verdi role. A challenge to the actor as to the singer. He was the doge of Genoa, like a king. It was a marine republic. He was a friend of Francesco Petrarca. You say Petrarch, the Renaissance man. Simon reads the letter to the council saying Venice and Genoa belong to the same country. I plead peace and love. Stop fighting. This was 1354, five hundred years before Garibaldi and Mazzini. That, for me as an Italian, is a good feeling. The aria he sings, "Plebe! Patrizi! Popolo!" is one of the most moving in all of Verdi. When they dismiss this opera, I feel sad, unhappy, insulted. I'm not talking about Tito Gobbi. Judge me as they like. But I don't like for people to dismiss Verdi's *Boccanegra* in this light way. With just a shrug.

As the interview ends, we are listening to "Plebe! Patrizi! Popolo!" as Gobbi murmurs, "He's a dying man. He's not shouting. It's his last plea."

I am immediately reminded of an interview I once did with Italian basso Salvatore Baccaloni. He said of Chaliapin: "He's the most great artist. When he sing the Boris, he go down in the street near to death with the scarlet fever and he tremble on the stage because he's a near to fall down. Many Boris today sing strong. What kind of sick man is this? Chaliapin was a no singer, was a no actor. When he was Boris, he was Boris."

GERAINT EVANS: THE OUTSIDER
1967, 1974, 1977

The doyen of Welsh opera singers. Though his repertoire included the classic baritone roles in Mozart, Verdi, and Puccini, his antiheroes in Alban Berg's Wozzeck *and Benjamin Britten's* Peter Grimes *(which he directed while playing Captain Balstrode) most affected me. Curiously (or perversely), it was his portrayal of Beckmesser, the awkward town clerk in Wagner's* Die Meistersinger, *that touched me more than the heroic Hans Sachs or the village's (and Eva's) lover boy, Walther. To get things rolling during our first encounter (having seen his Leporello, Don Giovanni's toady) I asked him to talk about the Don's remarkable number of amorous conquests, especially the distraught Elvira, a rejected lover.*

Leporello would sell his own grandmother. This suits the Don, who needs someone to bully around and play games with. And to do his dirty work as well. I try to play Leporello as a dog because that's how the Don treats him. I also did the Don for one season. It was a great decision for me, having already done Leporello, to find out really whether I'm going to play the Don or I'm going back to the dog. When people think of Don Giovanni, they think of a tall, elegant Ezio Pinza, who's a great Don. And of John Brownlee, who was a tall, handsome man. I thought, I'm a little too short. So I put on lifts and this, that, and the other. After that performance I had a long chat with Otto Klemperer, the conductor. He said, "Geraint, you know, it's better to be a very good Leporello than a good Don."

I was fortunate in my early days to work with the conductor Fritz Busch and stage director Karl Ebert. I'm indebted to those two great men. It was Busch who said, "Geraint, you should concentrate on Mozart. Be successful in Mozart, and then the other things will come your way." I love going back to Mozart after singing, say, Wozzeck or some other role, because you cannot cheat in Mozart, you've got to sing. And it's always fresh. I've performed Figaro around five hundred performances, and it's still as fresh as ever. Figaro is the exact opposite of Leporello—the new man who will not take any guff from the count. The most important thing, he was defying an old tradition, the rite of the first night. This is a revolutionary man.

Papageno in *The Magic Flute* is a naive character. I think of Papageno as my young son, now fourteen, who's beginning to have the pangs of growing up. He's beginning now to talk to girls. My younger son, who's six, came in the other day, and he said, "Mummy, Aaron kissed a girl just now." It was such a quick kiss, on the cheek. He didn't know why or what, but this was the growing up.

Almost like Cherubino in a way.

I play Papageno exactly like this: "I want something, I don't know what it is. I want a . . . I want a . . . I want a girlfriend, is what I want." And it has to be played with great sincerity. He's a bird catcher and maybe one day he'll be able to catch a wife, too. The only thing is now I'm getting a little large to play Papageno. [Laughs] I'd have to diet a little bit before I play it again.

One of your great experiences was directing Benjamin Britten's opera
Peter Grimes *and playing the observer of the tragedy, Captain Balstrode.*

Peter Grimes is about an outsider. He doesn't conform with things that go on in the village. He is the odd man out, anything that he does is noticeable. He is a fisherman who lost an apprentice—the boy died. It was shameful in those days—the time was about 1830. They were twelve-, thirteen-, fourteen-year-old boys. He falls foul of the village. He's a man of many moods. Jon Vickers, who is a marvelous Peter Grimes, portrays him as a poetical man, sometimes a violent man. I think had Grimes an education he would have been a poet. When I directed it, I based my interpretation quite a lot on the character of Alban Berg's Wozzeck. There's a similarity here. Wozzeck himself, he has dreams, sees things that other people don't see. These are two people who cannot express themselves. Therefore, everything explodes.

The crowd wants to see Peter Grimes hung from the yardarm. There's no mercy. Not so much because of the circumstance, but because of the man himself, because he doesn't conform. They are annoyed that he's not hanged or sent to prison for murder. He embarrasses them. These are people who are fighting the elements all the time, people who have lived by the sea. Maybe they are afraid of him because he is as wild as the sea. There are always these great waves of storms, yet the people still stay there. Grimes lives in a hut that is a converted old boat on top of a cliff. He is a very good fisherman because he has the strength, and his aim is to make enough money so he will be able to marry the widowed village schoolmistress, Ellen Orford. It was not difficult for me to relate to these characters. I come from a mining village. It could just as well be a seafaring village. My grandparents were seafarers anyway. You have Mrs. Sedley, the person who looks from behind the curtain as you're passing, and the gossip. She says, "Drink? I wouldn't dare go to a pub." Yet she drinks laudanum, she's on the fix. There were many there against drink, but they had their so-called medicinal brandy in the bottom drawer where they used to have a little tot occasionally. Balstrode is an old retired sea captain. Therefore he's lived outside the village. These people have never been outside the village. Britten could have ended that opera with the death of Grimes. He ended it in silence. The villagers go about their daily work as if nothing has happened. The whole thing is forgotten until another Grimes comes along. In a sense, Balstrode is like Hans Sachs in Wagner's *Die Meistersinger*. Not as great a person as Sachs, but he has great wisdom and tries to separate the crowd from Grimes, and to reason with Grimes. He reasons with him in the first act: "Why aren't you hiding from the storm?" But for Grimes, the storm is within and not outside. He can battle with the storm outside, but he cannot battle with the storm inside. And it's the inside that's eating him away.

There is a moment in *Die Meistersinger* where unless you feel sorry for Beckmesser, I feel like I failed in the part. He is a pathetic character, not a villain. The songfest of the Meistersinger is going to happen in the next few days. Pogner announces that the greatest prize he can give is his daughter, Eva. I feel that Beckmesser is, inside, a good man, having looked after his elderly mother. And now his elderly mother has died, he's not married, he feels he's been left on the shelf, and he would love to get married. Unfortunately, he has no way of addressing himself, of meeting people, how to say things. And he's always on the bad side of people, because of his personality. Here's the chance that Beckmesser has to win Eva, and therefore he enters the competition. But he always puts his foot in his mouth. He's an awkward man.

He's the odd man out. And he's always so meticulous. Beckmesser sticks by the rules. It mustn't go this way or that way. He's so technical. He has the mind of a bookkeeper, keeps figures, and therefore doesn't allow for the richness, improvisation of art. He respects Hans Sachs very much, too, and he would love to be Hans Sachs. This is sixteenth-century Germany. There are guilds of all kinds of craftsmen. Hans is the master craftsman. They all respect him because he's so open. He has great wisdom. Here comes the knight, Walther, who's introduced into the guild. And he has to prove himself in the first act. Here's a man who's going to really compete against Beckmesser, and he has a good chance of winning because he's young, he sings marvelously, and his verse is good. And Beckmesser sticks really rigidly to the rules. He cannot communicate. When I play this part, I try to feel myself small, to feel myself mean. It took me quite a few days to find the right pair of shoes to wear. They must be rather tight on my feet so I've got a pinched feeling. I start creating this character from my feet up. I keep my elbows into my body and play it in a rather effeminate way to this small feeling, this pathos. When I play it, I'm so sincere. I don't think of comedy at all.

What were your beginnings? Your Welsh background, theater, music . . .

We Welsh are a theatrical people, no matter what our profession or job. I was born in an industrial area, South Wales. My father was a miner, my grandfather was a miner, my great-grandfather was a miner. I was brought up in the sense of people in a small village. The entertainment was created by ourselves. I could sing before I could talk. The first time I went on a stage, I was about the age of two and a half, I sang a verse from the Bible. So there was music, folk songs, and oratorio. We'd never seen opera. To go to the theater—never. I remember my grandfather, when I went into this profession of singing, he said [deep-voiced], "Do you think, my boy, you are wise to go and mix with these type of people?" He was still living in the past where I was going into the land of the devil, sinful.

When I was about six, seven years of age, a minister was giving his sermon when the town opened a roller-skating rink. In the midweek, instead of coming to the Band of Hope or another religious meeting in the chapel, the young people were going down to skate on this new rink. The minister was saying [ominously], "You can't go to hell quick enough these days. You'll all be going to hell. But you won't walking or running, but going on wheels." [Laughs] Every child in that village who could go onstage to recite a poem in Welsh or in English, because Welsh was our first language, could go on to sing a folk song. And you'd get boys, when their voices had broken at twelve or thirteen, there was no stopping, there was no pausing, they would be singing an aria from one of the oratorios. Handel was the music of religion outside hymns. Handel was the greatest messenger of God that we knew in Wales. We even considered the Welsh language part of our religion.

The Welsh language was spoken by 70 percent of people living in Wales when I was a boy. I began to learn to speak English when I went to school, and I was beginning to master it at the age of seven or eight. After a few years the war came, and many, many young people, especially the boys, never went back home. They'd been out of Wales for the first time in their lives. I was the age of thirteen when I went to Cardiff first, which was only fifteen miles away. I was sixteen when I had my first ride in a car. All our lives were developed around the village and the town and the mines. This is still inborn in us. A few of us get together now, if one or two of us are performing in town, Welsh boys, I mean, people like Richard Burton, Stanley Baker, Emlyn Williams. We might meet in town and say, "Come over to the flat tonight." We might have something to eat, a few drinks, and before the evening is out we're singing. We can go on singing for two hours. You can't stop us, it's like something that's in our blood. We are very emotional. It's like when we sing folk songs. Our boyhood emotions take over.

∾ **Liebestod** ∾

JON VICKERS
1974

The Canadian singer, often described as the heldentenor of his day, had mixed feelings about Wagner. In fact, he was a man of many controversial opinions, fighting what he thought was the money machine that was taking over the arts. Aside from his Wagnerian roles, he may be best known as Benjamin Britten's Peter Grimes, the outsider. Incidentally, he was a magnificent actor as well as a singer. During our conversation we were listening to his aria Dio! mi potevi scagliar *from Verdi's* Otello.

To me, it's exactly the kind of music I like to make because there is such smoothness to it. There's no artificiality, no bombast. To me, it is just creamy. *Otello* and *Tristan*, the peaks of Italian and German opera. My voice teacher, an Englishman who had a career of sorts in Rome where he used to sing the Wagnerian roles in Italian, said to me, "A good big 'un is better than a good little 'un." I've always had this big sound, and I worked very, very hard to master the *messa di voci* that you just heard in the Italian. He used to also say, "There is no such thing as a German tenor, and a French tenor, and an English tenor, and an Italian tenor. There are only good singers and bad singers, and you must learn to be a good singer." The thing that separates German, French, and Italian singers, each from the other, is simply a matter of linguistic style, or in certain cases musical style. So that if you become a musical stylist and a linguistic stylist, then it matters not what language you sing in. A good sound, in any language, is produced in the same way. I'm talking about an understanding of style, and it's ironic, so often amongst the laymen, particularly on the North American continent, they will pick out an example of very bad Italian singing and say, "Oh, that's great, that's terrific." And then they'll pick out a very, very bad example of German singing and say, "Oh, that's really great German style." And what is the mistake? The mistake is exactly the same in both: it is cheap exaggeration and melodramatic use of the language, and vocalizing it instead of singing it.

You're reputed to have said that the Italian repertoire caresses the voice, whereas the German exploits it.

Yes, generally speaking, that is true. Certainly the Wagnerian repertoire, I think. Now, there are exceptions in the Wagnerian repertoire. I think this is not true of his *The Flying Dutchman*. It was very much under the influence of the Italian school, and I happen to be of the opinion that it is probably his greatest work. There are, of course, magnificent moments of lyricism and cantabile in *Tristan und Isolde,* in *Parsifal,* and in *Lohengrin.* I'm not denying that for a moment. But the mercilessness, relentlessness of so many of the Wagner parts; Tristan is just inhuman in its demands. The anguish of the man has to be portrayed, but in the third act of *Tristan,* when he says [says in German, then repeats], "The drink, the drink, the terrible drink," and he describes how it goes from his heart to his brain and drives him to insanity, this is an example of just how this kind of music can tear at the voice.

Who is Jon Vickers? We think of Canada. Canada is something different when it comes to the operatic stage.

Yes, it's true. Many people ask me how in the world I ever got into opera when I was the son of a schoolteacher with seven brothers and sisters in northern Saskatchewan. And brought up in the Depression years, of course. I hope we're not heading into another one. People ask me, "How'd you ever get into opera?" And my answer really is, I don't know. My career just growed [chuckles], and it just became a natural development. All my life I've sung, since I was a little boy of five. My whole family was deeply involved in church work and all of us were musical, we all played instruments, we all sang. We entertained the prisoners in the federal penitentiary and the local jail. I used to go up and sing for people in the insane asylum, as we used to call it in those days. I would sing anything. They were in the form of church services. My father was a lay minister and he used to preach to the prisoners. They used to whistle at my sisters. [Laughs] And they'd cheer me in the middle of a church service if I sang. It was marvelous. The end of my schooling was just at the end of the war. I came out the same year as all the boys came back from overseas. It was very difficult getting into university, and the university asked me to defer my application and reapply in two years. I was a very impatient boy, as I guess I still am. I just said the heck with it, and I went into the business world. I'd only been with Hudson's Bay Company for about six months or so, when suddenly I was offered a scholarship in Toronto. It was hardly a scholarship; it was a very, very meager amount of money. But I was young and I thought it might be fun.

My life has always been very music-filled. In fact, in many ways, it sounds funny to say, but it was more music-filled as an amateur than it is as a professional. I loved music as an amateur because it served me. It's the great transition that has to be made from amateur to pro. The pro has to learn the rigidity and the discipline and the heartbreak of serving *music*. It's the icy coldness and loneliness that the person has to discover in the transition. When you become the professional, music is your job, and then your love of music really has to be an *intense* love or you'll forsake it. It's a tough taskmaster. The line of demarcation between the amateur and the professional is very difficult for me to draw. The big step was when I was offered the first big contract at the Royal Opera House Company. Back in the fifties, there was a Canadian Broadcasting Corporation Opera Company, and a great oratorio field. In those years when I was a quasi-professional, I sang thirty-three oratorios—*Israel in Egypt,* and *Solomon*, and Haydn's *The Creation*, and *The Messiah,* and *Judas Maccabeus*, and all these things. I had sung twenty-eight operatic roles before I ever joined Covent Garden in London.

There's the mastery of language itself. You are Canadian, and there's French, Italian, German in your repertoire.

You just have to stick your nose to the grindstone. There's no shortcut. A lot of people believe that this profession has to do with luck. There's no such thing as luck. There's a basic talent that I devoutly believe is a divine gift, but it's a terrible taskmaster too. People say, "Oh well, he was just born to sing Peter Grimes." Other people say, "Oh yeah, he's just a natural for Siegmund." That's stupid. Peter Grimes and Siegmund are light-years apart, interpretively and vocally. If I have made a success of those two parts, it's because I've learned to do it. There's great music in language. The composer Janáček, for instance, who wrote *Jenůfa*, used to wear big, wide cuffs on his shirts. He used to take a pencil and he would notate the musical line of conversation. He's got this peculiar, stunted style of composition where he has very, very short phrases. He based a lot of his composition on the music of language, and it's the music, unfortunately, of the Czech language, which I don't understand. But all language has music. All you have to do is listen to a great actor, like Sir John Gielgud or someone, and you realize what unbelievable music there is in the English language.

So we come to Peter Grimes, *Benjamin Britten, and you.*

It's a strange marriage in many ways. Britten wrote this opera for Peter Pears, who is a very lyric tenor. I happen to feel that *Peter Grimes* is not really for lyric tenor because he's a big, rough, tough fisherman, and it should be a bigger sound. And it was a strange thing to sort of discipline myself into that kind of work. But back in my studies in Canada, I started out with Britten's folk song arrangements, and then I did his *Serenade for Tenor, Horn, and Strings*. Eventually I was invited to sing *The Rape of Lucretia* at the Stratford Festival in Canada. That was terribly successful. After I joined the opera house in Covent Garden, they tried many times to persuade me to sing *Peter Grimes*. I always deferred it because I felt the name Peter Pears was so synonymous with the opera, certainly in England, that I did not choose to expose myself to it. When the Metropolitan changed houses from the old to the new, Rudolf Bing [general manager of the Metropolitan Opera] phoned me and said, "Would you like to do *Peter Grimes*?" And I said

I'd love to. I'd sung in the chorus of *Peter Grimes* when I was a student up in Toronto, in the forties.

All opera to me is only interesting if I can search out the facets of the personality that I'm trying to portray. I bury myself in the parts I sing. *Grimes* is a great opera because anyone who sees *Grimes* must go out of that opera with all kinds of misgivings about their attitudes to other human beings. The person of Grimes is a timeless man, the opera is a study in human rejection. Every living human being knows what it means, really, to be rejected. It's an agonizing thing to experience. *Grimes* puts a message across to every human being that we really should do unto others as we would have them do unto us. He is not a success as a fisherman, because success—alas, in our society success is measured by dollars and cents. He tries to be. He says, "I'll win them over, I'll earn a lot of money." And it's tremendously pertinent to our society today. People are accepted because of the dollar signs they wear. When you study a role, you study it in relationship to society and what it has to say to elevate the thinking and root out the things that are foul in our society today. I'm sorry, we are headed down a very dangerous track. It is the PR man determining that the greatest opera singers are the ones who have become household words, like Ex-Lax or Coca-Cola or something: a product. They're a hunk of meat that's sold.

Now we come to the Iliad, *an ancient theme, the Trojan War. Berlioz's* Les Troyens.

You're using more than just a Trojan horse, and I like very much what the conductor Colin Davis said about it: "We need to listen again and again to the warnings of Cassandra." Because it was that mechanized thing that destroyed them. And here we are, and we're choking ourselves with our automobiles and with our computers, and with all our mechanization, and we're choking ourselves to death with it, and we're crushing out of ourselves all of the ability to live. We've got to listen to the warnings of Cassandra today.

We haven't talked about your repertoire, the breadth of it.

I was *determined* that I was not going to be shoved into an area of specialization. As soon as I opened my mouth on the big stages of the world, because I had this big voice, they said, "Ah, at last we've got somebody who's going to sing the Wagner style." And I said, "In no way am I going to sacrifice my life and my enjoyment of music to singing a half a dozen Wagnerian parts. I can't think of anything more boring, I can't think of anything more soul-destroying, I can't think of anything that would absolutely destroy a vocal technique. And besides, I just don't think Wagner has that much to say." [Laughs] Wagner was a great personal friend and admirer of Nietzsche. And the Wagnerian operas are all absolutely crammed full of Nietzsche's philosophy. And the genius of Wagner in many ways makes it diabolical. *Tristan und Isolde* is the epitome of that. Tristan and Isolde, they were not nice people, neither one of them. And when they talk about this as the greatest love story ever written, it may be a great love story between two quite horrible human beings. Don't kid yourself. They were not nice people. And the Nietzscheist philosophy that is inherent in the whole of *Tristan und Isolde* is what makes it, as far as I'm concerned, an evil and a wicked work.

Boy! And you are one of the great Tristans of our day.

I have no time for any of Nietzsche's philosophy. When you look at the life of Richard Wagner himself, and you look at *Tristan and Isolde,* and you really digest it, it comes out that he wrote *Tristan und Isolde* really as an attempt to justify his own behavior. I'm sorry, as far as I'm concerned, it didn't justify it. Okay, I've sung it, I've digested it, I've interpreted it, and I've had some pretty good things said about my interpretation, too. As a matter of fact, the greatest compliment I've ever had about my interpretation of *Tristan und Isolde* was when a young woman who I knew who was very closely attached to the Bayreuth Festival in Germany—who absolutely fell under the spell of Wagner, fell under the spell of Nietzsche's philosophy, and absolutely lost herself because of it— she came to me after my interpretation of Tristan in the Salzburg Festival and she said, "John, I've fought with you about your thoughts about Tristan. After I saw it tonight, I came to the conclusion that it was a wicked work because it made me want to go out and take my own life."

The great theological philosopher Paul Tillich talked about what art was and whether people can argue or not about the aesthetic, whether really the aesthetic can be discussed, and what aesthetic means. And Tillich said you can dig up a vase of 3000–4000 B.C. and you can discuss whether or not that vase is a work of art or not. The criterion by which you judge whether it is a work of art is whether it serves the absolute. That's a very interesting phrase.

I believe that Johann Sebastian Bach served the absolute. I believe that Verdi served the absolute. I believe Berlioz served the absolute. And I think it's the responsibility of singers and opera managers and conductors to serve the absolute in art. And when it's corrupted by a PR attitude and a PR philosophy, and when we have it crammed down our throats of the greatness of this singer and that singer, because of the fee that they made, then I'm very saddened. We forget that the Metropolitan Opera company and the RCA recording industry, those two great institutions, were founded on the great heart and the great generosity and the great talent of *one* man. The presidents of RCA today, who when they try to negotiate with us say, "Oh, but we don't make any money out of classical recordings," should *remember* that their corporation was founded on the voice of Enrico Caruso.

BIRGIT NILSSON
1961

Though others had discovered the fact that this little girl in a Swedish town had a remarkable voice, her father objected to the idea of her pursuing singing as a career. He'd rather she ran a family and a farm. It's from the Swedish peasants who worked for her that she learned many of the folk songs she came to love so much, which in fact led to her singing other, more serious songs. She was the Wagnerian soprano of her day.

What do you remember about your childhood?

I think back to my childhood. I'm singing about a true love and riding away with him on the horse, very fast through the country. I was born inside Sweden, a place called Bolstadt, a small village. One of the most wonderful places. Our king, Gustav VI, was always there every summer, also Gustav V, who died so many years ago. I used to sing for Gustav V at the church before I became a singer. I always wanted very much to be a singer. I sang very early. I sang before I could walk. I walked very late. [Laughs] Sang very early. My parents at that time were very proud of me. I spoke clearly at one and a half, and I sang all the songs that my mother taught me. When I was five, my father bought an organ for me, not very expensive, but I learned all the melodies.

I could sing and I played the organ. It went on until I was thirteen; I was singing in school, all over, and then I got a brand-new piano and I began to take lessons. I never liked to play piano very much but anyhow I had to. It was love songs with about thirty verses. Sometimes in the night I dreamed about the songs and I'd sing thirty verses in my dream. [Laughs]

We had a lot of work on our farm and of course I learned songs from the workers. I remember once when I was six years old I had to sing in a big Christmas celebration. My mother was with me. I had to stand up in a high chair to sing because I was so small they couldn't see me. They liked it very much; I sang children's songs I had learned, but I thought there should have been a little more applause. I remember singing a love song about two people who were in love with each other, but a third one was very jealous and he killed the other boy. It maybe wasn't too good for me to sing it. [Laughs] Just a little kid. My mother, she was holding me, and she forbade me to sing it for many years. My mother, she got horrified and said it was the last time she would let me sing it.

Did your parents encourage your singing?

No, they did not. My mother had a very good voice, my father was very proud of me when I was a child and he had me sing, but then when I was getting older and wanted to take lessons and become a singer, he didn't like it very much. He wanted to have me home. I was an only child and he thought I could have quite a good life at home and take over the farm. I sang in church choirs when I was fourteen years, and was soloist very often. Then I met a singing teacher and sang for him. I was eighteen years old, and he said, "You are going to be a great singer." I didn't believe my ears, I was so happy. But I thought, well, it's not so easy to be a singer. But I continued to take lessons from him. He then sent me to the Royal Academy of Music in Stockholm. My father thought, you go to Stockholm, the big time and everything, it's very dangerous. Forty-eight of us auditioned for the Royal Academy. Only two got in. I was the first one. When I heard all the other forty-six, I thought, oh-h-h . . . Everybody was singing so well, they came from everywhere, and they had sung in France and Italy, all over. I was scared because I had only sung in the country. So I decided to sing everywhere. [Laughs]

My parents could very well have paid for me in Stockholm, but my father didn't like it and he said, "Well, it is only a waste of money. It costs a lot of money, and you will never become anything." I thought, I will try to make it without his money. I sang in choirs and I sang at funerals. Sometimes I came home to Sweden with two cents in my purse for vacation, and I was very proud I had made it myself. It was very hard sometimes, but it went quite well.

When you read the libretto and when you sing the words, you must have the right feeling. In the beginning it was very difficult to combine all these things at one time, and then to look to the conductor, and to sing the right notes at the right time, it was very difficult. But after some time you have a routine. Once on an opening night I forgot to open a window—at a certain bar in the aria, I had to open the window. I completely forgot. I was so young. That is why I'm not singing new operas, new roles. I never feel I really conquered my old roles. I sang Isolde eighty-five times and there's still much to learn there. I'm quite sure I can sing this role two hundred times. It is wonderful. You will never finish with a role. In the beginning I had too much hate. More hate than I had love. I don't think it should be that way. Because Isolde is a poor woman who just was too much in love with Tristan. And, of course, while she loved Tristan so much, she hated him at the same time because she didn't know that he had the same feelings for her. [She sighs] It's a wonderful opera. Like Strindberg. He always combines the hate and love. They are very close to each other. Tristan is dead at her feet and she lies down there and looks at him, and she cannot really believe that he's dead. She just thinks in her mind that Tristan is still alive. She sees him, he's smiling at her, and she feels his heart and sings about how he loves her and how she still sees him before her eyes. It's hard to come down to earth at the end of the "Liebestod." The opera is art. It's very hard to be a normal person again. Oh, the music, it takes so much from me. I mean, I love it so much.

In all of these roles, I assume, you're always seeking, probing. Leonore in Fidelio *is wholly different from Isolde's relationship to Tristan. She's the faithful wife.*

Oh yes, yes. I compare Fidelio to Tosca, but Fidelio is more a fighter. Oh, they are both fighters. Tosca kills Scarpia to, she thinks, save the life of Cavaradossi. Leonore is ready to kill to save her husband's life. They are very like each other, but she understands more than Tosca. Yet they're also very much like Isolde. It's a pity Beethoven only wrote one opera. It's wonderful to sing. My husband doesn't recognize my *Fidelio* now—I first sang it in 1954. He said, "I can hardly recognize how much you have changed."

I feel I need to sing more than one composer because otherwise the voice gets a little stiff and heavy. I would like to still have a certain flexibility to the voice. I sometimes do recitals and sometimes Italian operas. And one gets the vocal cords to work a little bit finer. As for Wagner, you need lots of volume to it. If you concentrate on Wagner, something happens to the voice that makes it difficult to do Mozart or Puccini. When young singers start out, they immediately want to become a new Tristan, a new Isolde, in their second or third year they are singing, and then they go on singing only Wagner. You can hear the difference after only four or five years. The voice, the luster and the beauty of the voice disappear very easily if you don't stay aware of how to handle the voice.

Now we come to Mozart.

I made my debut as Donna Anna in *Don Giovanni* in 1949. So here's Donna Anna and she's furious, her honor has been defiled by the Don. She swears vengeance. And he killed her father, too, who challenged him to a duel. Well, just before Giovanni appears, he doesn't want to show his face for Donna Anna. As he tries to seduce her, she resists. Later, she sees that it is Don Giovanni who has betrayed her and killed her father, and she gets completely out of her mind. Her boyfriend, Don Ottavio, is at her side.

A critic wrote: "This Donna Anna of Birgit Nilsson is a worthy opponent for Don Giovanni, whose sensuality she confronts with the iridescent armor of an avenging angel." [She laughs.] In interpreting Donna Anna, you see her in many lights, don't you?

Yes, of course. Coming out of a more dramatic tradition, like Wagner, maybe I make her more dramatic then the more sad singers who come from the lyric repertoire. I don't like women who are only going around crying and being sad and being left alone. I would like to take some action. [Laughs] So I think something should happen. I have very difficult time to just sit and be lonesome and cry and be unhappy. I like to do something about it. You know, we have to struggle. A human being, I think, is born to struggle a bit, to feel that you can succeed and you can solve problems. It makes you stronger after a while.

Many young people today are brought up to think that they should get everything they wish for, and they have nothing to wish for anymore. They don't know how to work hard, to struggle for a living as many of us have done. It's a big challenge to get a good role, but you should never be satisfied with that. I have sung many roles two and three hundred times, and I never try to stand still, I always try the next time to make it better than before and go on and on. I always have the feeling that if you stand at the same point, then in the public's eyes you go backwards. You have to find new things, to get the voice more polished. Otherwise you become mechanical after a while and that is very dangerous. To be satisfied with oneself is the greatest danger in an artist's life.

We know you as the operatic soprano. Do you find the challenge different as a concert singer?

It is like night and day. You cannot compare these two arts. It's so good for the voice. You keep the voice much, much more under control when you sing lieder because you have to be careful about every note. Maybe in the opera, in some operas at least, if two or three notes are not so correct it's not so important. But in the recitals every note is important, you must have everything under control. And when you are making a whole program of twenty songs, you have to be twenty persons, just to get the right atmosphere in the song. In an opera you only have to play one person.

∽ Salzburg ∽

JOSEF KRIPS
1964

If there is any one musician responsible for bringing forth the works of Mozart anew following the devastation of World War II, it was Josef Krips, the Austrian conductor who founded the modern Salzburg Festival, dedicated primarily to the work of Mozart. It was he who said, in his cracked Viennese accent, that Beethoven was heavenly, but Mozart came to us from heaven. It was that moment of genius that elevated all of us in our lives. And it was he who in creating the Salzburg Festival brought forth Elisabeth Schwarzkopf and Irmgard Seefried and Erich Kunz. One thing about Mozart he made quite clear: you can't fool around with him. That is, you can't make any mistakes. People will detect it immediately. If you make a mistake with John Cage or with Stockhausen, who would know the difference? To him it was Wolfgang Amadeus Mozart who represents the genius that is in the human species.

People think that I'm a Mozart specialist, and for all the Vienna classical composers. I was born and brought up in Vienna, and Vienna always was the town of Haydn, Beethoven, and Mozart. I have a special experience with Mozart because after World War II, 1945, when the Vienna Opera was burned down and then bombed, we had to play in a very small opera house for only eleven hundred people in the audience. So we tried to do a repertoire that fitted there. I thought the time had come, really, for a renaissance of Mozart. Mozart was always loved and appreciated in Vienna, but never too much.

Before the war I was already conducting the Vienna Opera and I don't recall that we had very many *Figaro* performances, four or five a year, and not many more *Don Giovannis*. I remember even a time when *The Abduction from the Seraglio* was not in our repertoire for about twelve years. The same with *Così Fan Tutte,* sometimes five or six years not in the repertoire. After the war, we started what was called a Mozart renaissance. We had our wonderful young ensemble. That was the time of Irmgard Seefried, Elisabeth Schwarzkopf, Richard Tauber, and Erich Kunz. They were very young. We really started from scratch with Mozart. For *Figaro,* there were not more than twenty-nine people in our orchestra. It was like chamber music. Everything was clear and transparent. We worked it so that the voices really blended. That is a difficult thing to do. Sometimes you find great singers and each of these singers may have sung his or her part already a hundred times. But to sing together in the ensemble it takes a long time until the voices really blend, the same as with an orchestra or a string quartet. If you brought together the four greatest string players alive, they wouldn't be good enough until they rehearsed and worked together. The great singers at that time were not stars, they were just artists, and we all tried to build an ensemble to serve the composer. For me, it is the worst critic who goes out of an opera performance and says, "Wasn't Miss Tebaldi or Mr. Del Monaco wonderful?" What about the other performers? Either you are moved by an opera performance or you are not moved. If you want to hear just one aria of a singer, then it is best to go and listen to him in a recital or listen to a gramophone record. But an opera can be the highest form of art. It is great music, great poetry, great painting, great singing, great playing, great acting. With everything together, it can be a great experience.

Mozart is especially difficult to perform, because in Mozart everything is open. You can hear the slightest mistake. Even people who are not so enormously musical can hear that something is wrong. In a work by Wagner or by Richard Strauss, there are many things that happen where nobody will notice. And I will not even talk about contemporary music. Who could say in a Stockhausen or a John Cage piece what was wrong and what was right? [Laughter] Mozart—that is the highest because Mozart is the expression of eternal truth. I always say that Beethoven reaches heaven, but Mozart comes from heaven. There is an old saying that thirty-five years is one second in eternity. So Mozart was an angel who was sent for one second to our planet. He arrived completely unnoticed, and he disappeared. Up to now nobody knows where he's buried. He just disappeared. Whatever he wrote he never made corrections. What he wrote was written for eternity. His music came out as a whole. And it went so fast. The whole of *Don Giovanni* was done in maybe three months. Imagine, he composed the overture the night before the first performance. I couldn't imagine an orchestra playing the *Don Giovanni* overture without any rehearsal for the premiere! In Mozart's music, he starts maybe on the floor, but after two seconds he's up in the air. Take the overture to *Magic Flute,* the first three chords. [Sings] With the third chord you must have the feeling we have arrived in the country of *The Magic Flute.* If you have not this feeling on this third chord, then it was not *The Magic Flute,* it was just the flute. Therefore, when I come to an orchestra I say always, "Everything is by Mozart." That means it has to be played as if it were Mozart or else it will be a bad performance. That means so clearly that you can hear all the inner voices of a piece. There is always a perfect balance between string players, woodwinds, and brass. That is what I call Mozartian. The clarity is such that the man in the second balcony, even though not a music fan, would know something is wrong. The same with the tempo. If you take a wrong tempo in Mozart, everybody will realize there's something wrong, because there is only one right tempo.

I was very early on attracted to Mozart, but very soon I found out that to conduct Mozart is the most difficult thing to do. It was in 1926. I was invited to guest-conduct for the position of general music director in Karlsbad, which was one of the old court theaters with a great tradition. Even Richard Wagner conducted there. The program that I chose was the G Minor Symphony No. 40 by Mozart, something by Strauss, and Beethoven's Fifth. I made a success of it, but after the concert I said to myself, "My God, will I ever again be able to conduct this G Minor Symphony?" In my opinion, it is still the most difficult piece of music ever. So I didn't perform it for the next few years. I had two scores of it in my home—one on my desk and one on my night table. I studied the piece nearly every day, and you know when I did the second performance? In 1951. This G Minor Symphony is the most mysterious piece that exists. There's a saying that when a person dies, just before he closes the eyes forever, he has the grace of God to see once again, maybe in one second, his whole life. Like a kaleidoscope. [He hums a phrase from the G minor.] You must feel it. When you just start this movement with the violas [tootling], then it's not the G Minor Symphony. The second movement, that's a piece between heaven and earth. Just in the air. You have to be a conductor for at least twenty years until you get the drama of this symphony. That is a real challenge. Mozart speaks to everybody. Everybody must come and sit down and be willing to listen. When you listen to Mozart, it's like relaxing and listening to your inner voice. Everybody has such a thing as an inner voice. Only many people don't take time to seek it out. But they should. What is the inner voice? That is the music of Mozart.

When I do a Mozart opera, I say always I have two orchestras: one around me in the pit and one onstage. I do not want a singer just to follow me because he has to. No, the work has to be rehearsed until the whole thing gets so natural. The singers and musicians should not have the feeling that there is somebody who leads and somebody who follows. Also, you should not ever have the impression that you are in an opera house. The public has to feel that everyone is a part. We make music not with our arms and legs; we make music with our breath, with breathing. Imagine when I give the upbeat and sixty people in the orchestra take the breath together with me, ah . . . Then comes the unity. And then that goes over to the singers. In a really good performance, after twenty seconds the whole public takes a breath with us, and we are all together, we are all one body. That is the goal we try to achieve. Eternity. That is eternal . . . good and bad and everything. You have the feeling you experience the peace of true humanity. That is in reality the goal of art. Art is not entertainment. Art is a gift of God. It should give uplift. It should be able to give consolation. What you get from it, you can't count in dollars and cents.

How did you come to be this particular conductor?

I was a pupil of Felix Weingartner, and I first studied theory with a professor who was a friend of Brahms and Bruckner. In 1924, when I was twenty-two years old, I went away to a tiny place in Czechoslovakia—in those days Czechoslovakia was German. With a little orchestra of thirty-six, I conducted my first *Lohengrin,* and my first *Seraglio.* I was there only one year, then I went to Dortmund in Germany. Here I had an orchestra of ninety-two people. Then I spent seven years as general music director in Karlsbad. During this time I was guest-conducting many times in Frankfurt and in Berlin and Munich. In 1931, I conducted the first time as a guest in the Vienna State Opera. I stayed there until Hitler came, then I went to Yugoslavia. I did all kinds of work. I have no regrets for that. Maybe for the first time I learned how to treat people, how to live with people, how to give people support. After the war, I revived not only the Vienna Opera, but also the Vienna Philharmonic. I remember a Saturday morning during a Philharmonic Orchestra rehearsal, then in the afternoon a concert from three till five, and then at seven o'clock conducting *Fidelio.*

In those days we had nothing to eat. I weighed about forty pounds less than I do now. And we had no transportation. There were no buses or trams for the first months. Sometimes I had to travel up to three hours a day. I had two suits and an overcoat and some rugs. In the cold winter, I slept in them. Our windows were paper. It was quite harsh. Our money was worth nothing. The fee for my monthly twenty-eight performances was four pounds of lard. Thank God, my fees are now a little bit higher! But still I wouldn't have liked to have missed that. Because that was the time when you could see what music in reality can mean for people. When we performed the first *Fidelio,* in the first act, Irmgard Seefried had tears coming down her cheeks. The three others in this quartet also had tears. All of a sudden, I saw that the orchestra musicians had tears. And you could feel that the whole audience had tears. In this music, they lived all what they had gone through. It was a consolation, and they were grateful. The quality of the performances, I would say, was higher than nowadays because today everybody knows he's now here in Vienna, but that next week he maybe has a concert in Boston, and everything is easy. But at that time music was really the *only* great thing that was left for us. I will not forget that.

Art is a gift of God to mankind. Somebody who says, "I don't need art" is a second-class individual. If you hear somebody making music, you will know at once what kind of man he is. In real music, there is no lie. It is not possible. Music is an essential part of life.

IRMGARD SEEFRIED
1964

She was at most five feet. She entered, sat on the couch, and plunked her feet on a footstool. Tiny she was, and yet on the stage she loomed impressively large.

Many people have quite beautiful voices. But behind these voices there must be much more. It's the humanity as well as the vocal cords involved. In *Don Giovanni*, Elvira is the only person who really reveals the true Don to the audience, his personality and his power. I don't believe in the Elvira that you usually see—the woman scorned. I believe that Elvira is the only real partner for Don Giovanni. That's the reason why he's running away from her all the time. Because she knew him through and through, because she loved him deeply. It would be frightening for Don Giovanni to be all the time with Elvira. That's the reason why he would like to kill her nearly, because he knows, "If I stay with this woman, I have to change myself." That's why he's scared of her, because not only is she close to him, but she's like him, too. She is exactly the mirror of him. Some men, they are just like that. [Laughs] Frightened by the woman who is most like themselves.

Aside from being an artist, you are an observer of the human condition, of human nature.

It's my life. How can you separate life from art? Mozart's characters are all taken exactly from life. It's not like Wagner: Wagner didn't pick the people out of life but out of mythology. *Die Meistersinger* is an exception. But Mozart was always deeply, deeply involved in the human being. Now we come to Fiordiligi in *Così Fan Tutte*. Fiordiligi is a different kind of person. She is a deeply warm woman. She's the only one of the six people who is really very intelligent. The funniest thing for her is that even if you are intelligent as a woman, you can, as it shows in the second act, change your mind. This is wonderful and difficult to act. In the aria *Per pietà, ben mio, perdona*, she would like to say, "Excuse me. Can you forgive me for all I have done?" She reproaches herself for having sent her beloved man away, thinking he is another man. Sometimes you see a person and you think it's a different one. That's the way it is in life.

Mozart has always been in my life, all the time, and Susanna in *Le Nozze di Figaro* was my most favorite role. [Laughs] Oh, she's quite a person. Somehow just like a *régisseur,* you see. She's the director of the whole situation. She knows perfectly well how to handle these things. Most people always sing her as a coloratura. I was one of the first of the lyric sopranos, and since that time Susanna has quite changed. You have to bring out more than only the happy side. It's not only baroque rococo, as most people think of Mozart. Mozart is much more. Mozart is a very deep, emotional composer. You must have a special color in your voice. In this case, it's like Wagner. If you don't have a Wagnerian voice, you just can't do Wagner. With Mozart, it's not only the joy, it's sometimes the *tristesse,* the real sadness.

Your feelings about Bach's St. Matthew's Passion, *which you performed after World War II.*

I did it the first time in Leipzig, where it was very difficult to do. It was exactly there in Bach's St. Thomas Church. I sat on the grave of Bach and I placed my hand over it. We had to record the whole night through. It was so cold I had to wear fur coats because they had no heat. It was a moment I will never forget. Those boys there, the chorus, were very hungry at that time, nothing to eat. It was quite a moment. It was the music of Bach that kept me warm. The aria is not just a prayer, it's a sigh, let's say, of the soul. A sigh for all humanity.

Now we come to the Russian, Mussorgsky. "A Children's Song."

[She emits a sound between a roar and a sigh.] I remember the first time I sang it in Vienna. It was after the birth of my first girl, she was then two, and while I learned it, she came and watched me. When I saw that she couldn't understand the words, I had the feeling of aha, I have to do it more clearly. Until I could see that she could really understand the whole story. So I went on the stage and did it just that way. There was one critic in the hall, he slammed the door as he went off, furious! [Laughs] He thought it was too much to hear somebody doing Mussorgsky's *kinderlieder* just as a child speaks. When I was singing, I was just changing the voice. A real lieder singer is a *character*. You don't even need to speak the language. I did it in German. When you hear the music, you can do it in *your* language with exactly the same color as it should be in Russian. I sang it for a Russian and he came afterward and said, "The funniest thing happened. I thought you were singing in Russian." Two years old. To make this genuine, my daughter had to understand it. Mussorgsky was writing this for children. Why should I sing this for people who think this is just a song and it's only for them to understand? They must have a child in their mind, as we all must have.

Consider Mussorgsky's song "Evening Prayer." How different this is from Bartók's "Lullaby"? Different, yet so related.

Mussorgsky is the child who speaks. Bartók is the wise mother. A real deep feeling of mothering. You hear it, this fear of death: she knows what's coming for this darling, beloved child. I thought it's a good idea to show these two moments: this happiness of a child who speaks the little ba-ba-ba-ba-ba. And the mother who knows what will happen: the child must face life in this terrible world, and eventually will die.

You are in Chicago now, playing the young composer in Ariadne auf Naxos. *He's the second young man you've interpreted of two Strauss heroes. The other is the handsome young Octavian in* Der Rosenkavalier.

I was waiting, nearly crying, to get the part of Octavian, but it wasn't happening, something went wrong all the time. I wasn't absolutely ready. I'm quite sure that if I had done this earlier, it would not have been right. Octavian, ah, it's just my whole life. Strauss wrote these two young boys for women's voices, for sopranos, because there is no young boy, young man, who would have the wisdom to do this. Most intelligent women have both parts in one body, the understanding of male and female.

There is a beautiful scene where Octavian meets and falls in love with young Sophie and she with him, when he presents her with the silver rose.

That's a great moment. Every performance is the same feeling for me. It's totally down to the knee. [She makes a strangled sound.] This is your moment for what you were studying and doing and working for all the time.

Who is this young composer in Ariadne auf Naxos?

Now, in my mind, I always have the feeling that the young composer in *Ariadne auf Naxos* is the young Beethoven. Absolutely. Rebelling. And he's bringing out his whole being. For me the part is so difficult because you don't have enough time to build it up. You must in one hour depict the whole life of a man. You have no time just to go on slowly. You come on and directly jump in the middle of the whole thing to show that you have to say something in your life.

It's just a little prologue. The story itself: a rich man is having this opera performed, the story of Ariadne, and he is saying it's too dull. Therefore, this young composer is suddenly surrounded by philistines who want to jazz things up.

Exactly like today. You find it everywhere; they don't like to have only one show. The rich man thought, "Maybe I could, with my money, have two shows in one." For the serious man, this is too much. This makes him absolutely furious. Going up to heaven and going down to hell from one second to the other. This is maybe my favorite moment, when I can say the prologue: "Music is the holiest art which unites in sacred bonds all who can dare, like cherubim guarding a radiant throne. That is why of all the arts, music is the most holy, the holy, holy art." [She repeats it in German.] I sang when Strauss was there.

He heard you?

Strauss heard me! He came in and clapped. I was terribly shy. I said, "My gosh, is something wrong?" He looked at me and he said, "My dear girl, I never knew that my composing was so good." I sang with him lieder, too. He was at the piano. That was maybe the most moving experience of my whole life. With this young composer, no matter what the obstacles, music will always be part of his life. And mine.

ELISABETH SCHWARZKOPF
1960

Elisabeth Schwarzkopf, the German soprano, may be best known for being a founding member of the modern Salzburg Festival, following World War II, which specialized in Mozart. Her Mozartian heroines are among the most highly regarded. But she was renowned for her lieder singing as well. One word to describe her approach toward her art would be ease. There was a quality there in which not only did she appear comfortable to you, but you felt comfortable listening to her as well.

The role of the Marschallin in *Der Rosenkavalier* is very difficult because there have been such great artists singing it, like Lotte Lehmann. People who have seen her will always remember her in that part, though I have never had the luck to see her in this role. I have approached *Der Rosenkavalier* from the Hofmannsthal libretto, and from my own possibilities, vocally and physically. There exist some letters between Hofmannsthal and Richard Strauss that say that the Marschallin should be thirty-three, thirty-five years old. I hope I can still make that believable. I did it just the other day in San Francisco. Lotte Lehmann came around and brought me a little box with roses to remember this *Rosenkavalier*. I've always been lucky that great artists have always been helping me.

It is very sad when any woman sees that her great love affair is drawing to an end. The Viennese have a feeling that is quite sentimental. I use the word *sentimentality* as something different from *sentiment*. In Salzburg this year, a new production of *Rosenkavalier* was filmed. The actress Elisabeth Bergner was there all the time with Hugo von Hofmannsthal's book. She said, "Hofmannsthal says in his letter on the libretto not to be sentimental. Don't you think you could convey this?" The Marschallin would not be sentimental in the crying sense. I used to end the Marschallin's monologue with just, let us say, a teardrop. Now, after having been talking the thing over with Bergner, I

don't cry anymore. The more one works at it, the more you change it. It grows
with you.

Wasn't your beginning as an oratorio singer?

I started out with everything at once, doing opera, oratorios, lieder, anything.
You have then to be very sure, to know what you do with a given piece. You
cannot just let your voice speak for yourself. Out of necessity and out of
some things which we German-type voices do not possess, like Italian voices,
we have to make do with other things. That perhaps accounts for developing
a sense of style, a sense of acting. I was really fortunate in becoming a lieder
singer, where with each lied you have to find a new color of the voice, a new
expression, a new range. In opera it is necessary as well. But not for the Italian singers, because with a voice like Tebaldi's, they just speak or sing for
themselves. The conductor Josef Krips was quite right in saying that Mozart
comes from heaven. Professor Krips is an old friend of all of us singers because he was the one who after the war really built up the Vienna Opera and
the Ensemble of the Vienna Opera. He rehearsed hours and hours on end
with every one of us. You can still see something which is so marvelous with
him: if a thing goes well, and you can see it in his face, he's enjoying it. For
us, the supreme moment is when we know we've done a good performance.

Wasn't Elvira in Don Giovanni *one of your earliest roles in Salzburg?*

That was also my first role I performed in Covent Garden with Professor
Krips, when we all went with the Vienna Opera for the first outing after the
war. It was in 1947, I believe. I remember the very special occasion when
Richard Tauber, the very famous tenor, asked to sing Ottavio in the performance with the Vienna Ensemble once again. None of us knew that he was
already a dying man at the time. Two days after the performance he went into
the hospital, and four weeks later he was dead. I still have the performance in
my mind when he sang the two Ottavian arias. You know how difficult those
are, the breathing of those coloratura phrases is just excruciatingly difficult to
perform. I have never heard it sung better. We all knew that he had been doing very many light operetta things in his last years and we expected that this
might have been straining his Mozart style, but it had not. There was not one
operatic slur that you do in operetta. He came through in true Mozart style.

Aside from opera and lieder, operettas and folk songs challenge you.

Folk songs are dear to every German and Austrian's heart. We all lived with them. We grew up with them. We have hundreds of folk songs in Germany and Austria that make the holy family into just peasants. Ivogun even gave it to me on the original piece of paper that she used to sing from. I still carry it about with me, and it's in tatters, every poor accompanist has to read it from the little torn paper. But they all get awed when they see the name Maria Ivogun on it. As for operetta, I hardly enjoyed anything as much as recording some of the operettas. It is some of my best singing. And it is not easy to sing operetta well. It has to sound very easy, very conversational, with greater charm than anything else you sing. There is nothing more difficult. You may know it from the great comics. To seem casual is really a very difficult thing.

Lieder is an entirely different medium. In the concert you cannot use anything else but your voice and your face. You paint with a very much finer brush than you ever have to do in an opera. In a lied, you can go down to the very finest threads of pianissimo, which you cannot do on an operatic stage. You have to find so many colors which you never could employ when you have to cut through an orchestra. Poetry comes into it, style. You have to have a feeling for poetry. It happens very often that even in a lied which you sing ten years, twenty years, you suddenly come across a dot, and that dot will alter surely something in the way you express that word. Even though you've sung this one lied time and again, there is always the discovery of some nuance. You are alone with the pianist, who is the true partner, who I always regard as really my other half there. Everything is rehearsed to the last detail. I do not improvise at all on the lieder. Gerald Moore is my favorite accompanist. He is, I should say, my colleague. We have many great pianists, but you have only a handful of great accompanists. Furtwängler played for me, my very first recital in Salzburg. One day he said, "Have you got an accompanist?" "No," I said, "I haven't." "What is it going to be?" I said, "It's all Hugo Wolf." He said, "Would you accept me?" And this great man went to work, all through the first half of the Salzburg Festival, practicing scales. Every time you went past his little castle where he was staying, he was practicing, practicing, practicing, like a beginner. He wasn't easy, but it was wonderful.

When you were a very little girl was it always your idea to sing?

Not to sing, but to make music. I started to learn various instruments when I was quite young. I always sang, naturally, but I always played all kinds of instruments. I learned the piano and the viola, I played chamber music, I played the organ and the guitar, and I even played the timpani. I played all kinds of things. I wouldn't do it now. [Laughs] I'd rather sing.

∾ Diva ∾

ROSA RAISA
1959

Rosa Raisa, a soprano out of a Polish ghetto, was the jewel in the crown of the Opera Company of Chicago during the glory years of the twenties. It was she for whom Puccini wrote the role of Turandot in the opera that he did not finish. After its first performance, shortly after Puccini died, Toscanini lay down his baton and said to the audience: "Here is where the maestro died." And they cut it there. But her roles—Norma especially, as well as Aïda—were as though written for her and were among her great performances.

I was born and raised in Bialystock, Poland, it was then under the Russian government, it went back to Poland after World War I. When I was fourteen, I emigrated to study in Naples at the conservatory with a great teacher, Barbara Marchisio. She was at the time of Adelina Patti and was a wonderful singer herself. She knew Maestro Campanini, and she said, "One day when

Raisa will be ready, I want you to hear her." I remember when I made audition for him in Milano. He was sitting there in front of a big wardrobe with three mirrors. And I, with the tail of my eye, could see the impression I made when I started to sing. He had a habit of touching his nose with the index finger, and he looked in the mirror, and showed his wife how he pleased he was. So he squeezed his nose with satisfaction. The first aria I started—what did I start with? *Casta diva* from *Norma,* one of the most difficult things to sing. Then I sang another aria for him and he said, "That's enough, that's enough." But I said, "Maestro, would you hear me in another aria? I want to sing for you." One from *A Masked Ball,* which I love. So I sang that. I wasn't full age. We just shook hands, and he said, "I engage you for America, for Chicago. Prepare your repertoire that I'm giving you to study for Parma." One of the most difficult cities to sing in. The first opera he suggested was of Verdi. It was understood that when he came back from America, I would make my debut at Verdi's centenary. That was September 1913. Verdi was born in 1813.

I made my debut in the first opera of Verdi, but I was young, I didn't realize how important it was to sing in front of such a difficult public. Madame Campanini said, "I'll come tonight before the opera starts. I'll be there around seven o'clock." [The opera started at nine.] "I'll make you up. I want to meet in the dressing room with you." They told me that eggs are very good for the voice: big eggs, with sugar and marsala wine. I was sitting there and eating the two eggs. All of a sudden, I realized it was about quarter of eight. Madame Campanini went to the dressing room and she didn't find me, so she came as quickly as she could to my home, and there I was, quiet. No sense of responsibility. We went to the dressing room, she made me up, and I was ready. I could hardly wait to go out and sing. There I was in the wings, waiting for my cue. The stage coach was in the wings, and the maestro told him, "Please, you hold on to this one. She's like a young horse. Like a little filly." So he held me by my arm. I just couldn't hardly wait to go out to sing. I didn't feel that it was my debut; I just went out, not conscious. Young, no responsibility, nothing to worry about. I thought, I'll try to do the best I can. After all, they won't kill me. If they like me, that's all right. If they don't, I'll try to do my best, that's all. I did pretty well, I think. In those days, an artist that used to go to America had to be pretty good. So the next day the papers, they're all beautiful articles for the promising young girl we heard last night. And here I am, after all these years.

We used to start our season in Philadelphia. For two weeks. I think those days a season was between eight and ten weeks. There would be a long, long tour to the coast and back. I made my debut here on a Saturday afternoon. It was November 1913, in *Cristoforo Colombo*. Then I sang *Aïda*, Campanini conducting. I opened in Chicago at the Auditorium. In my days, a soprano had to sing everything. I sang *Norma,* and then I would sing *Il Trovatore*. I was trained for it. First my teacher made me study coloratura work, and I hated it. I was a young girl, I didn't know how very important it was to study coloratura work. She made me study *The Barber of Seville,* which wasn't my temperament. I wanted to sing dramatic roles. She said, "My dear child, you probably will never sing *Sonnambula* and *Lucia* and *Barber,* but this will train you for the operas that you will sing, *Norma* and *Trovatore*. It will give you flexibility." She was right. I still bless the memory of Barbara Marchisio. I studied for five consecutive years: three times a week I would study at the conservatory in Naples, and the other three times she would invite me to her home to study. During the summer, I would go to her villa, which was near Venice. And I would take a lesson every single day. I can still remember. It was a beautiful villa with a big arbor with lots of pears and apples and grapes. I would go out in that arbor and pick a pear. It was hard to swallow it in a hurry when she used to call me, "Raisa, come on! Come on and study." And then I would swallow that pear and run. For a whole hour, every day, I would study. She taught me Italian, and she taught me how to live on the stage, how to live like an artist should live. Take care, and not go dancing the night before, or sing in a room full of smoke, or eat something that is not good for the digestion. Or go out . . . Discipline. Live a decent, fine, healthy life, which goes with a healthy career.

When I made my audition for Maestro Campanini of the Chicago Opera, he asked me my name, so I said, "My name is Raisa Burstein." He said, "Raisa Burstein? You'll never become famous in America. That's too long a name. In America, they like short names." So I said, "Maestro, what do you want to call me?" He said, "What does it mean, Raisa?" I said, "It's like *rose* in Italian." "Well, then we'll call you Rosa Raisa." That was really euphonic and quick. When I sent for my father in 1918, right after the first war, I was singing in Chicago. Naturally, the first thing, I called him up and I said he should come out and hear me. He heard me when I was a little girl, and always, since I can remember, I always sang. I would run after all the organ grinders in Bialystock singing with my full voice all over the place. And in the woods, I would go out and sing. I like, in the woods, I liked to hear my voice from a very great distance. The echo. My girlfriends would come with me and yell, "Raisa, sing, sing!" So my father, when he heard Rosa Raisa, he said, "Oh, Raisa, why did you take off that beautiful name, Burstein? It's such a beautiful name." One night in *Otello,* when he saw in the last act how the tenor chokes me to death, he got out of the box, yelling, "Oh, no, no, no, no." I remember another time, in 1921, I was singing *Gioconda* with my husband, Giacomo Rimini. The last act, we had a very dramatic scene. He would pick me up at the very end of the act, whispering a few words, and then he would raise me from the floor. I already lay down there dead. I didn't do like many other actresses—after they die, they get up and they thank the public, and then they die again. So while I was lying there, Rimini raised me, just kept me straight in his hands, the whole body rigid. He would whisper these few words to me, and then he would let me go and I would fall on my back. My father, when he saw that, he just walked out of the box. After the performance, there was my father, sitting on the couch, waiting for me, kind of moody. I thought maybe we gave a bad performance. So at last, I decided to ask: "Papa, how did you like the performance?" He said, "One thing I didn't like, that your husband should let you fall like that and break your neck." I said, "Papa, this is the thing I have to do." He said, "Well, I don't care. You have to do it, you don't do it. Still, he is your husband. He shouldn't throw you to the floor." Right after I finished my first season in Chicago, in 1914, an English impresario engaged me for Covent Garden in London, and I sang there with Caruso in *Aïda* in 1914. I remember he gave me his caricature. I still have it. He wrote: "I wish you the great career which I'm sure you'll have." I sang with him in Cologne and Buenos Aires. Singing with Caruso was, of course, a great thrill for me. Believe me, he was an inspiration. If you gave 100 percent, with Caruso you had to give 200, because he was so great that one had to be good to really sing at his side. I remember, at the beginning he was always nervous. He had to warm up. But what a voice, what a thrilling artist! Oh, it was a joy. His voice would blend, that voice would give you really gooseflesh, and you had to do more. I will remember those performances as long as I live.

In 1924, Toscanini cabled me that he wanted me to create the role in *Nerone* by Arrigo Boito. I was so honored. It was a great event. It was performed after Boito's death, just lying there for twenty-five years, never done. When Boito was on his dying bed, Toscanini promised him he would one day do it. It was a world event. People came from all over to hear that performance. In 1925, I went back and I sang *Trovatore* and *Faust* with Toscanini, and I did *Nerone* again. I remember that during the rehearsals of *Tosca*, Puccini came on the stage. He wanted to listen to the rehearsal. Toscanini said, "Giacomo, I would love to have you to listen to the rehearsal, but I want this to be a surprise to everybody until the final rehearsal. There isn't anybody allowed on the stage." I felt so sorry to see that big man going away. I took him to the back door of La Scala, and I said, "Maestro, I feel so sorry that you can't stay for the rehearsal." He said, "Raisa, I'm writing an opera, and I can just see you and hear you, and I want you to be the one to create it." Then he got sick, he went to Belgium for a very serious operation, and he died. So *Turandot* wasn't finished.

A year later, Toscanini wanted to give that opera at La Scala, and he cabled me—I was on tour with the Chicago Opera Company. Would I be there ready for rehearsals in April? So I cabled back: "As much as I would love to, and as much as I feel honored by your wonderful offer to create *Turandot*, I cannot be released by the company because we are on tour and I won't be free until May." He cabled me that he would wait. The first performance was very sad, I'll never forget it. I was standing there at the end, while Toscanini left the podium, put down his baton, and he turned to the public after the death of Liù, and he said, "And here the maestro died." I can remember the feeling. I just stood there and I could feel the air of grief in the whole theater.

In my days we didn't have radio. Now, life has become much more difficult. Everything is rush, rush, rush. They want it overnight because they want to make money. On television and radio, you don't need that very long, wonderful training. Now, they just know how to whisper a song with the radio, you know, it's amplified. They can do miracles now! If I had in my days a little, what do you call it, tape recorder, how much work it would have saved me. To make a record, you rehearsed with the orchestra. Then you made one record and listened to it, to see whether you liked it or not. Then they would make three masters. By the time one made a record, the artist was exhausted. If the violin wasn't so, or the trumpet wasn't so, we had to repeat ten times the same thing, the *whole* thing ten times. Now you just put in a note if it didn't go with something, and that's done. Now, the young singers have all these possibilities, but I think an artist today, even being musical, even with a beautiful figure, even with talent, needs three to five years of constant study. It is not only the technical work necessary to prepare mentally, physically, emotionally. Today, how many talents have become famous overnight and then died overnight? Overnight sensation, and that's that.

There must be that sense of responsibility. My first *Norma*, my first *Aïda* with Caruso—the next day, even after a triumph, next morning, I would still go back to the piano and would say, "Oh, I can improve that, I can make it better. I can use pianissimo here, or forte there." What artist nowadays does it? After the performance, they take the plane and fly to Alaska. Next it will be to go and sing to the moon. [Laughs]

EDITH MASON
1966

Edith Mason was an American singer when there were few of them, back in the twenties. She was a strong figure in Chicago's opera company, at the time headed by Campanini, and later by Giorgio Polacco, the man she married. Mason was a combination. The voice was described by one of the old opera critics as a light, lucid, sparkly soprano, poised like an angel in flight. Yet when she spoke in conversation she was raffish in nature. Slang words and words not necessarily elegant came forth. She was a very amusing companion as well as a remarkable performer. Her portrayal of Madame Butterfly was especially moving. She once said, "A couple of those times when I was a delicate little Japanese aristocrat, I tipped the beam at about 250 pounds!"

I was born in St. Louis. When I was seventeen years old, I knew I wanted to sing. It was with my grandpa Salisbury down in New Orleans, and I heard some sort of a light opera. I said, "When I get to be a big girl, I'm going to be a singing, acting woman like that one was tonight." My mother said, "Oh, no." You see, she was a college graduate here, and then she went to Zurich, and then she even went to Heidelberg University. But we're not German at all, pure Irish. She wanted me to have a higher education. My mother spoke nine languages fluently and was a professor when she came back, at Iowa State University. She wanted me to go right along with that. I said, "No, I want to be an opera singer." I'd heard Caruso and Farrar.

I sang with him, Caruso. Gatti-Casazza was married to Frances Alda. I had signed a five-year contract with him. I was being paid the magnificent sum of $50 a week. He was paying three women at $350 each a week. Oh, I could say so many things about Gatti. I stepped in because I had to learn about fourteen or fifteen roles, at my expense, that hot summer in New York. I'll never forget. It was the summer of 1916. Anyway, I learned all these different parts. And one of them was the Micaela in *Carmen*. Frances Alda got sick and I went onstage and sang it without any rehearsal. I spoke a little bit of Italian, not much. Farrar was Carmen, and Antonio Scotti was the toreador. So here was I, a little saphead, you know, debutante of the worst kind. And I went on and sang. Caruso was very sweet to me. Our nice little duet in the first act went nicely. He said, "Mason, that first act went very nicely." I shook hands with him and his hands were sweating, just like a faucet had been turned on. I said, "Signor Caruso"—now I'm thinking in Italian again—"is it possible that you're nervous, you're scared?" He said, "Well, certainly, Miss Mason, I am. Those people want me to give 150 percent out there. I can't give 100 percent." After he sang "The Flower Song" [she sings a line or two] so perfectly, he was just like a kid out of boarding school. He was wonderful. Then I, oh, I had an awful row with Gatti. I was a page in *A Masked Ball*. Caruso was in that, too, you know. Gatti said, "Mason, you go upstairs and try on the costume." I said, "Gatti, do you think I'm going to wear those tights like that with my fat thighs? You have another thing coming." He just knew he had to give up, you know. "Well," he says, "go upstairs." I had turquoise blue velvet, a little bloomer effect, with pearls and things, and the jaunty little cap and a little cape. There stood Gatti [she growls] and I kicked my leg at him. [Laughs]

Once Giorgio Polacco and I and Gatti, and that dear Rosina Galli, were on a boat together. Oh, I'd sit up until three in the morning with Gatti. At that time, I spoke fluent Italian, ungrammatical, and said the things I shouldn't. At that time, we'd become friends again, but I had to go over his head to get out of my contract. I had to go to Otto Kahn [banker and funder of the Metropolitan Opera] to let me out. He didn't want to let me go. I wasn't satisfied. Gatti said that I had to sing Musetta in *La Bohème*. I'd learned it, of course, but I didn't want to sing it. I went to Gatti and I said, "I don't want to sing Musetta." "Well," he says, "what do you want to sing?" By that time he knew I was a tough one to handle. [Laughs] I said, "I want to sing Mimi." He says, "Where have you sung Mimi?" I said, "I've never sung it." He said, "Would you pay $50 to a man for the first pair of shoes he's ever made? You wouldn't, would you?" I said, "No, Signor Gatti." "Well, then, that's it." So I went out and there was dear Caruso. And I was crying. Caruso said, "*Cosa c'è?* What is the matter, Mason? Is somebody dead? Why are you crying?" He was so dear, Caruso was. I said, "I didn't want to sing Musetta." He said, "Mason, you can read?" "Yes." "You can write?" "Yes." "You read your contract?" "Yes." "And you signed it?" "Yes." "Then why are you crying?"

Caruso used to come here years ago. And one fine day, *un bel giorno,* eh, he called me on the phone. He had been arrested. He was in jail here. He said, "Mason, for God's sake, come and get me out of jail." I said, "What did you do?" "I didn't do anything, but I was going down on the bus and there was a very charming lady, and I just pinched her fanny a little. And she had me arrested. And I'm in jail." I went down and said to the top man in the jail, "This poor saphead didn't know any better. Let him out this once, but if he ever does it again . . ." I talked in Italian and English both. I said, "You'll stay in jail a thousand years. I'll never come and bail you out again." Oh, he was so darling.

I also knew the bass Virgilio Lazzari. Bless his heart. Do I remember? Do I? We were on the boat once, and I was sitting at the right hand of the captain, at his table. Of course, this was many years ago. And just across from me was this Cesare Formichi, and all of a sudden, these friends of my husband, they're perhaps the top family in Chicago, saw me get up and throw a glass of champagne in this man's face. They said, "Bill Ragland, you're never going to live with that woman if she's got a temper like that." He said, "I'm going to ask what happened." I'll tell you. This Formichi, I'd had plenty of experience with him—I had to have concert tours with him also. He was talking Italian, and he said, "I'm taking away $80,000 from America. They're just a bunch of asses, they don't know anything." The Irish came out and I just got so mad I threw champagne in his face. I always am and will be. One friend of mine last year said, "Are you still as energetic?" I said, "Yes, I guess so." She says, "You know, I think that when you're dead, you'll kick the slats out of your coffin." [Laughs] I was so infuriated at that Formichi.

I wanted to go back to Europe to study. Gatti said, "That's the trouble. You Americans have a little bit of success and it goes to your head and you get swell-headed." I said, "It isn't the case. I want to go back to Europe and study some more and have some more experience." I had to go over his head to get me out.

The first voice lessons I ever had in my life were in Paris. I was working with Edmond Clément. Do you remember that delightful, small, lovely voice? I was coaching Manon with him when they asked me to sing it at the Comique. I studied, heavens, with twenty-five different voice teachers. I'll never forget my debut at the Met, *Der Rosenkavalier*. I was Sophie on a Saturday matinee. A man called me on the phone and he says, "How much are you going to pay the claque?" I said, "What is the claque?" My mother was going to be there that day, too, bless her heart. He says, "Well, it's the people that clap for you." "Well," I said, "this is the day for me to find out if there's anything worth clapping for. I won't pay one penny." And I never did. And dear Charlie Hackett, the tenor, bless his heart. I sang a lot of performances with him. We decided, this claque, you know, we'd give them $10 each, see. So I said, "Go on, Charlie, now you go out and get your ten bucks' worth." [Laughs] That's a business, I suppose, like anything else. But I can't see it. Sour apples, really. [Laughs]

Toscanini heard me over the air, when we used to sing in the Auditorium, these Saturday night broadcasts. He wrote me a letter and he asked me if I'd sing Mimi. They hadn't done it for many, many years at La Scala. I was thrilled to death. When I got to New York, I got the best *répétiteur,* that's a pianist. We rehearsed for about two months, day and night. They didn't like my costumes, and they sat up all night making new costumes. At the last minute, Toscanini couldn't conduct. He was having trouble with his eyes. I went to his office at La Scala, imagine, and he said, "If I die tomorrow, will everybody stop singing?" "Well," he says, "you go back home and think it over and come tomorrow." The La Scala dressing room for the prima donna has a beautiful little drawing room, a large dressing room, and a full bathroom. And he was there. When I came on the stage, just all this joy was gone because it was not Toscanini. Who should be there backstage, beating the tempo for me, but dear Maestro Toscanini, with a black bandage around his eyes, and he had this little wide-brimmed black hat on. He would stay in my drawing room while I was changing my clothes. At the end—don't think it's swell-headed because it's not—I had a lot of acquaintances and a few friends who'd come to speak to me afterwards. It was at least three-quarters of an hour after the opera was over. I walked on the stage and there was one light, and there was Toscanini, Carla, Wanda, and the son. He started applause for me. I was just so thrilled.

Toscanini had rehearsed Gounod's *Faust* forever. He sent for me and he says, "I just want to hear what you do at the end of the 'Jewel Song.'" I did it exactly the way it's written, and that was all right. Then he asked me to sing Nannetta in Verdi's *Falstaff* at Salzburg, many years ago. I remember, Angelo Minghetti was the tenor. In the first act, there's that kiss [big smacking kissing sounds], one side and the other. Poor Minghetti couldn't get it like it should be. So Toscanini was so infuriated, he gave the baton to the hand of his first violinist. He said, "You conduct." He came up on the stage and showed poor Minghetti, mwah, mwah, on each side, a sandwich, as you say, kiss. A year ago last summer, we were back in Salzburg to hear some opera. One evening he was so pleased, Maestro was. He came out for curtain calls. He was in the same hotel as I was. He said, "Edita, will you come and have supper with me after the opera?" They start late, you know. I said, "Yes, Maestro, if you've got plenty of money, because I'm hungry. I can't sing on a full stomach, and it's going to cost you money." So he let me have everything from soup to nuts, and he didn't eat much. But he loves his champagne. I drank a little champagne; I never cared for that. They were dancing in this place, the finest hotel there in Salzburg. It wasn't this awful music that we have now, naturally. He sat there, didn't say anything. I didn't say anything. The man who was the headwaiter then, now he's practically the head of that hotel, he said, "I was there that night that you dined with Toscanini and you didn't say a word." Because at the end, Maestro said, "*È ora di andare a riposare*—it's time to go and rest." So he took me to the elevator and kissed my hand and thanked me for a beautiful evening. But complete silence—can you imagine that? He was the headwaiter then, now he's practically the manager.

Wow, I'll tell you something else. Carla and Toscanini, he was to conduct in Bologna, a big concert. This was under fascism. And they wanted him. There were three cars of us that drove from Milano to Bologna, and they wanted him to do that little "Giovinezza," the fascist anthem. And he wouldn't. When we drove up in our cars, this group of young men asked him if he was going to do that fascistic hymn. He said no. And one of them hauled off and was going to hit him in the face and instead hit Toscanini's younger daughter, Wanda, and knocked two front teeth out of her. Then the mayor of Bologna came and he said, "My dear, your friends, I cannot guarantee that you will not be killed. Now you have to go back to Milan." So he went back. He was a man of such character and strength, and such a seriousness of purpose.

I'll tell you who's somebody that I'm crazy about, haven't heard her lately, and that is Maria Callas. I met her many years ago when I first heard her in

Verona. She was very fat. She was the greatest phenomenon that ever lived, Callas. She sang coloratura superbly; lyric soprano, perfectly; dramatic soprano, magnificently. She's such an actress. She could do a Greek tragedy, you know. One night—oh, I must tell you this, this is true. I got off the boat, that's years ago, and I had a brown suit, tailor-made, made in Italy. There were about eight telephone calls from Francis Robinson saying that we should come immediately to the Metropolitan. Callas wanted to see me. It was *Norma*, it was after the first act. After the second act, he took us backstage. Callas was in the dressing room with a doctor. Francis said, "Edith Mason is here," because I'd known her. She's just plain Brooklyn, you know, the way she speaks. She says, "Oh, Edith, did you hear what I did at the end of the *Casta diva*? Did you *hear* that?" I said, "No, Maria, I was not there. We were out to dinner. We came the minute we got back." She said, "What's wrong with me?" I said, "I don't see anything wrong with you, but I'm going to tell you something. I've nearly *died* of the heat here tonight. It's so hot. All these fat dowagers with the blooms out and all the squillions of diamonds and rubies and emeralds." I told her that many years ago here Chaliapin used to be in our company, the great Chaliapin. Early one morning, he was going to give a recital at the Blackstone. He got in there, it must have been eighty or ninety. No singer can sing that way. He made them open all the windows and shut off the heat and put wet bath towels and everything. And he said to the public, "Now you can get out if you want to. You want me to sing, I'll be delighted." Because that dries the vocal cords, you see, and that was what was the matter with the Metropolitan that night.

Chaliapin was wonderful. He did *Boris Godunov*, and I sang *Mefistofele* with him in it. He would stage it too, you know. It was at the time when we had Prohibition. We had two trains, that was the good old days. He had his chef and he had his butler and he had his dresser, I don't know, half a dozen. He wanted to have his drink. So he'd have somebody go around in every town and get this bathtub gin or whatever it was. A temperamental person.

Now I'm going to tell you another one, it's the cutest thing. I sang in the Opéra Comique. The maid brought me in a calling card, I think I have it someplace in one of these seventy-five trunks. Monsieur Leduc, something-or-other, wanted to see me. Here's Monsieur Leduc and he said, "Madame Mason, I want to help you tonight." "Why, that's wonderful," I said. "God knows I need it." He said, "Now I have this opera glass, and I have a seat in the back, in the middle of the opera house. Now, I push this button, that's a red light, that means you're sharp. Now, on the other side, I'll push a green light, it means you're flat. When I push the middle button, it's white, and that means you're on the pitch. Now [in French] you can depend upon me and have no worry." Imagine. [Laughs] I look at the maestro and think about what I'm doing and hope for the best. He wasn't in a box, he was right in the middle of the house. I asked some of the other singers there, "What do you do?" And they said, "He was a *grand seigneur,* but he lost all his money." He must have been eighty. "You can't give him money, but you can put something in an envelope." The last performance he came to, he said, "Oh, you never sang off pitch once, it's all based on my opera glass." I gave him the envelope and said, "Here's a note from me and my appreciation of your great help." I didn't see his light at all.

❧ **American-Born** ❧

MARIAN ANDERSON
1961, 1966

Toscanini once said of Marian Anderson: "A voice like yours is heard only once in a hundred years." Ironically, most of us remember her best for being banned by the Daughters of the American Revolution from singing at Constitution Hall in Washington, D.C., in 1939. Because of Eleanor Roosevelt, who then resigned from the D.A.R., and others, she did sing at the Lincoln Memorial, and it was a magnificent, memorable experience, with seventy-five thousand people in attendance. She was the first African American singer to ever appear at the Metropolitan Opera, on January 7, 1955, in the role of Ulrica, the fortune-teller, in A Masked Ball, and that was long after her prime: she was fifty-eight, but received standing ovations for her performance.

Probably for as long as I can remember, music was important to me. That was a long, long time ago. My sisters and I had little chairs, children's chairs.

I remember my chair, which had a lid on the back which you'd flip over the top, and the food was put in front of one there. Very often the spoon would come out of the food and be banged on the table and we would sing at the top of our voices any tune which came into our minds. It didn't have to be something that was really melodic, just a noise probably, but hoping that it was a song. Later on, when we'd graduated from that stage, one would sit on a stool and play on the table with one's hands or with one's fingers, and then actually make up little tunes. When we were six years old, we were taken to the children's choir with my aunt. There we got an actual opportunity to sing with other little girls and boys, and not only just the melody but sometimes an accompaniment to a melody, and that would be probably two or three voices, maybe more, in a small chorus. A little quartet, a duet, anything.

In the Union Baptist Church, of which I was a member, every Sunday morning a part of their service was the singing of a Negro spiritual. And then in high school, the Negro girls very often sang Negro spirituals. And I was very interested, several years after we left school, to discover that the head of the music department, who was the one who was there when I was in school, came one day to call and wanted to know why the girls in school now were not interested in singing the Negro spirituals. But that is another thing. They are far removed from it. Like my aunt, too. I don't know that she looked down upon it, but whenever we started with Negro spirituals she said, "Can't you find something else to sing?" Now, my aunt Mary was a person who loved music, but this was an association with a time which was very unpleasant. The richness of it and all of that did not make a great deal of difference to her. There were other aspects of it that overshadowed any beauty there might be.

When did you discover that it was singing you wanted to do most?

As a matter of fact, I think we knew this a long, long time ago, before we ever sang in public, really. We sang with the children's choir at the Union Baptist Church, and it so happens that with this chorus we had a great opportunity because they became quite good, and we sang not only at the church but even outside of the city. When the distances were too great they didn't send the whole group, they sent a representative or two, and we happened to be one of that group. We were there every Sunday for the children's choir, for the Sunday school, and the fourth Sunday in every month, I believe it was, the children's choir sang. And then at thirteen or fourteen, my aunt took me with her to the senior choir and there, of course, one had the greater opportunity, really one's greatest opportunity up to that time, because the conductor was good enough to let us take the music home and we learned everybody's parts. And if there were special visitors at the church and the soprano wasn't there, he'd simply give me a call, or beckon to me, and point to the soprano's seat, and oh, I would be as happy as could be, and without any inhibitions would go along with as many high C's as they wanted to put out. It was a wonderful time, really.

I knew that singing was going to be my life when I was in fourth grade, where music was first taught to the students in the school. When we reached the third grade, we all sat next door to the fourth-grade classroom. I heard absolutely nothing in the room in which I sat, because my mind and my ears were in the other room. So came the day when we reached the fourth grade and we had our first singing lesson. Came also the day when the song that I liked most was given to us to sing. I just threw my head back and began to sing, "Sleep, Polly, Sleep." This was what I heard through the walls of the fourth-grade class of the year before. Pretty soon, there was a tap on my shoulder by the teacher, and she said, "What are you singing? Look at the blackboard." There were the words, "Peacefully sleep. Sleep, Polly, sleep." It was that little story which I remembered so well because I had waited so long to get into the fourth grade, where we might be able to sing "Sleep, Polly, Sleep." When I was a very young person in Philadelphia, Roland Hayes came to our church to sing. It was the first time I had ever heard anyone sing a group of German songs. At that time his program consisted of a group of Italian classics, German lieder, French and English art songs, and then Negro spirituals. It astonished me a great deal, what he was doing, and had the most profound influence on my life.

In 1955 you were onstage at the Metropolitan Opera. Your mother was in the box. Do you recall that moment?

Vividly. Mama had looked forward so many years to this time when I might appear with a regular company at the Metropolitan Opera House. And Mother, who was not a demonstrative person, that night had a glow around her that cannot be described. And as the family was there and a lot of people who shared one's dream, there was an electricity in the house that few escaped. The orchestra started up, and there was a thump/lump in one's heart that came straight up to the throat and made singing very difficult. But it was the realization of a dream. We had hoped that it might have been earlier, but it did come. And this is an experience that will always remain with me as one of the greatest moments in my life.

Toscanini heard you when you made your debut at Salzburg with Lotte Lehmann.

As a matter of fact, one had read a lot about Toscanini, but one had not seen him ever. And we knew beforehand that he was going to be at the performance, and of course, that doesn't make one so easy. And when it was over a woman brought Toscanini backstage. By the time he got back there, I was just about speechless. I know that he said something, but if anyone said to me, "Your life depends on these few words which he has said to you. What did he say?" I would not have been able to tell them. But it was a great thing that he did come, a great honor to us.

You were in Bangkok and you performed before some schoolchildren there.

In preparation for our visit, one or two of the Americans there had acquainted the children with the Negro spirituals, which comprise a part of every program that we give. And the children had rehearsed these for quite some time, I understand. On the morning that we went there, there was a lesson on the board and they were telling them the meanings of the words. Later, when they took their seats, they were very delighted to begin singing Negro spirituals. They had a feeling for them, which had been translated to them by their teachers. But probably even more than having heard them sing spirituals was the feeling that we got from them when they came outside. This was very unrehearsed. We sat in the car, about ready to leave, and these children who had stoic faces for the whole time that we were there, which was probably an hour and a half, came out and stood by the car, and the first one put her hand just across my fingernails. Then there was another hand up to maybe the knuckles, then another, until there were hands all the way up to my shoulder, and some girls were leaning almost into the car, and they looked at each other in astonishment and then there was laughter. I had never seen that happen before, and don't expect to see it again because there wasn't a single one of them who gave you the impression at all that there could ever be a smile on their faces. Now, so far as audiences were concerned over there, of the numbers that we did on the program, I think it was the spirituals they probably liked most of all, and particularly "He's Got the Whole World in His Hands." It was that spiritual that we needed to repeat without exception everywhere that we performed it.

Awareness is very important in any and everything we do. There happens to be sometimes a period of awareness in children, or lack of awareness in children, which will permit a person to play the piano in a fashion which, after they learn certain rules and regulations, she'll feel certain fingers don't belong on certain notes in relationship to other notes that she has to do. And when she doesn't know this, the finger works, but the minute that she knows it shouldn't be there, that same finger feels that it's committing a crime to act in the way that it had before. The understanding as well as the natural art must be there, too.

I think there are a lot of things we learn when we're younger that whet the appetite for wanting to know more about the thing that we've become rather interested in. If you have a basis upon which to build a good structure, it is very good. The raw talent today, which is in sore need of being developed, may in some instances never be developed. These people will, in order to live, have to make a second choice. Which means that you're not getting 100 percent out of the individual. Regardless of what happens to us, we find ourselves in need of making a living, and if one cannot get it at the thing that she most desires, she tries to take something else which is not too objectionable to her. Whether or not we will ever see the day when the people who have something to offer may also find the opportunity to have it developed, it would be a wonderful thing. It is a great task.

RICHARD TUCKER
1962

Richard Tucker, one of the most highly regarded of American tenors, was often taken to be Italian-born and -raised. In fact, he was a singer of cantorials at various synagogues, especially in Brooklyn, where he was raised. It was his debut in Chicago during the fifties in Lucia di Lammermoor *when he set the house afire. "Richard Tucker is an American, and yet he's the finest Italian tenor of our day." So wrote Howard Taubman, music critic of the* New York Times.

My training as a boy began in the synagogue choir, at the ripe old age of eighteen. I was very, very much in a hurry to get going. Although singing as a cantor until the age of twenty-one, I began my vocal studies seriously with Paul Althaus, the former Wagnerian tenor. He had a lot to do with my career. Although he was a Wagnerian singer, he never allowed me to take a German word into my throat at that stage. Originally Althaus was a lyric Italian tenor. It was just fate that changed Paul Althaus from a lyric tenor into a Wagnerian tenor. Because there was a tenor who was alive at that time called Caruso, Paul had no chance. So Giulio Gatti-Casazza, who at that time was general manager of the Metropolitan Opera, asked Paul how long it would take him to study the role of Lohengrin. Fate turned him from an Italian-wing tenor into a German-wing tenor. Not only did I never see Enrico Caruso, which I regret, but I never attended an opera in my life until I met my wife. We used to attend the Sunday evening concerts at the Metropolitan. This was my introduction. Of course, I heard the great singers on records. I have a great feeling for the Italian language and Italian opera. How come a nice Jewish boy like me should remember the great Italian tenor? When I was invited to Verona by the Italian government to come and sing, I was the first American to appear there right after the world war, 1947. Coincidentally, this is the place where Maria Callas made her debut with me. At that time she weighed 240 pounds. I had to hold her up for about two acts, the third and fourth, because she wrenched her ankle. But she was an eager beaver, so to speak, and young and very, very inexperienced.

The officials of Verona were very much concerned how an American would sing or speak Italian. The first-act rehearsal went by, where I didn't utter many notes. You must realize this is an arena that seats twenty-five thousand people. So they whispered to Tullio Serafin, who was the conductor, would he please ask me to please sing in full voice the second act of *La Gioconda*—I made my debut there in that opera. I complied with his wishes. When I got through singing the aria *Cielo e mar*, they all rushed on the stage and started to embrace me in the French and Italian way, with kisses on both cheeks, and everyone asking me, "Mr. Tucker, where did you learn such perfect Italian?" I said, "In Brooklyn." They said, *"Non possibile*. It isn't possible. Were any Italians living in Brooklyn?" I said, "Of course, there are Italians living in Brooklyn, but I only mention it as a jest because I was born in Brooklyn." Ever since then, this is how my name was referred to with respect. I've just returned from Italy. But for the past two summers, I used to sing at the Teatro Colón, in Buenos Aires, and there you really have to be on your toes because this is the greatest theater in South America.

Following your Veronese debut [1945], the Chicago music critic Claudia Cassidy says they lit candles for you, and said, "At this rate they'll be lighting bonfires." They gave you a triple-forte hurrah.

Well, I think it was because, number one, they enjoyed my rendition of the great aria *Cielo e mar* from *La Gioconda*; number two, because I was an American who just came over right after the war; and number three was because people knew I wasn't a prima donna, and they loved that. To show their appreciation, they lit little candles, like birthday candles. And when I finished my aria, you can imagine how I felt looking out into this vast audience, seeing twenty-five thousand candles. I thought I was at the gates of heaven. They were hollering the word *bis,* b-i-s, which means "encore." I thought they were hollering "beast." But when I saw the smile on Maestro Serafin's face I understood immediately that this was a great success, and he motioned for me to repeat the aria.

At the time of your first audition at the Met you were known as a rising young cantor. I heard that there were only a few people in the house.

There were perhaps four or five people sitting out there in the great opera house. It was very dark and I didn't see them. They always say that at an audition you either make it or you don't. I sang in the Metropolitan Auditions on the Air in 1944 and was practically guaranteed I was going to win because there was no one around to give me any competition. As fate would have it, I did not win, only the consolation prize. Right after my audition, I was ushered into the office of Edward Johnson [the tenor who became the Met's artistic director], and I met the man who was responsible for my debut, the conductor Emil Cooper. So I owe him a great deal. He taught me the rules, so to speak, of becoming an opera singer, the life of an opera singer. And Edward Johnson kept an eye on me and he said that with the proper study I couldn't miss. So you see, the old saying: quality never goes under. Somewhere, sometime it will rise. When I auditioned in the great 8H studio of NBC for Maestro Toscanini for the first telecast of *Aïda*, as Radames, I had never sung *Aïda*. I said to the maestro, "I never sang the opera. Do you mind if I read it from music?" He says, "No, go right ahead." After I had sung *Celeste Aïda*, he said to me, "Why don't you sing *Aïda*, you sing *La Gioconda* so well." I said, "Maestro, I didn't know that you listen to the radio." So it shows you that somebody always listens to you.

I can talk about Maestro Toscanini for days. He was really a great man to be around. I sat there at the rehearsals just as a student would, with my feet on the floor, so to speak, with chin up, practically drinking down every word he would utter. So he really taught me a great deal about this opera. There was not much humor. It was more work than anything else. Because when I used to visit him on his little island in Italy, he would always mention to me, in his harsh voice [he imitates, sounding a bit like Marlon Brando in *The Godfather*], "Tucker, you are really good." [Laughs] I really admired him, of course, as everybody else did. There was no two ways about it.

Rodolfo in *La Bohème* is one of my favorite roles. I think anyone would be amiss who doesn't enjoy *Che gelida manina*. This coming season with Lyric Opera, I shall have the privilege to sing with Miss Renata Tebaldi, one of my so-called soprano sweethearts. I really love the dramatic dynamics of Verdi, especially the aria from *A Masked Ball,* the *Ma se m'è forza perderti*. I remember singing it with the great European conductor Fritz Busch in Dresden. I remember during rehearsals one day, he told my coach to make sure that I sang properly the sixteenth and eighth notes, not thirty-seconds, when I sing *È scherzo, od è follia*, after the witch tells me that I'm going to die. After I had rendered this beautiful aria in the performance, and when the applause was really overwhelming, Busch turned to the orchestra and raised up his right hand and touched his heart, meaning that I sang it with so much heart, and I really deserved it, and I never forgot that.

At the age of six, I was led by the ear like all boys go, by their fathers, into the synagogue to become a boy soloist. I sang on the East Side of New York. I sang with a cantor for fourteen years until my voice matured and I had to stop. I started out again at the age of seventeen and a half to study as a cantor, and did so for a period of years before assuming my serious studies for the opera. I never gave up singing as a cantor because the love of liturgical music is in my heart and I guess it will always continue as long as God gives us all years and health. I have always refused engagements throughout the world that occurred during the High Holy Days, or on the Passover. This is because of the upbringing that I've had, to be together with my family, my wife and three sons. I am very happy and thankful that people respect my wishes and are desirous always of hearing me chant, not only in the synagogues, but come to hear me in the opera as well. I have gained many friends here in the Chicago area and of course throughout the country. They have followed me, even east, where I chanted for the past seven years at one of the most luxurious hotels in the Catskills.

What is the difference between training for a cantor and training for the opera? There's a very simple answer. The voice has to be trained, regardless of the language. What's the difference if we sing Italian, Hebrew, Greek, or Latin? The position of the voice is always the same. It's a question where to put the vowel. Even though I was studying to be a cantor, my teacher, Paul Althaus, always stressed that even to be a cantor, you have to have a great voice. As fate would have it, studying for the cantorate prepared me for the operatic field. Let's take, for instance, the composer Rossini. Where did Rossini get all the cadenzas? He couldn't get them out of the air. Or even Verdi. All these composers grasped something from the church, synagogue, liturgical music. The study, the preparation is the same. Of course, it has to do a lot with temperament. But that's secondary because you learn temperament when you learn the meanings of the words. Unfortunately a lot of our singers today don't study the meanings of the words and have no way to bring out the characterization. You meet it in every generation: the singers are too in a hurry to get there. You cannot become a great Carmen without suffering. You don't hear greatness from a person of twenty-four; you don't hear greatness of a young woman at twenty-one. Everybody wants to become a Deanna

Durbin [a star movie singer during the 1930s and 1940s] or a Caruso at twenty-four. It's impossible because nature has built us so that you cannot attain success and greatness till thirty-five.

CATHERINE MALFITANO
1992

Of our contemporary operatic sopranos, it is Catherine Malfitano who may be the most daring. Tosca is one of her perennials, but she can do La Bohème as well. Her deepest interest, however, is in the more adventurous roles, such as Alban Berg's Lulu, and playing roles in the new operas of William Bolcom, whether it be in McTeague, A View from the Bridge, or A Wedding, or Marc Blitzstein's Regina, adapted from Lillian Hellman's The Little Foxes. Malfitano is attracted mostly to those roles that draw upon her depths as a performer, and in so many aspects the subject of death is there, in how one faces it, in how one regards it. It is this aspect of it that Malfitano dares to confront. To watch her perform is to see a singing actress in the tradition, some might say, of Mary Garden, the mezzosoprano and, for a time, the artistic director of the Chicago Opera Company back in the twenties.

Some call you a great acting singer and others call you an actress who sings. How did this all come about?

Good genes, good family, good background. Growing up in New York. Many things went into it. Much of it is a mystery, remains a mystery, even to myself. I've searched and searched through many, many, many roles in these twenty-seven years of singing professionally, to find the real Catherine Malfitano. I find her in bits and pieces in every role that I play. There are so many people inside me. I live for art and I live for love, yes. I think they're one and the same—art and passion, art and love are one and the same. This is my search. It's probably the search of all artists to find deep spiritual understanding of the universe through art. Tosca is deeply spiritual, deeply religious. Even though I don't have Tosca's religion, I try to find meaning in my art and in my life with equal passion. Remember, when she stabs Scarpia, she puts the cross on his breast. But above all, life and art are fused.

Back to beginnings . . .

My father was a violinist with the Metropolitan Opera Company in New York. My mother was a ballet dancer. She was also an actress early in her life in Hollywood. My father gave solo recitals. So I experienced this unbelievably rich life in New York with them. I was at the Metropolitan Opera all the time as a child. I was in the dressing room with my mother when she was a dancer with American Ballet Theater. She worked with Nora Kaye, with Anthony Tudor, all these great people. She married very young, she was eighteen. They said that she betrayed her destiny because she was meant to become a great soloist. But she fell in love with the man who was the concertmaster. Growing up at the opera house, I heard a lot of singers. Unfortunately, I didn't see Callas. But, oh, Tebaldi moved me tremendously. I was a very critical young child, I have to say. Even though the music moved me tremendously and I *loved* the singing, I was highly critical. I didn't believe what I saw onstage. Something was missing. For years I was singled out for my voice, but I never thought about it seriously because something was missing for me. I was moved by ballet, I fell in love with ballet dancers. My mother had the dancer's eye. She taught me to see dance, to feel the emotion of dance. Because I started to feel music as a dancer, it became a part of my body. I sang my first Salome in 1990. I totally understand Salome and her monstrous act. You have to understand people who are driven to awful acts in their lives, I mean even serial killers. There is always a story behind this monstrosity and there is a place where we can find compassion. So I developed a great compassion for Salome. Through playing Salome, I've learned that human beings do awful things usually because there is something awful in their background. When I approached Salome, it frightened me tremendously. How do I get inside the skin of this woman? The minute I got inside, I started to see what she was about. She's beautiful inside. She's poetic inside. She's searching for a love that she never had. She's trying to appease a huge hunger that is besieging her whole existence. When you come at her from that angle, that this is a love-starved teenager who's misunderstood, who's not loved, you start to put the pieces together. You realize that she is not a monster. This is about a great catastrophe, a family catastrophe, a dysfunction of the family.

With that it became a search for meaning, this desire to possess Jokanaan, the prophet. It is not so much about her sexuality, but more about finding love from another human being.

My four-year-old daughter and my husband were at a rehearsal when I was doing my first Salome in 1990. We were unsure whether we even wanted her to see this opera, but then thought why not? It's a story, after all, and there are many horrific fairy tales that we tell our children. This is a fairy tale and there are many symbols in there, and children get it. Even when they're frightened, children get the symbolic meanings. When I was rehearsing the scene with the head, my husband turned to Daphne and said, "What do you think about this? Is this right or wrong?" She said, "Oh, no, it's not wrong. She loves Jokanaan, and besides, she doesn't know he's dead." I thought to myself, God bless her, this is the key for me: the disassociation in Salome, this poor young teenager who doesn't really put two and two together, doesn't put a decapitated head together with the knowledge she's killed this man. There are moments in the monologue when she goes quickly into a very romantic space, a kind of spiritual space.

After my first performance as Salome, I received a letter from Ljuba Welitsch, the Bulgarian singer, the great Salome of her day. She was in Berlin. She saw me on television. I was *stunned* when I saw [the name] Ljuba Welitsch on the back of the envelope. I opened it and it said in German: "You are the greatest Salome I have ever seen. Give yourself to the people and you will get much in return." So I wrote back to her and said, "Thank you for this wonderful, wonderful letter that I will treasure for the rest of my life. I don't know how you can say that when I feel that *you* are the greatest Salome that I've ever known. I'm going to Vienna in a few months. May I come to visit you?" She wrote back and said yes. So when I arrived in Vienna, I called her on the phone, set up an exact appointment with her. She said again on the phone, "You are the greatest Salome I have ever seen." I came to the door, she opened it with great flair, I handed her some flowers, and she said, "Catherine, you are the greatest Salome I have ever seen . . . after me." [Laughs]

Now the dance. In some cases, Salome disrobes entirely.

Well, I did that the first time. That's on the video. It has this sticker on it with "Beware of . . ." What does it say? In true American fashion, beware of nudity and violence. [Laughs] We, of course, don't know anything about violence.

My father was really my teacher early on. He took me in hand at a point when he felt that I was not getting enough training at the university, where teachers really only have one hour per week to work with a student. So he decided to teach me the Garcia-type method of working. Manuel Garcia was a great voice teacher of the last century, and he trained his students on a daily basis for years. My father also worked with me for two or three hours every day for about three years in order to give me a foundation in technique, but beyond that, to give me an incredible foundation in interpretation, in expression. We even had exercises in expression, as actors do. Picking up a telephone book and trying to express anything you're reading with a certain kind of expression, with an ecstatic feeling, with a sad feeling. We also did recitals together. We looked for music that was just for voice and violin. Then we made a recording in 1973, and this was really the beginning of my career. This recording is, for me, a kind of love poem with my father. It expresses the wonderful relationship we had, musically and personally. I think there are feelings that could not be expressed in words but could be expressed beautifully in our music making together. It was a heightened language.

I think my crazy, wonderful family gave me this unbelievable sense of daring and confidence. It's just something inside of me. I really discovered it through working on Leoš Janáček's *The Makropulos Case*. That's an opera that has the strongest spiritual message of all operas: enjoy the life you're given. Life means something because death is so close. It is about this woman who lives to be 337 years old. She doesn't choose to, she's forced to. That's why risk is so important in my life, although I don't think of it as risk in a wanton, unprepared way. It is risk with discipline. That's very important. It is to have that sense of adventure and risk in life, which I think is something we all need to do, whatever we do. I do it with singing and acting, and I do it in my relationships, too. I think that one has to always have the sense that death is right next to you. I've made a friend of death all through my life, and it started when I was about eighteen. Actually, it started with the first kiss of the first man I fell in love with, because I thought I would *die*—I thought I could die on that first kiss. It was the beginning of my relationship to death that has been really wonderful because it has made me aware that death is obviously going to be my final destination, and until that moment I want to taste every aspect of life that I possibly can. I found my credo in that opera. People always ask, "Which is your favorite opera?" I've always said I could not be unfaithful to all my loves, so I can never choose. Now I would say, at this point in my life, that I've come to realize that the message inherent in *The Makropulos Case* is the message I have in my real life.

It is your attraction to amoral heroines that interests me. Your Lulu in Alban Berg's opera was a real knockout at Lyric Opera.

The amorality has *nothing* to do with it. Lulu is a kind of pure individual who is simply what she is. I see now how much I love this character because I often say about myself as an artist that my task is to be a vehicle for the audience to travel through, to journey through, and to be able to experience all of humanity and all of the emotions that humanity is capable of. I'm a mirror and I reflect back to the audience elements of themselves and experiences of the human condition. Lulu does that, too: throughout the whole opera she's this incredible mirror. They attack her for being this or that, but they are really only seeing themselves through her. For me, she is also another abused young child. She doesn't create anything, she just *is*; she's absolutely pure and untainted. Others taint her.

Which brings us back to William Bolcom's McTeague *and you as Trina. Your love scene with those gold coins is so horrifying and fantastic—only you could do it so well.*

[Laughs] What does that say about me? What does that say about me? I don't know. Trina was a real challenge. I can't tell you how I used to feel at the end of those performances. Normally I feel very uplifted by almost any character I play, whether it's Lulu, who goes through unbelievable stuff—after all, she's murdered by Jack the Ripper at the end. But I still felt uplifted by Lulu. Salome, after having this man decapitated and singing to that head, I felt uplifted afterward. After *McTeague*, I could not feel uplifted. There is nothing uplifting in the act of loving an inanimate object, especially when it's money. It's kind of akin to Jenny at the end of Brecht-Weill's *Mahagonny*. There's something empty in that emotional experience of being so in love with money or fearful of being in love with others. Trina is the embodiment of this kind of avarice. To have a scene where you can be in bed with all your golden coins and just let them fall all over your body like the gentlest caress of a lover is frightening beyond belief. She's alone in her room. She's no longer living with McTeague, and she's now just a mere cleaning woman. This is a woman with $5,000 who could have invested it and been doing pretty well in her life. But she chooses to save and hoard that money as if it's the mother lode; it's her lover, never to be touched. She takes this money out, she puts it on her bed. She forgets all about her exhaustion, her pain, her cares as she gives herself over to the magic of the sound of her golden babies. McTeague comes back; he crashes through that window. We hear the fabulous sounds of the money, the crash of the window, the twisting of her neck, and then his scurrying out over the glass on the floor. He takes the money with him. She's dead, her life lacked all meaning.

What a contrast to Trina, Lulu, Salome, and Jenny is your Madame But-terfly, Cio-Cio-San. Hers is the moral strength that defies convention.

The key to this woman is her willingness to turn her back on her society, to change her religion, to risk being ostracized. Not many women could do that in her time. She holds this strength for years, believing her Western lover will come back, believing in his goodness. When that's all shattered, what is her choice? She offers her child up to what she believes would be a better life. She has no money, she has no friend except for Suzuki, her maid, and no chance to survive. It's hard to understand because of our Western way of thinking. I had a lot of exposure to Japanese culture in my childhood through my parents again. One has to love these other cultures. We may not under-stand them, but we have to go inside them to try to see what is miraculous and unique. We say Cio-Cio-San's a stupid woman; she should just take the child and go off somewhere else. Where should she go? She has nothing, ab-solutely nothing. I love to get into characters who must find their strength in the worst of situations.

∾ The Instrument ∾

ANDRÉS SEGOVIA
1978

It is the morning before his Sunday afternoon concert at Chicago's Or-chestra Hall. It is, as always, sold out. The guitar had, ever since antiq-uity, been regarded as a folk instrument, nothing more. It was Segovia who single-handedly brought it into the world of classical music. He is the nonpareil of classical guitar artists: the maestro. An air of bonhomie pervaded our talk; he was in a whimsical mood. During our casual warm-up conversation, there was an allusion to Vladimir de Pachmann, the ec-centric piano virtuoso, celebrated at the turn of the century.

I knew de Pachmann in Rome. He was very funny. He was more popular for what he did during a concert than for his playing. Once there was a lady sit-ting in the first row. She was fanning herself very quietly in two movements, like this. [He demonstrates] De Pachmann lifted himself from his stool and approached the lady. He shook his finger at her. "Madam, you are fanning yourself in two tempi, and I am playing in three. That is absolutely impossible. Stop it!" He would frequently talk to the audience during his concert—most often to chastise them. At times, when he didn't play well, he struck at his left hand to punish it.

Wasn't Fernando Sor one of the very few—before your time—who composed for the guitar?

Fernando Sor was the best, to my knowledge, for the well-being of the classical guitar, because he was in London a long time and was better known. One of the great French critics called him the Beethoven of the guitar. I think that is a little exaggerated. The quality of Sor's music was noble, but he was no Beethoven. Francisco Tarrega was a great master. I did not know him. He died when I was fifteen years old. He could not give the guitar the popularity it deserved because he very seldom gave concerts. He played for a gathering of friends, and each gave him a little money.

With so limited a repertoire for the guitar, why didn't you, as a small, gifted boy, take to a more established instrument: the piano, the violin, the cello?

It's true, I may have been born with the vocation for music. But the musicians who played in the little village where I was raised, near Granada, were very mediocre. I rejected the violin, the cello, and the piano because they sounded so terrible. A friend of mine used to say that the piano was like a rectangular monster. He yells when we touch his teeth.

So you taught yourself?

I heard the guitar played by people with very rough hands. Despite that, the sound of the guitar by itself, its melancholy, moved me more than any other instrument. I heard always around me the flamenco guitar and I didn't like its sound. I wanted to discover the true musicality of the guitar, to find its delicacy, its grace. Notice the curves of the guitar, so feminine. [He half shuts his eyes, smiles, as he caresses the imaginary guitar.] The guitar is descended from the ancient kithara, Greek. There were two gods, Hermes and Apollo. Hermes invented the lyre and Apollo the kithara. Hermes found it in nature:

the form of the lyre assumes the shell of the turtle. The guitar was more advanced with its curvaceous sides and flat bottom.

*I'm bowled over by your vision as a small boy in Linares. You sensed in the
guitar possibilities not yet tapped.*

Exactly. I guessed them. I didn't experience them because nobody played it
the way I wanted it. So I became my pupil and my teacher. The pupil dis-
turbed the master very much by asking him things about the music and the
instrument that he did not know. [He chuckles softly]

You were carrying on a dialogue with yourself. . . .

And never we quarrel too much. We continue living in mutual admiration up
to now. [A laugh] Today, we are still very good friends. I respect the master
and the master loves the pupil.

*I read somewhere about José Ramirez, the guitar maker known as the
Stradivarius of the instrument. When you were a kid of sixteen, he heard
you play and gave you the guitar as a gift. He wanted no money, he just
wanted you to play it.*

Exactly. I was seventeen. I longed for a good guitar. The one I had for my first
concert in the Athenaeum in Madrid was made in Granada by a good craftsman, but he had no money for acquiring good wood. I asked Ramirez to lend
me one of his guitars for the occasion. He was so pleased with the idea that he
said, "Take her, she's yours." You see, the professor of violin at the Royal Conservatory had heard me and praised me to Ramirez. I was very moved. I told
him, "This is something that has value but no price."

I was fourteen when I made my professional debut at the Arts Center of
Granada. The night before the concert, a flutist who did not know me asked,
"Do you know the young guitarist who is going to play?" And I said, "Yes, he
is an intimate friend of mine." He said, "I was told that he's talented." I answered, "No. You are going to see for yourself. He has no talent at all." He
was very indignant. "You say he's an intimate friend of yours and he has no
talent. Are you jealous?" After the concert, he approached me. "You are right
to be jealous of that young man. But not to the point of denying his talent."

What about your encounter with Toscanini years later?

It was at a dinner with Toscanini and Olin Downes [classical music critic of the *New York Times*] in New York. Toscanini had never met me. He knew my name because I had already played many times in Italy, France, London. But he thought it was not an instrument to be taken seriously. He needed to be convinced. He had me send for the guitar. I played for him. When I finished, the maestro marched over, embraced me, and kissed my hand. Downes said, "Oh, I'm going to make a marvelous article about this moment." I told him, "No, I don't want to convert this thing into publicity, propaganda. Don't tell anything. Let the public hear me and judge for themselves."

You are now eighty-five, Maestro. Your debut in Granada was seventy-one years ago!

This year is the fiftieth anniversary of my first concert in America. I'm still traveling and playing and finding much joy in it, as much as ever. I feel I have accomplished my purpose, which is to make the guitar *known* and beloved by the world public. By traveling so much, I have felt the roundness of the earth under my feet.

You have often said you will never play down to an audience.

No, no, no, no. Never. I have too much respect for the guitar. And for the places where I play it. I have had three wives in my life. I have had three guitars. I have flirted with other guitars, not with other women. I have four missions in life. The first is to redeem the guitar from flamenco amusement. The second is to make the guitar well known through the world of music. The third is to create a repertoire to rescue it from its confinement. And the last is to influence all the academies and conservatories to open their doors for teaching the guitar with the same level of dignity as given to the piano, the violin, and the cello.

Our conversation began in listening to Fernando Sor, who composed specifically for the guitar. Now you suggest Bach—a transcription of a chaconne he had composed for the lute.

A transcription is a very curious matter. There are no known theories of composition for the guitar. At the beginning, composers who are my contemporaries—Castelnuovo-Tedesco, Villa-Lobos—did not know how to write for this instrument. I had to adapt, arrange, suggest.

Castelnuovo-Tedesco said you gave him all sorts of directions.

Exactly. I told him the way to compose it. They have composed something beautiful, indeed they did. But it was impossible to play it that way on this instrument.

You were, in a sense, a collaborator, a co-composer.

May I offer you my idea of the composer and the instrumentalist? Jesus went to the tomb of Lazarus. He said, "Lazarus, stand up and walk." From that moment, Lazarus belonged as much to Jesus as he did to himself. The artist goes to the score and tells the music, "Stand and walk." From that moment, the music belongs as much to the artist as to the composer.

It occurs to me that had Bach been alive today, he might have composed Segovia variations for his contemporary, the harpsichordist Goldberg.

That is possible. I have never tried to make a transcription of any work unless it could produce a deeper emotion in the guitar. I think Bach wrote the chaconne originally for the ancient lute, but I felt it had less purity than the guitar. I experimented with this transcription so many times, in so many different ways. I even examined a Busoni transcription of a Brahms piano piece for a single hand. It didn't work. I even experimented with a chaconne transcription for violin and orchestra, but, no, it wasn't right. The poetic soul of the chaconne can be captured by no instrument as beautifully as by the guitar. It is not because I am a guitarist, no, no, no. It is because in the violin, it is impossible. The chaconne is larger than the violin. It is so pure. It should not have so many dresses to cover it. It is the *simplicity*.

This may account for such rapt attention in the audience when you are alone on that stage with the guitar and a footstool, nothing else.

Exactly. The silence of the public in the concert hall for the guitar is more than for any other instrument. In listening to the piano, for instance, you may sit like this. [He slouches.] In listening to the guitar, you lean forward . . . and in absolute silence. A great friend of mine, a philosopher, was lecturing in a large hall. Somebody came up to him to tell him, "Please speak a little louder because we are having difficulty hearing you." From that moment, he spoke lower. [He whispers, delightedly.] And everybody helped. They listened even more intently. All the masters thought that it was impossible to hear the guitar in a large hall: Francisco Tarrega, Sor, everyone. That is one of the reasons why the guitar did not advance in the consideration of the public. I am playing always without amplification. I am every two, three years in Ann Arbor in the auditorium of five thousand people. I don't push the force of my guitar farther than I do in my own room. And it is absolutely heard. Electrification takes away completely the poetry of the sound of the guitar. All the nuance has to be there. The intimacy. You always find a new nuance with each performance. If this intimate connection with the audience is not there, the interpretation is a little cold.

Some of your most gifted disciples speak of your generosity of spirit.

I have many such students. Christopher Parkening, Julian Bream, John Williams. From South America, I have a grand-disciple of mine, because he is a disciple of a disciple of mine. So he's like a grandson. They have fine careers, all of them, but they must always work more. Do you know that at my age, eighty-five, with my knowledge of technique, I have to practice five, six hours per day? Technique is like the dictionary. All the words are there, but you have to combine them to give it significance. Out of the significance, the soul appears.

Five, six hours a day you practice? Even now?

More than ever. I have to keep the flexibility of the fingers. Nature is *very* bad sometimes and the fingers become stiff if you do not exercise them. Like the legs. If you remain seated all the time, you lose the flexibility of the muscles. Another idea why it is necessary to work. Do you know Jacob, the ladder of the biblical Jacob? The angels went up and down every step, even though they had wings. They could have flown, but they needed the exercise. It is necessary to go up and down, *every step:* to prepare the finger and to polish every difficulty in the composition. The guitar is polyphonic. It offers the illusion of an orchestra. The flute, the brass, the cello, the violin—they all make me think of the guitar. It's like an orchestra observed through the reverse side of binoculars. That is, a smaller orchestra. One of my friends, the philosopher Salvador de Madariaga, once said, "The Spaniard has such a strong individuality that, by himself, he is a society." And I say he has elected the guitar because the guitar is in itself an orchestra.

RAVI SHANKAR
1961, 1969

Ravi Shankar is to the Indian sitar what Andrés Segovia is to the guitar— the nonpareil. The sitar, though part of India's culture, high and low, had not been too well known in the rest of the world until Shankar came along. During one of Shankar's Chicago concert series, he and two colleagues [Mr. Dat, tabla, double drum; Mr. Malik, drone] entered the studio dressed in Indian garb and settled on the studio floor to talk and demonstrate their artistry. Shankar was full of vitality and in good humor.

Namaste.

Come again?

Namaste is the greeting in India. It means hello, good morning, goodbye, anything—an all-purpose form salutation. Just as the raga is India's basic musical form: it is adapted to every mood of the day, every mood of the season and life. The ragas are actually based on scales. We in India have—like the major and the minor here—seventy-two full-octave scales. Seventy-two, mind you. On each of seventy-two scales, there are quite a number of ragas. This means we have hundreds and thousands of ragas. Each of these ragas is associated with a different phase of the morning, day, noon, afternoon, evening, night. Each of these ragas has its own sentiment, its own mood. In the olden days, they signified different pictures, different paintings from different epochs. But the artist, while performing, either singing or on the instrument, always has some liberties to give his own version. Based on this scale, this raga has its own ascending, descending movements. I'll just give you a little example. [He plays] This is equivalent to the major scale, for instance. [He plays] On each of these scales, we have got hundreds of ragas. [He plays] What I'm playing actually are the skeletons of the ragas, known as the ascending and descending movements. The moment we start playing a raga, there are a lot of other things, like using the slide, and little quarter tones. We make usage not in a static way. For instance, we won't use a note like this [an instant ping] but we will use it as a catapult to heighten the emotion. [He plays] Just slide it, yes, in quarter tones that is. . . . [He demonstrates] In India, actually, we play ragas of the particular time. We don't play the evening raga in the morning, or vice versa. After choosing the raga we have to bear in mind the duration of the performance: whether I'm going to perform for one and a half hours, or two hours, one raga, or whether I'm going to perform it for three minutes. For instance, in the 78 phonograph discs, I perform for fifteen minutes. Once we know that, we can start the recital accordingly. It can last for three hours, four hours, in the hands of a good musician who really has experience. And in India, I never play a raga less than one-and-a-half hours.

A raga has its own shape. Each raga is like a different personality, different person. Some of them are very playful, some of them are very erotic, some of them are tranquil, some of them are full of pathos. Once we decide the raga, we have to, as much as possible, keep the personality of the raga intact. The artist does have a bit of freedom to give his own touch. Having decided on the duration of the raga, we do the improvising accordingly. The usual procedure in our music is to start slow, and get faster and faster and end in a climax. Like making love. There are three steps to the raga. The first is the invocation, the solo sitar playing. That is how we start. It is a very slow, soft, sitting movement. I would say it is very spiritual and very introverted. It is not one of those extrovert-playing-for-the-gallery things. It is completely emotional. The second movement is where the element of rhythm is added. There's a lot of slowly growing excitement. Improvisation is occurring all the time. Yet it is like being bound down in a rigid system. When we choose a raga we cannot go out of that specific one. But at the same time we have all the freedom in the world within that framework. Even when we call it solo, you always hear something else in the background. It is known as the drone instrument. It is this tamboura. [Mr. Malik plays] These three strings are keeping the tuning all the time as you hear it. This is also known as the hypnotic drone because it continues all the time being played in the background. It builds an atmosphere that is very important to us, the musician as well as to the listener. It keeps in the mind the constant pitch. We never change this pitch in our music. In Western music that's very unusual, and that is the reason why most of our Western listeners after some time feel that our music is a bit repetitious, which is not true. We keep the tuning all the time the same. We go on changing the ragas, but the tamboura is always behind, maintaining the pitch. Harmony is not present in our music in the sense that it's understood here. But it's there in a very subdued, subtle way. The tuning of the tamboura itself is a harmony. It's the hypnotic drone. After some time you start getting the illusion of hearing the harmonics of that tuning.

The sitar is a big instrument, nearly four feet in height. In the base, below, it is a gourd. The upper part is made of teak wood. It's completely hollow. There is a small piece of gold on the top, which is also serving as a resonating chamber. There are four strings, mainly for playing, and two for rhythm, making it six. [He plays] Below, there are thirteen sympathetic strings that resonate. Altogether nineteen strings. [He continues playing, demonstrating what he describes] This instrument can be played vertically as well as horizontally. This gives the effect of vocal music, the human voice.

Now, about the drums known as the tabla. But the tabla is in reality two drums. The tabla is tuned with the hammer. When the drummer plays a solo or accompanies a sitar player, it is the sitar player who chooses what he's going to play, whether he's going to play a slow piece or a medium or fast one, and in what rhythmic cycle. The main thing is that the tabla player has to know the starting point. Unless we keep track of that starting point, one, or the sum, you really cannot enjoy the music, because we always improvise and come back on that one, something our experienced listeners know, and that's why they enjoy the byplay. There's a language of the drums. Anything that can be played can be spoken. In India, when the music goes on, actually we don't wait till the end to applaud; even the audience, when there's something very exciting and interesting they shout, "Aha, va-va," and this helps build the enthusiasm of the artist, too. We have another sign when we are at times silent, but we sort of shake our head from side to side like this. It has been misunderstood many times by our Western listeners, as if we are disapproving when we do like this, but actually it means appreciation. It's like saying "va-va." Very nice, wonderful.

Our music, you see, is basically aural and not visual. That's the main difference between the Western music and our music. And our music has been handed down from one person to the other through generations. We have our notation system, which is like the so-fa system. Each of our notes are like do, re, mi, fa, so, la, ti, do. We call them by names. We have short initials for each note, either in Hindi or Roman letters. That's how we write our notation. We only use it for keeping records, mostly of old songs, fixed pieces. Also, in the new forms, like film scores or ballet music or different orchestral pieces. That has to be written down because it's not improvised music, it's fixed music.

Your music for the film trilogy The World of Apu *really knocked me out. It was the masterwork of Satyajit Ray [best known for the Apu trilogy: Pather Panchali, Aparajito, The World of Apu]. In the first one of the three,* Pather Panchali, *you did the sound track. There was one moment that was indelible to me. The little girl dies and the mother screams. We did not hear the voice of the actress. We heard your bowed instrument. Boy, oh boy. It brought to mind Münch's painting* The Scream. *It was a grief so profound, it dared not speak its name.*

When Satyajit Ray asked me to do the music score, he actually wanted me to take three, four days at least, for recording and singing. After I had seen the whole film once, I was so moved, and really, it got me so deep in my mind. I immediately had this theme music in my mind, which perhaps you remember. It came to me spontaneously while I was seeing the picture for the first time. In the nighttime, starting at ten o'clock, we began to work. I had only three musicians with me. One flutist, one bowed-instrument player, one drummer. And myself. Four. I had everything completely in my mind. I utilized the theme music as much as possible, again and again, on different instruments—on solo instruments as well as together. It was just done on the spot, after seeing the film only once. I think it's an all-time record for finishing music for a whole film—in four hours and fifteen minutes. And when the mother in the film screams, you hear the bowed instrument, and it's as though you heard her voice even more than if she actually screamed. Beyond reality.

Up till now, our music has been thought of as purely ethnic or exotic, rather like a museum piece. But I tell you, our music is alive, full of life. It is not like many oriental countries' music that has a lot of folk tunes. Our books mention our music as at least three thousand years old, probably older because it came directly from our old texts, the Vedas. In the Western music, of course, Gregorian chant was associated with the church. In the same way our music was very deeply associated with old spiritual religious life. In the case of Western classical music, the approach has been more intellectual. In the olden days a musician had to be a great yogi also. So yoga, music, religion, all are spiritual aspects. Everything was connected.

In the very old days, the music was also popular because classical music was attached to the temple. You know how old our temples are. They were the center of all the creative art, this culture, this painting, the music, the dance. They had their own stage, their own huge backyard where the people used to come and see the dance and hear the music. Later, especially in the north, music was brought into the palaces. It was shut in, rather, for the aristocrats and the maharajahs and the rulers. Little by little, in the north mainly, the common people lost the contact with our tradition. I would say the same thing was done in Europe. Remember the days of Mozart and Wagner. It was the archdukes and counts who were privileged. So it was very much the same. It is only since the last fifty years or so that some of our pioneer people in India, especially in north India, have tried to arrange music festivals, get all the musicians together to perform, almost like a jam session, one after another. The duration of each artist is much more because there we are actually supposed to play each raga for at least one and a half hours. Not less than that. Especially after the independence, our music has become very popular through the radio, as well as through festivals all over the cities, like Calcutta, Bombay, New Delhi. It's a common thing to see a huge pandal, which is like a big tent, in open air. You see five thousand, eight thousand, ten thousand people sitting all night till the early morning, about seven o'clock, and again repeating the next day. This goes on for seven, eight days. And such festivals you have at least twenty, thirty of them in each big city every year, in the cities. All-India Radio has done a great service. I was in All-India Radio for many years.

It's also been exciting to me that young people in America have become interested in our music. It has been a wonderful experience. I was coming almost every alternate year, playing before small groups. Each time I was feeling that my audience was growing, growing, growing. I always had the students in the campuses and jazz-loving and folk music–loving people. Toward the end of 1965, I was playing a lot for the folk clubs and smaller houses in England. The Beatles were the rage at that time. George Harrison became very interested in sitar. He came to a number of my concerts and he wanted to use the sitar as a new sound. So did other pop groups like the Rolling Stones. That immediately created a great interest among the young people. Sometime in 1966, George met me in London and expressed his desire to take sitar lessons from me. I said, "If you want to learn the sitar, you have to give a lot of time, you have to come to India." I gave him two or three lessons in London, and I went back to India. Then he came to India and spent six weeks with me. In him I found a lot of humility, which is a great quality. He practiced as much as he could in that short time. This is nothing really, nothing. We believe it requires eight to ten years minimum of training and learning from a guru. Since then, I have been meeting him once in a while, sometimes for three lessons, four lessons. But he has really not been able to do much for the reason that he has so many other commitments. But his interest boosted the whole thing and there came this sitar explosion. So from that time onwards, I had larger audiences of younger people, and it went on growing.

There was the Monterey Pop Festival in June of 1967. Monterey was one of those very unusual experiences in my life. I was very strict. I wanted a separate sitting of my own, not in between the other pop artists, because I knew there would be a different vibration. Atmosphere has to be different. So they give me a segment in the afternoon, with no artist before me or following me. It was between one o'clock and five-thirty. I played for four and a half hours. It was so wonderful because there was no disturbing that particular vibration that was created there. A give-and-take between the listener and the musician is very important in Indian music.

Then I had a lot of problems. On one side I became very popular, almost like a pop star, being chased in the hotel corridors by young kids. It was absolutely something I didn't like at all. In the beginning they were coming to my concerts with an attitude they are used to having at a pop concert, you understand? Very flippant, very superficial. It was like a fad. Then they wanted to smoke along, listening to the program, or sip through their beer cans, or start necking with their girlfriends and everything. From the very beginning, I sat down with my sitar and said, "I won't play until you sit properly and listen to me as the music should be listened to, the same way as you listen to Bach or Beethoven." It did irritate them a little, and hurt them maybe, but slowly they started understanding, and things have changed since then. Believe me, I have gone through such a strain because I was criticized back in my own country, and by friends who have known me always as a classical musician. They were wondering, Why is he going for this cheap popularity, as they called it, and trying to impress the young people? What has he got to do with the Beatles? Why are all these hippies getting to you? After the height of this frenzy for Indian music, or Indian anything—this was almost the end of 1967, the beginning of 1968—many of them dropped out. To them it was really more of a fad. But those who remained are still there. I find them today as some of my best listeners. They really understand, they appreciate, and they inspire me. Slowly they began to understand how much more complex our system is, how old it is, how traditional, and how much discipline it requires. That's why many of the jazz people even started learning Indian music. I gave lessons for quite a number of them. Many of them have since tried to do something based on certain raga patterns or on some of our complex rhythms. Many of the young very quickly took to Eastern philosophies. Music was something which gave them a better chance to understand. They wanted to find gurus. There came that big period of Maharishi Mahesh Yogi. But the sad thing about it is that they tried to follow some of the big personalities. For instance, they took to Mahesh Yogi because the Beatles did it, and some of the famous people in the films. [Sighs] It was not so much of their own personal urge or seriousness. That also became like a fad. There are still a lot of young people who are very much interested in the Indian approach to religion and spirituality. But those superficial ones dropped out. I do understand a lot of problems and reasons they have, but still, drugs were another way for the young, you know, an easier way out. The whole drug thing is beyond me. Some famous, self-appointed gurus in this country, Americans, are irresponsible people. I have myself heard them say that in India everyone takes drugs; that you have to take drugs to meditate or to say *om* or to listen to music or to make love. This is very sad, because the kids believe that. I meet many of these kids who go to India. I meet them in Bombay, the streets of Calcutta, New Delhi. It is so sad to see them begging on the street, or completely gone out of their minds. They think they are doing a great spiritual experience, and they are ridiculed, they are laughed at, they have lost their health, they are diseased. Oh my God, it hurts me so much. They go to India, and instead of really finding a true person, they make a beeline for those peddlers on the street, and those religious people now are not really religious people. They are the showmen who have big beards, the original hippie. They provide them with hashish and that's the end of it. Why go to India at all? That's what makes me very angry and very hurt. Why do they take the

excuse of India? Our basic training is to make people free from any intoxica-
tion because we believe in being high without drugs. The music has such
strength and intoxicant power that it can turn you on, and I feel very cheated
when I see you are already turned on and sitting there with your eyes completely glassy. It's not their fault because they have been told by these really
"learned" people. . . . I don't believe at all that you can get anything easily. It's
not possible at all, in music or spiritual awareness or anything. You have to
work for it.

ALFRED BRENDEL
1981, 1991

Chicago Tribune, *April 20, 2004, Michael Cameron: "It may have been
a grand piano on stage at Symphony Center that was coaxed, coddled and
caressed by that grand poet Alfred Brendel, but his recital of works by
three masters was in fact a celebration of the human voice." Brendel is
one of our most scholarly concert pianists. His repertoire is a broad one,
from Bach to Schoenberg. As a writer, his interests are not merely music,
but all art forms. His book* Musical Thoughts and Afterthoughts *is a
case in point.*

Schubert and the piano. It is a relatively new field of discovery. Some of his
smaller piano pieces were known, but most of his sonatas have been played
only after the last war. Artur Schnabel had done it in the twenties and thirties. There are a number of younger artists who embarked into the discovery
of these pieces. It seems to make a great difference when one can discover
something, or whether there is an enormous file of experience you have to
reckon with, as with the Beethoven sonatas. Many younger musicians particularly love this music, and the public has taken to it. One of the greatest joys
of my career is to have observed how the public got used to these pieces. I
have done whole Schubert cycles of four evenings in large halls. This would
not have been possible a few years before.

*The resurgence of interest in Schubert, especially by the young—how do
you explain that?*

There was a large area of Schubert's music that has not been highly enough esteemed in the past. It has something to do with Schubert's very short life span, with his character as a musician. He was a performer who played in large halls. He only performed the songs with an excellent singer. So people knew about his marvelous songs, but they did not realize until this century, and particularly until after the last war, what Schubert sonatas mean. There was a great artist like Schnabel who played some of Schubert's sonatas, and triggered something that came to fruition after the last war as far as the large audiences are concerned. Many people suddenly discovered this music and felt familiar in a quite unusual way. This was a parallel development to the rising popularity of Mahler's symphonies. I asked myself if these two composers have something in common, and gave myself the answer that it may be that there is something about the form of the pieces. You're never quite sure where the music will go. It is like walking in the forest where you lose your way. It may reflect something of the basic feeling of people who live in our time, who cannot cope anymore with certain important problems that would be important to solve in order to save the world. There is a sense of being frightened, of not being able to cope. Not in the way of artistic failure, but in the way of voicing basic feelings about life. That was close to the Romantic heart.

You imply that things more and more seem beyond control. You speak of going out into a forest as dangerous. At this moment, the music of Schubert may fit the time.

That's what I was trying to tell myself in thinking about Schubert and Mahler's music. When Schubert's sonatas were composed, it was just after Haydn, Mozart, and Beethoven, who gave music a terrific sense of order. And whose music reflects in a way the belief of the Enlightenment that there is a sense of order that's prevailed, that we can find out if we are patient, that the world is good or at least could become so. With the Romantic thinkers, things changed. They realized that such a sense of order is not available, and that one had to find a sense of order in oneself, or create it.

Liszt still is, unfortunately, somebody who is regarded as more interested in bravura than in music, and as a personality without a backbone. There is a strong prejudice, I think particularly here in the United States, which may have been nourished, amongst other things, by a very unfair book by Ernest

Newman [the doyen of British music critics at the time]. He must have been taken very literally here. On the other hand, there's an enormous amount of evidence by people who knew Liszt which points to the contrary. If I would have to choose one single composer with a particularly noble mind and a particularly magnanimous attitude towards his colleagues and toward the music of others, it certainly would be Liszt. I don't usually look for the quality in composers as people from whom to get illuminations about their music, but with Liszt, it seems to work. I find this largesse and nobility in all his good piano pieces. Even if they are very small and brief, there's always this big space and generosity. There is not only the Mephistophelian side, the diabolic side, important as it may be. There is also the Franciscan side. I think Liszt is the greatest composer of religious piano pieces. No other piano composer has revealed more about the piano, about what the piano can produce. Nobody can teach the pianist more clearly. The notes, the brilliance as such does not count. To be turned into music, it has to sound meaningful. He was a very lonely man musically. His music was not appreciated, even by somebody like Wagner, who was a close friend. He was, as a composer, very uncompromising. One forgets that if one listens to some of his more popular pieces. He was experimenting from beginning to end. That's what I meant when I said he was a revolutionary. He was looking for new possibilities of composing. He had an inkling of where the direction of music proceeds. He had the nose for it more than any other composer of his time. Some of his late pieces have more to do with twentieth-century music than with that of the nineteenth.

Beginnings. In Graz, Austria. You were not, as many concert artists are, a child prodigy.

No, and I did not come from a musical background. There was not a single musician in the family. So it took much longer to develop whatever talents I had. It meant that I had to find out things for myself, which suited me well. I did several things at once in my teens, apart from practicing the piano and giving my first concert at age seventeen. I painted, I wrote poems, like everybody else at that age. I read an enormous amount of literature. And I composed, although I would never consider myself a composer. It has remained very important for me that I did compose and have some inkling what it is to put a piece together, of what it means to observe a composition as a unity which goes from the first note to the last. I have remained in the habit of trying to look at pieces of music from a composer's point of view. There are pieces where one should see. For instance, in Liszt's "Les Jeux d'Eaux à la Villa d'Este" there is water and there is light and there are colors. There is also a spiritual side; it is a religious piano piece as well. Although I'm not a believer myself—I'm a skeptic by nature—I am delighted to enter the train of thought of a composer if his music persuades me to do so.

The question of Bach and the piano has prevented me from playing Bach in the concert hall for several years. I have done so rather late in my life. I have, for a long time, listened to old instruments and seen how the players mastered them. If somebody writes music for the keyboard instrument, it's usually a reduction of other matters. It consists of orchestral or vocal ideas, ideas in various ensemble, which are put onto the keyboard instrument to compromise. There's one player who masters the whole piece alone: there are no other players around to disturb him. In a composer like Bach, I feel that a lot of potentially different music, of latent orchestral or vocal or organ music, is present in his keyboard works. And that's why I feel that it is perfectly legitimate to play his pieces, or some of them, on the modern piano, which is more able to bring out some of the latent things. Often he did a fantasy and a fugue, and the fantasia is as unpredictable and liquid as the fugue is firmly built, solid, and architectural. Always in a really great composer, there are many sides. You cannot easily put them into drawers. The single masterpiece is inexhaustible, a powerhouse of energies where one can discover new things all the time. This is one of the aspects that make my life so interesting.

With Mozart, the case is contrary to Liszt's. There are a lot of letters and some evidence, but he is one of the most elusive personalities as a man among the great composers. Mr. Shaffer has written a brilliant play [Amadeus] with marvelous roles, extremely effective. In the first part, for me, it was extremely funny. But people who leave the theater afterward and think they know more about Mozart are gravely mistaken. What happens in this play is that through focusing on one little segment of Mozart, the Mozart of a certain series of letters which he wrote to his cousin, rather indecent letters, he has become a cartoon figure which governs the first part of the play with a lot of comical zest, but for me, gets very shallow in the second part when things are more serious and Mozart nears death. One could say that the figure of Mozart is observed through the eyes of Salieri. As a matter of fact, one doesn't learn more about Salieri's personality either. And even less about Josef II. [Laughs] It is a play about ideas, and I think that plays should be about human relations. What I mind is that in the play there are always authentic quotations to make it seem historically correct and exhaustive, which it is not. I have seen too many people leaving the theater thinking, "Now I know more about Mozart."

If I were able to be lyrical in words, I would become lyrical now about Mozart's piano works. The piano concertos are certainly one of the peaks of the whole literature. Mozart himself must have been the most natural of pianists. One of the things which attracts me so much about his piano music is that it is so vocal. I have always conceived piano music as vocally as possible. For me singing is one of the basic ingredients of music. No composer shows it more clearly than Mozart does. Some of his slow movements of the concertos, some of his episodes in the rondos, seem to me like operatic scenes. I often conceive of the sound, even in passages, from the point of view of the singer. Sometimes from the point of view of an oboe player, who would articulate runs in a very minute manner, to make them alive. But it is always, with Mozart, the singer who is in the foreground of my thoughts.

As a piano composer, Haydn is still the one great personality who has to be presented to the public. I think that the public has not yet got the message. It is one of my aims to spread the gospel the best I can. No composer has given me more pleasure in the last ten years than Haydn. I'm always looking forward to studying some more of his sonatas. Also, with some of the pieces, to make the public laugh. I'm also very interested in the comic aspects of music, and some of my colleagues obviously are not. There is one very famous Beethoven player who maintains there is no comedy in music and that music cannot express humor, and I couldn't disagree more. There's nobody who can demonstrate my disagreement better than Haydn in some of his pieces. I try to look at the pieces of absolute music where no words come in, where the music has to prove by itself it is funny, not what the listener expects, sometimes even to the extent of being complete nonsense, of being downright irreverent. I'm sometimes trying to reflect about music, that what makes a work of art is its organization first and foremost. There is, of course, the raw material, the *feeling,* from which everything comes, and to which I hope a good performance may then return. But feeling in itself is too chaotic to amount to anything: it is the sense of order and the mixture of order and random that makes the work of art what it is. It's a sort of polarity between understanding, trying to pin down what things are about, and the sense of wonder that is inherent in each masterpiece because somebody was able to put something together that is so convincing, that remains so fresh when you deal with it over the years, that it is a constant source of rejuvenation of the artist. It is a cooperation of the two, intellect and wonder. The better you understand, the greater the sense of wonder can be. The word *staunen* cannot be quite literally translated. It's somewhere between "wonderment" and "awe."

If we hear a piece by Beethoven, we invariably think of you. You have recorded all of the Beethoven piano works. I suppose when it comes to staunen, we think of someone like Beethoven, don't we, and your approach to his work?

Yes, that's very fair to say. He has, in some of his slow movements, been able to carry the listeners as near to mystery as music can achieve. I don't usually like to talk about these things, but I pursue the matter in the way the Austrian novelist Robert Musil pursued it in his great work *The Man Without Qualities*. One tries to know everything that is possible and encircle what cannot be known.

Silence, I think, is the basis of music. You notice it very strongly if you go to a concert and the audience is not quiet. I notice it even more. [A small laugh] All important music incorporates silence. There are pieces where one can notice it very distinctly, that generate out of silence, or they end, like the last Beethoven sonatas, in silence. There are sometimes telling silences, not interrupting the music, but rather as a partner. There are movements of Beethoven where there is a musical soliloquy, and then the silence replies to it. The last three of Beethoven's piano sonatas, I think, lead into silence, whereas all the ones before close up the piece with the last chord. There is a connection between silence and good music, not with Muzak or also not with pop music. I don't want to criticize pop music, but it is simply a quality pop music does not have, this connecting with silence. When you go to a serious concert, you hope that the audience is able to create the necessary silence and the concentration because one would think that they come to a concert to listen—not to their coughing, but to the music that is made. There is a general increase of noise. I observe it in the hotels that I stay in. In restaurants, many are noisier than they used to be. There are air conditioners. There are sorts of gadgets in the bathroom, or refrigerators, or all sorts of things that you didn't used to have—the TV of your neighbor. That makes life very much more difficult. I think it is so among the young people, and one hopes that after a few years of excessive noise, they will get sick of it. I just hope that by then they will not have lost some of their hearing.

You're aware that there have been surveys made about their hearing, and it has been affected.

I know it will be a slightly deaf generation for which I have to play in ten or twenty years, and I'm not sure that I will raise my noise level for them. [Laughs]

This is a crazy question to ask: about the matter of your experiences as an accompanist, because Schubert naturally brings to mind Dietrich Fischer-Dieskau, the great interpreter of his songs. Before that: when you play Schubert, or whatever you interpret, you, Alfred Brendel, are living in this twentieth century. . . . Is it a different interpretation than Alfred Brendel who may have lived in another period?

Necessarily so. On one hand, we try to do what the composer wanted. On the other hand, we have to play for audiences of our day, and take into account certain habits of listening, certain halls, instruments, and nervous systems that are available today. Going back to Fischer-Dieskau, I would like to correct you, if you'll forgive me. I do not consider myself an *accompanist,* but rather a partner, and there was nobody more instrumental in making a pianist a partner than Fischer-Dieskau himself. He has really brought about the big change. He was always looking for the partner, for somebody who would also give him a certain amount of inspiration and lively musical ideas that he then would take up, because as authoritative as he is in his own thing, he's also marvelously able to listen.

If you were able to listen through all those enormous boxes of all-Schubert or Brahms or Schumann recordings that have been issued from the beginning of the century up to the forties or fifties, you will see with amazement how unbelievably alien to what the whole piece has to tell those contributions of accompanists used to be. Of course it was the singer who wanted them to be like that. It was the singer who often obviously had not even looked into the score properly to see what the pianist has to play. When the pianist plays alone he seems to be hurrying over his lines to be as unobtrusive as possible.

When the singer comes in, things get two or three times as slow, so that the singer makes his point. [Soft chuckle] It is very interesting to observe how in the thirties, forties, with the help of collaborators like Gerald Moore and Paul Ulanowsky, and some more enlightened singers, the lieder singing has changed.

With regard to improvisation, we know about a jazzman improvising, but how does one improvise in your world?

There are two different things. There's the improvisation of notes and of the music itself that the jazz player does and that a performer of Baroque music these days sometimes will do when there is a single melodic line that can and should be adorned. There are instances in Mozart's piano concertos where the same can happen, and there are fermatas that have to be filled in. There are gaps in Mozart's own notation where he hasn't finished things for print and where the performer has the right and the pleasure to fill in something of his own that sounds like Mozart. When I talk of improvising, I mean actually something else: to play the piece that is written down, that has its own sense of order, that conveys its own rules, but that also allows for a certain amount of freedom while it is played. There may be people who have everything figured out, like a computer, and will repeat their performances almost literally. This is something I couldn't do even if I wanted. I have usually prepared each piece very thoroughly, but there is, at the same time, a certain amount of space for what we come in at the moment. It's a mixture of controlling yourself and associating freely with the different half of your mind. It is only if both things come together that a really good performance will emerge.

I think one can strive for perfection if one realizes that it is not of the ultimate importance and that it is something that will never be quite fulfilled. I am also talking about technical matters. There are of course listeners who want something to be completely flawless, who are actually waiting when they listen, in the concert or even a record, for something to go wrong: "Am I not wonderfully clever to spot it where it goes wrong?" There are also critics who cannot refrain from writing it down if one or two chords have gotten wrong. It sometimes disturbs me very much if something goes wrong, but it will not kill me, because I remember some of the greatest performances I have heard in my life and many were very far from spotless. When Cortot played, or people like Furtwängler or Bruno Walter conducted, it did not necessarily mean that there was absolute perfection. What was there was this feeling of rightness. The essential things were presented to you. It is sometimes thought that complete technical perfection is the basis on which those essential things then can emerge, and that is not quite true.

GARRICK OHLSSON
2001

Garrick Ohlsson may be the best unknown pianist in the United States. Back in 1970, he won the Chopin Competition in Warsaw, and from then he was on his way. Ohlsson's interest is not merely in exploring Chopin as no pianist of our time has ever done, but also in exploring composers—both older and contemporary—who have been taken for granted and neglected through the years. His discovery of their genius makes him, along with Alfred Brendel, both a scholar and a virtuoso.

In 1970, you were the first American to win the Chopin Competition in Warsaw, but you refused to become a "Chopanzee," as you put it. Ten years before that, Van Cliburn won the Tchaikovsky Competition in Moscow. Something happened to him, tragic in nature, that you avoided. He became almost exclusively the Tchaikovsky man.

I can only offer my version of it, my understanding of what happened to him. I was ten when he won that prize in Moscow. It was 1958, I believe. I didn't know much about the world, but I knew it was the Cold War, I knew it was an exciting time. An American had beaten them. They had beaten us with Sputnik at that point. It was a very different world than it is now. There was a perception that they were going to beat us in lots of ways. It turns out to have been absolutely not true in retrospect, but I didn't know that then. We, as Americans, had a cultural inferiority complex about classical music at least, if not other things. It was somehow a sense of national pride. Here goes this apple-pie American boy over to Russia and beats them at their own game, a Texan of all things. In fact, he came from a very sophisticated background. Labels are very dangerous, as you know. He played brilliantly, and he won the hearts of the Russians and of the distinguished international jury as well. He came back home a folk hero. No classical musician has ever had the reception that Van Cliburn got when he returned here. Not even Horowitz had a ticker-tape parade down Broadway, not even Lenny Bernstein. It was an awesome thing. It was political, it was public relational. I feel that he got a little stuck, being the Tchaikovsky man. In other words, he became a public commodity. People wanted him to be this hero and everybody wanted to hear him. I heard him shortly after he won. He played the Tchaikovsky, and there were screaming teenagers. Was the situation simply too overwhelming? A lot of musicians say that he should have resisted more. I don't know. If that happens to you and you become the vortex of all this activity, it's hard to know what's coming from outside, what's coming from inside. It's like some of those opera singers who get very famous. Then they play kings all the time, so they start to think they're the king. [Laughs] I don't know the inner workings of him at all. There was a marvelous, a great pianist, a wonderful artist, who seemed to burn out.

You heard Rubinstein at Carnegie Hall when you were eight. There are accusations that he was cold, and that was said of Heifetz, too. But you say far from it, he played with tremendous passion.

Yes. This is another funny thing I've learned over the years in my field. I don't know about the interpreters of the nineteenth century, but all the dominant twentieth-century interpreters were considered cold and modernist in their youth. Rachmaninoff was. Horowitz not so much, although they said he was cold. Heifetz, Artur Schnabel. All these people were considered modernists. Toscanini. They were wiping away the barnacles of tradition, and they were accused of being too modernist. As time went on, they matured and the public matured with them. Now we have a tendency to think back on the great Rubenstein of his old years with the glorious sound, and we think of what a wonderful old guy he was. In fact, he was a Young Turk, he was full of fire, and yet all these artists were accused of being too modern or too cool, if not cold. Actually, I think *cold* is a red herring with an artist like Heifetz. He looked cold when he played. If you listen to the playing, it doesn't sound cold. People sometimes have a problem with the demeanor of the artist. Some are very flamboyant and some are very reserved. I don't subscribe to either theory as being right. I think *vive la différence*. I think we should have everybody be what they are.

Your teacher, Rosina Levine, was a devout Chopin admirer. At the same time, she marvels at what you've done. You became interested in Webern and in Bartók and in Samuel Barber.

She actually encouraged that; she felt that was healthy. She was also the teacher of Van Cliburn. She felt that he had fallen into the trap of his own success, although she always admired him very much. She implied that Van was young and not quite ready. He didn't have a big repertory, and he didn't have the inner strength to withstand all this public acclamation. Of course, nobody ever had to withstand that much, either, so I'm very empathetic. But like a good teacher, she said if success strikes you, don't be a one-trick pony, be ready to be the full artist that you can be. It was a bit of a warning. How shall I put it? There's art, and then there's the business of art. Art is a pure, sublime communication. It's one of the best things we have on earth. Unfortunately, to get it to people, there has to be a commercial aspect to it. Not all the famous people are great, and not all the great people are famous. [Chuckles] You have to have an enormous ambition to keep ahead of the crowd, because there are lots and lots and lots of pianists, and why should the folks at Ravinia want to hear me instead of John Smith? They don't know who John Smith is, but they know who I am, so they're interested. For me, the most important thing is that it brings people into the musical experience. I can help them in my way, bring them into this unbelievable world so that they can have their own experience.

Your repertoire is an adventurous and dangerous one. Before we come to your interpretation of Chopin, there is Liszt. You've taken two composers, wholly misunderstood for years. We, offhandedly, think of Liszt and bombast. Let's go back to how it all happened. How did music and the piano enter your life?

In a very normal way I showed signs of being interested in music when I was a kid. This was in White Plains, New York, a metropolitan area ten minutes from the Connecticut border—a prosperous community with good schools. I'm an only child, and there are no professional musicians in the family. Both my parents were squarely middle-class folks; they had had piano lessons when they were kids, and they felt it was an important part of growing up. I picked out tunes on the piano and did all that stuff. When I was eight, it was time to get piano lessons, so I got piano lessons. I was hooked after one or two lessons. All I wanted to do was rush home from school and play the piano. My mother would have to chase me outside to play with other kids. She said, "You have to go play with the kids for an hour." After thirty-five minutes, I'd be knocking on the door and saying, "Can I come in and play the piano?" [Laughs] It's a dream. It's the opposite of what any parent who has to force their kids to play has to deal with. I was crazy about it. I had a good teacher. He was the first man of musical culture that I knew, so he was like a musical father for me. He instilled in me his belief that music, playing the piano, is not about just manipulating the machine; it's about something that's bigger than you are. It's about a communication that transcends yourself. It's not just about showing off how fast you can play, or how beautifully. It's not just about your success, it's about you having a life with this great art, and communicating that to other people. He said, "Oh, they'll admire your technique anyway. Don't worry," he said, "but it's much bigger than that." It sounded so simple then, I grew up with it.

When I went to Juilliard, I realized there were many kids who were not raised with that as an ideal. It was about "me and my career and my octaves and my thunders and my victories." I'm exaggerating for effect, because nobody is that simple. Everybody has that communicative desire. But it was really, for me, it was a question of being immersed in something bigger than myself, and serving it. It also serves me. It's very gratifying, too. I'm a lucky guy. [Chuckles] I get to spend my time with Beethoven and Chopin and Liszt and Rachmaninoff in a sort of intimate relationship. I get to know them in my nervous system.

Chopin is much bigger than his popular image. We have this very romanticized idea of this poetic, this frail, consumptive Polish artist dying young, an expatriate, a tragic life, a Romantic. They're all true, of course, but he was much more than that. When he left Poland at the age of twenty, he didn't intend to go abroad and get ill and die. That's nobody's goal. He intended to prosper. He had a genius in him that was astounding and recognized from the earliest age. Interestingly enough, although he was the quintessential Romantic composer, at the beginning of the Romantic movement he considered himself a classicist. The artists of the time were working toward a very modern conception of the interrelationship of arts. He just didn't have it. He was actually a little bit boring on the subject. They said he talked like a dry kapellmeister; this man who drove people to distraction with his music was actually quite meticulous and even pedantic when he spoke about music. He felt that music had its own meaning. He said it's not about thunderstorms or candlelight or swooning. Nevertheless, people did swoon—even the greatest musicians and minds of his age swooned when Chopin played. They were driven outside of themselves, knocked out by his music, and the forward-looking qualities of it, and the intensity. In his music, he was misunderstood badly throughout the nineteenth-century music world for one very interesting reason. This was the time in European music when we began to develop a canon of great works, the way we have in literature. Particularly in Germany, there was a whole movement to publish, for the first time in the history of the world, complete works of the great composers of the past: Bach, Handel, then Beethoven when he died, Schubert, and so on. Shortly after his death, they took on Chopin, too, and canonized him as a great composer. Brahms was one of the editors. What a time. Unbelievable. There was a misunderstanding in a lot of Europe because Chopin's work was contained in piano music alone. A couple of concertos, a tiny bit of chamber music, a couple of songs, nothing much else but this great body of piano music, and most of it short. It took me ten years to record all of it. Altogether it's several hundred different works. It covers thirteen volumes of CDs. He didn't write large public music: he didn't write big symphonies, he didn't write operas, he didn't write masses, and he didn't write string quartets. Even when he was a kid in Poland, his teachers said, "You must write these great pieces and show the world what a genius we have here in Poland." But he knew himself: he just went his own way. We know, in retrospect, he was right, but he was misunderstood, even by the musicians, because they said, yes, he's exquisite, but he's a miniaturist. Now we know that in a miniature there can be depth and profundity. His forms seemed so wild and modern that even great musicians like Schumann misunderstood them. He supposedly said of the Second Sonata that Chopin had "here yoked together four of his maddest children." Musical analysis has advanced tremendously since then. Now some of the greatest critics of the twentieth century call Chopin's Second Sonata the thirty-third Beethoven sonata. He is really a monumental master of the form.

He was a fragile physical person; he never weighed a hundred pounds. I've always been more than twice his size. [A hearty chuckle] I'm six foot four, too many pounds. [Laughs] Two hundred plus too many. Frail Chopin has this tremendous depth and strength. There is the miniature quality. In other words, Chopin can say, in a half-minute prelude, something that will affect you for the rest of your life, but it is a small form. I'll say, in defense of all the romanticism, if you don't have a little bit of the swooning of Chopin, you're missing something really important. He's not Le Corbusier, he's not a stark modernist. He is a great romantic, and his music is some of the greatest perfume and some of the greatest pastry in the musical world, and it shouldn't drive you crazy. But it's not only that.

One of the luckiest things in my life was the fact that I won the Chopin prize in Poland in 1970. I went back to Poland almost every year ever since. And as you know, they had a lot of history that happened in the last thirty years there. I was in Poland during the Solidarity movement. I was there during martial law. I was on an airplane with guys with machine guns pointed at us as we sat there. I saw these all-night vigils in Warsaw. People were open, people talked to me because of my connection, because I came back. Not only the chambermaids talking about Chopin, but I met all kinds of people that I wouldn't meet giving concerts in most places. I was lucky enough to just have a little inside understanding of what their lives were like. That gave me more of an insight into their modern history and their ancient history than any book I could read.

The Poles are known for their sense of irony. They were walking a tightrope during the Cold War, certainly during the Soviet Union's existence, and the United States—two powers, antithetical to one another. They're on the tightrope, therefore they had to develop this sense of irony.

That's right. A tremendous sense of irony, and of double meaning in order to understand what is behind the words that are spoken, because they would have to read their own censored press and figure it out.

As American slaves used, during slavery, code words.

They had to be incredibly clever and even slippery.

Now, concerning Liszt: Liszt is one of the most fascinating, multidimensional personalities who ever lived. His biography is like fiction. The greatest pianist of the nineteenth century, the greatest interpreter, and one of the first major sex symbols, too. He was incredibly good-looking. He was sort of an early rock star. There was a sexual frenzy, practically. Women fought with each other to get a lock of his hair or to get his cigar butts—they would put

[them] into their bosom and treasure them. He had a magnetism and excitement. He did have bombast also. He had excessive talent, and excessive brilliance, and excessive genius. He was all over the place. But he was also one of the most devoted people. In those days, there weren't radios, we didn't have TVs, we didn't have CD players, we didn't have tapes. You either made the music yourself or you went to a concert and you heard the great Franz Liszt. He would play music by the great masters you couldn't play. He was disseminating the world's greatest music all through Europe, in addition to his own brilliant compositions and piano playing. He was not above putting on the best show in the world; he would just knock you out. He was a virtuoso, and he did go over the top, all the time. He was the first person who played all of the Beethoven sonatas. He was a missionary for the cause of music and a great interpreter. Once again, just as Chopin drove all the greatest musicians wild, even Liszt's enemies in music had to admit there was nobody like him. Clara Schumann even said, "I really hated the way he played that piece, but I wish I could do it that way myself." In other words, I may not approve of it, but it's a force of nature. His understanding of music was so deep. Yes, there're a lot of baubles and bangles in his music too, and he probably cried all the way to the bank. He's a multisided person: part saint, part sinner. In his greatest music, he has a relationship with the great tradition of music. He is a truly great creator of music, and a great master of form also. He has a titanic strength, and a power, and I admire him second to none, although there is so much music by Liszt that is very showy and fun. I would not be interested in playing all of Liszt because there'd be lots of stuff that was composed just to wow the public. Chopin never composed just to wow the public; Liszt thought it was just fine. He was a public orator and he stirred them up. But what an important creator he was. He advanced the musical language, he pointed toward the music of the future, he developed this chromatic language, pushing toward atonality. All of these composers were swimming in the current of the time, but they altered the current.

You've used the phrase "organic music." The only person who used the word organic *that way was Frank Lloyd Wright, the architect. He was talking about the automobile being anti-organic. It isolates the driver from the others, prisoners in their cars. Yet Wright's Imperial Hotel was one of the few buildings that withstood the horrible Tokyo earthquake of 1923. It did because his building was organically connected to the Japanese soil. So to you the music is organic, connected with the very nature of life.*

Yes, and to understand that this music that comes from certain places has roots, it has a connection. There's a reason why when you go to Prague and you hear Dvořák, it sounds right there somehow. I'm not speaking sentimentally; there's a danger in that. But there's a real feeling. It has to be, as you say, consequent with the environment. That was an excitement for me, because I was an American kid, twenty-two years old. I knew a lot and I didn't know much. You know how we all are when we're twenty. We're sure of things, but we don't know much about the world. My travels, especially in Poland, gave me an insight into history and people's connections, and what music can mean in a multilevered way. The other thing that was very moving for me in that society, where there was censorship, is that the great thing about instrumental music is you can prohibit it from being played, but if you allow it, you can't censor it. You can censor the words, even of Beethoven's Ninth Symphony—they took the word *God* out of it in those places. You weren't allowed to say *God,* so they just rewrote the words. But you can't rewrite the music. People have their own musical experience. So in a time of repression, think of the spirituals, too, of the slaves. These are things that come from a deep inner need. So there was a connection and a need for this music in that part of the world that really did transcend my own experience, the depth of it. It was palpable. Because we as musical artists have this connection to music, and to have it in a whole culture, that's pretty powerful.

You sometimes sing while playing.

The piano is a box of diminuendos. You strike the note, the hammer strikes the string, it begins to vibrate. That's the strongest impact. The tone develops a bit and then dies away very beautifully. That's all piano can do. Everything else, all the illusion of growth, of sustaining, is all what we do as magicians. Every good piano teacher has said to his students, "Make the piano sing, don't make it sound percussive." In other words, make it suggest something else. It's an instrument of suggestion. A violin really makes the note grow and wax and wane. A singer can do that, a wind or a brass instrument can do that. We pianists have to suggest it, and somehow people have to get the idea. Singing at the piano is not just a matter of playing the notes in the way that they're heard, it's a way of connecting them so that they sound songlike. You know, of course, who the greatest master of that was—Chopin. His music actually has a vocal quality. Yet the paradox is that if you try to sing Chopin's melodies, they're absolutely unvocal, you can't do it, it doesn't lie in the voice at all. But he creates the illusion of singing on the piano.

What challenge awaits?

In terms of music, nothing radically different than what I've done already. My goal as an artist is to continue not only developing my repertory, but stretching my limits. I feel that I'm so lucky with my work in music because it's almost a meditation. I don't sit and meditate when I practice, I work very hard, but it's a kind of internal work with the music—getting myself in touch with what I feel is the essence of this music, and then being able to communicate it. I want to just continue learning the greatest repertory for my instrument. The piano has some of the greatest repertory in all of music. Music of our time is written by people who are alive now, who have got the same problems and the same issues in their lives: they're paying their taxes, and they're reading the paper about campaign finance reform, and having whatever feelings they have. These people live our lives, they are our contemporaries, and if we don't hear their music, it won't exist. Music in a score, that's just notation, that's not the music. Music exists in the air; it is something that's alive that goes from me to you. It's the best thing I can give you. It's the best thing I know how to do. I think we really need to hear music of our time, as well as music of the previous century, which is still not understood very well. It's fascinating. It keeps it going and it keeps us alive, keeps me alive.

NICOLAS SLONIMSKY
1988

Nicolas Slonimsky was gifted both as a conductor and as a classical music historian. This interview took place when he was ninety-four—he lived to be 101. Born in St. Petersburg, he described himself as a failed wunderkind. Aside from his being a historian, he conducted and encouraged the works of avant-garde composers such as Charles Ives, Edgard Varèse, and Henry Cowell. It was John Adams, composer of the opera Nixon in China, *who called Slonimsky "a character of mind-boggling abilities, who has a completely eidetic memory and can recall with absolute precision the smallest detail of something he's read forty years before." An all-around, highly gifted character.*

Your family itself was immensely gifted in so many ways.

Well, there were so many geniuses, but you can't separate genius from the just mentally unbalanced. You know, there is a theory that genius is a form of insanity. Max Nordau published a book eighty years ago on genius and insanity, and of course he gave examples of Nietzsche and others who became insane, and they were geniuses.

Your grandfather is credited in some quarters with having invented the telegraph.

[Chortling] Now this is a big joke. He never claimed any such thing, but he improved the transmission of telegraphic messages. And so what happened, you know, the Soviets claim that they invented everything: you name it, they invented it before anybody else. And so they discovered that my grandfather had something to do with the improvement of telegraphic messages. It came out in their papers that my grandfather invented the telegraph. Well, anyway, it got into American newspapers. I'll never forget that day. That was in 1951 when I bought an evening paper and there was a letter to Joe [Stalin, who was still living]: "Dear Joe, you say that a Muscovite named Slonimsky invented the telegraph. Could be. But we think that you are a champion, because after all, you invented Slonimsky." Now that certainly got my goat. I said, what do you mean Stalin invented Slonimsky? I exist. Here I am: one-quarter of the genes of my grandfather, whom I never met. He was born 1810, died in 1904. I mean, that's quite a life, particularly in the nineteenth century, because people died of common diseases.

You've lived through a century. You were born in 1894.

I'm afraid so.

The changes you have seen.

Of *course*. When I was a boy, no electric lights, certainly no automobiles, airplanes. I mean, I read in the papers about the Wright brothers, and then I watched the first airplane in Russia. I had to pay a ruble just to watch that plane go twenty miles an hour.

I'm thinking of you when you were five, six. When was the recognition that you had perfect pitch?

Well, this is an innate capacity. You don't have to be a genius or anything. I mean, you get born and you just happen to be able to name any note played on the piano or any other instrument or sung, just the way ordinary people name colors. It's still a mysterious thing because many great musicians didn't have it. And many not-so-great musicians, including myself, did have it. But anyway, it's an extraordinary ability that cannot be trained, no matter what anybody claims. You can't do it.

You were known as the wunderkind. Now here you are, ninety-four. Your life has been that of a wundermann. Of course, throughout you've always been a revolutionary in music, haven't you?

Well, sort of, yes. I invented all kinds of things in music that sounded crazy, but now rock-and-roll musicians use my book as a manual. Frank Zappa has, and John Coltrane, the saxophone player, discovered my book forty years ago, *Thesaurus of Scales and Melodic Patterns*. John Cage as well.

Let's go back to when you were a young man. You were there during the revolution.

Absolutely. I was right there in the center of things. You see, just when the first revolution took place, I met Kerensky, who was the head of the provisional government, on the first day of the revolution. There he was, the only socialist in all of Russia, the first one, whom they called "the nice one"; the revolutionaries were all in Siberia, and Lenin was in Switzerland. I played at Tarakanov's services because I was close, not to the revolutionaries, but to the sort of moderate, progressive people. Naturally, I was very much involved in this.

You were also witnessing the counterrevolution; certain generals were pogromists, too.

Yes, yes. Terrible people. As a matter of fact, my chance of survival during the Russian civil war was not good—the odds were one in twenty-five—because I was of draft age, and I just decided not to go to all those generals and ask them to classify me. So I just paid no attention to all their proclamations. I suppose it was an act of passive courage. I have no active courage; I don't believe that I could go into a cage of lions or something like that.

So you survived in the manner, say, of the Good Soldier Svejk.

Yes. Except that Soldier Svejk was in a civilized country—I mean, it was Austria, they had rules. But those generals, the White generals in Russia, they had no rules.

You leave, you wind up in Constantinople in 1919 for a time before you head for Paris. And what did you do in Constantinople?

I played in movie houses and in restaurants. That was before radio, before records, so they had to have live musicians. There were a lot of émigré musicians from Russia. And there were Russian restaurants and Greek restaurants, all kinds of restaurants, but they had to provide music, you see, and so when I landed, you know, the customs officer asked, "Who can do what?"

There were people who would say, "I'm a poet." "He's a poet. Go to the left. . . ." Meaning . . . [chuckles] disposable. One said, "I'm a painter." "Are you a house painter?" which is a good thing. "No. I'm a modern painter." "To the left you go." I said, "I'm a musician." He said, "Can you read music?" So I said, "Yes. Not only can I read music, I can *write* music." And he said, "All right, to the right." Because they knew they could place me. And so it was extraordinary how much money I made. My first job was for fifty cents an hour. For fifty cents in Constantinople I could buy a dinner.

Then I went to Paris, where there were many Russians in the early twenties. And so I found a place I could have company. I was a good accompanist for singers. And then Koussevitzky was a famous double bass player before he became a conductor. He needed a pianist to play those difficult scores while he practiced conducting. There were just four-minute records and practically no records of classical works. There was no radio; there was no way of creating music except by actual playing. And so he hired me to accompany a singer and he thought I was good at the piano. And for several years I was with him being a surrogate orchestra, so to speak. I met Stravinsky and Prokofiev, and all those legendary people. Bartók, too. There was no question about Béla Bartók. He knew what he was doing and he certainly heard everything. When he was my soloist in Paris, believe me, I was nervous. I'm never nervous. I was conducting his piano concerto, with Bartók at the piano. That was a responsibility. And then he found something was wrong in the way a percussion player hit his suspended cymbal. So who cares? Bartók wanted him to hit it from below and this Frenchman hit it from above. And the Frenchman says [he speaks French gibberish] . . . the way the French talk. So what's the difference? So Bartók said, "Yes, there is a great difference." And so he went to his stand and he proceeded to show how to play it. In the meantime, I was losing time, and then there was a certain disintegration in the orchestra.

I had to learn about conducting by just trying to conduct, and at first I was very inefficient, because I may have heard all the notes, but that was not the point. It would be just like, let's say, a proofreader reading James Joyce. So James Joyce has all kinds of made-up words, so the proofreader would find out that a word was misspelled, but this is the way James Joyce wanted it. The trouble with old-fashioned conductors is that they were completely unprepared for new works—Stravinsky and Prokofiev, long before compositions by John Cage or Charles Ives or Carl Ruggles or Henry Cowell. That kind of music was completely barred, so to speak. Charles Ives really belonged to the past century. But he created music that was not even music of the twentieth century, it was music of the second half of the twentieth century, though he died before hearing a lot of the performances of his work. I was the first to conduct his major works. He appreciated me. He wrote repeatedly to various figures in music saying that I was the greatest conductor in the century. He said so. It so happened that I was the only conductor whom he ever heard. [Laughs] He just believed that I could do something that no other conductor could do. In a way it was true, but who wanted to do all those things? I myself have always been interested in what could be done with musical tones. See, here I had this extraordinary collection of musical tones. It was just like peas or beans or something. And I thought of arranging them in a new way. And I myself published some music of this sort, quite different from Ives and others. But I didn't have the genius of Ives.

Now, the most revolutionary work ever written in the twentieth century is Edgard Varèse's *Ionisation*, which is really the process of atomic fission. I understand that my recording of *Ionisation* was constantly played during the creation of the atom bomb in Los Alamos. I was told by scientists that they had that record for inspiration and for relaxation. Oppenheimer, too. *Ionisation* is written for percussion instruments only—no violins, no cellos, no voice, nothing—percussion and the tone clusters of the piano. Meaning something played with forearms, fists, and elbows in order to cover more notes. And two sirens! So it was really possibly the most modern work of the century, and nobody would *touch* it until Varèse gave it to me. He dedicated the score to me. And I conducted the piece at the Hollywood Bowl, which was at that time financed by a number of old women who didn't care for music—they were deaf anyway, most of them, but they gave money. So all those dowagers heard those sounds, they said, "What's going on?" The audience walked out in droves. But then there was the nucleus of a new audience that thought it was a remarkable thing. John Cage told me that he attended *every* concert of mine in Hollywood. And, eh, what they wrote about Stravinsky's *Le Sacre du Printemps*! There was a poem that a writer in the *Boston Herald* wrote about *Le Sacre du Printemps*. She said, "Who wrote this fiendish *Rite of Spring*? / What right had he to write the thing? / And then to call it *Rite of Spring* / The season went on joyous wing / To birds' melodious carol sing . . ." And so forth. . . . Now, that was 1924, and it's one of the most famous compositions in the world. But I've collected other reviews of twentieth-century works in my little volume *A Lexicon of Musical Invective*. I will take just thirty seconds to quote one review—which I believe was the best, I mean from the viewpoint of extraordinary invective and insults—against an American composer named Wallingford Riegger, who wasn't even such a revolutionary composer. [His] piece, *Dichotomy*, was in dissonant counterpoint. This is what one critic wrote: "It sounded as though a pack of rats were being slowly tortured to death, and from time to time a dying cow would moan." Well, I thought this was beautiful, and it was just like a surrealist painting. The pack of rats were being *slowly* tortured to death. Wallingford Riegger was accused by McCarthy of actually recruiting members of the Communist Party between Thirty-second and Fifty-seventh Streets in New York. Maybe he was involved. He was not a member of the Communist Party. But anybody who was anywhere near anything that was progressive was accused.

You knew the bass Vladimir Rosing, who apparently had George Bernard Shaw and Ezra Pound among his fans.

He thought that a singer had to impersonate the subject of the song. So when he sang the *Songs and Dances of Death* by Mussorgsky, he would just screw up his face and look like a skeleton or something. Then when he sang the song of the flea, he actually scratched himself. Don't forget, that was sixty years ago, and people were pretty gullible for this sort of thing. Also, he believed in all kinds of psychic phenomena, and now it's coming back. So he told his students to flex the muscles of the brain. So finally our mutual friend Rouben Mamoulian, who became famous as a film director, so he finally told him, he said, "Listen, there are no muscles in the brain." So he said, "Nonsense. If there were no muscles in the brain, how could we concentrate?" And he was some kind of a fool, but a very lovable fool.

Gershwin complained to me the last time we had lunch together, on the day of the first performance of *Porgy and Bess*, that people complained that he couldn't write music. Many so-called composers really couldn't write music. That didn't prevent them from being great composers of sorts. For instance, Irving Berlin, who celebrates his one hundredth anniversary, could never learn to read or write music, but he composed great songs. So what? And Mamoulian had this ability to direct. There was a group—Mamoulian, myself, a young writer named Paul Horgan, who was subsequently a Pulitzer prize winner—and we called ourselves geniuses. We formed a society that was called Society of Unrecognized Geniuses. And then a few years after, I had to disband this society, and I wrote the members, I said, "This society is hereby disbanded. Reason? Said geniuses have become recognized."

You once called yourself a diaskeuast.

Well, this is a word that I found, believe it or not, in a crossword puzzle. It means a lexicographer. *Dia* means "through" in Greek, you know.

You and Latin and Greek. Your daughter's name is Electra. You were talking Latin to her. She said, "What a childhood. With Nicolas Slonimsky as my father."

Well, you see, I have an idea that children are much smarter than adults. There's one thing that until this day is not solved: why can any child learn any language without trying, and yet important scientists who go to another country cannot learn that country's language? It's extraordinary. Nobody offers *any* kind of theory.

You've just revealed one of your secrets. Has anyone ever said to you, "You have never lost your sense of wonder"? You speak of the child and the child's imagination and sense of wonder. And you have never lost that. That is true, isn't it?

That is a very good definition. I'm delighted, and with your permission, I will use it someplace.

∾ Composers ∾

VIRGIL THOMSON
1965

The day of the interview, Virgil Thomson was in a dry, whimsical mood, which was usually the case. Aside from his work as a music critic, he was renowned as a composer. His memories that day were devoted primarily to his work with Gertrude Stein.

You're from Kansas City. The music critic Harold Schonberg described you as the Parisian from Missouri. It seems as though you work in double dimensions as a critic and as a composer, as in your life you are continental and midwestern. Do both reflect you?

Missouri and France are both agricultural states. [Laughter] In both, they play a great deal of attention to religion and cooking. From the beginning I felt perfectly at home in France. I could identify the whole thing with Kansas City, and with my great-aunts. [Chuckles] I suppose everybody can identify

Paris with something in his own life, because Paris contains everything and consequently can remind somebody of anything. You're more American when you're in Paris. The city is like a litmus paper. It has a way of accentuating the talents and the failings you have more than any other city. A great deal of American literature has been written in Paris. I met Gertrude Stein there, though I knew her work before that. I'd read everything that was published and I'd even put some of it to music.

I was brought up in the generation where our most admired artists were Pablo Picasso, Ezra Pound, James Joyce, the hermetic writers in general, and particularly Gertrude Stein.

Four Saints in Three Acts came about because I said to Miss Stein one day, "Why don't you write me an opera libretto." She said, "I think it would be a fine idea." So we sat down another day and came to an agreement about a theme, about a subject. She wrote a libretto and handed it to me, and when I took a look at it, I thought, "Oh my, what can I do with this?" I couldn't tell stage directions from speeches or her own meditation style. I took a second look and thought, "Really, it is quite wonderful and I think I'll put the whole thing to music, including the stage directions," which I did. And we had the idea of using the voices of black singers because of their beautiful way of articulating words, they love words and they sing them so well. Of course, they have beautiful voices, too. In addition to which they look wonderful on the stage. They don't stand around like lumps. They stand alive. Also, you see the black people took quite naturally to a religious subject matter because their own background is so full of religious feeling and experience. They completely understood Gertrude Stein's text. They had no resistance to it. They knew what she was talking about. Within a week after the rehearsal started they were all conversing with one another in quotations from this libretto. The funny thing is that neither Miss Stein nor myself was a particularly religious person. We'd been brought up in religious enough backgrounds, but not Catholic, although the subject is Catholic saints. Gertrude was Jewish and I was Southern Protestant. But this is our story. We were both so delighted with *Four Saints* that she asked me to suggest another theme. For operas, it was always I who had the idea of something that would make an opera. The first time it was about the lives of the saints; this time about nineteenth-century political life and Susan B. Anthony—*The Mother of Us All*. Gertrude was very amenable to ideas.

In Paris I studied composition with Nadia Boulanger [the influential

French teacher, pianist, and composer] who, independently of the techniques of composition she taught me, managed to put me at ease in front of the music paper. I'm grateful to her for that. She made me understand that I wasn't, for every little piece I wrote, in competition with the ghost of Beethoven or Brahms, that it was more like writing a letter; I had something on my mind and could perhaps say it clearly, and that was quite sufficient. We're old hat, my generation, because today's young composers have jumped into either electronics or imitations of *Saints,* and so they're much more aware of one another than they are of folks like us on the shelf. I don't know, they might wake up in the middle of the night and worry about it. [Laughter] I don't know. And of course, some of us wake up in the middle of the night and worry about them. I can't tell you how many composers of my generation, and even sometimes ten or more years younger, are frightfully worried that the whole kind of thing they are doing will be put on a shelf forever. It's hard to remember that everything really goes on always at the same time. At the 1958 Brussels World Fair, Varèse created an electronic composition, *Poème Électronique.* Varèse was a far-out composer from his earliest days. But nobody can be an electronic composer until electronics exist as a possibility. Electronic tape was invented in Germany before World War II. The invention was stolen by Americans and the French at the end of World War II. Nowadays, of course, all God's children got tape. All gramophone recording is done on tape. It all began when unoccupied engineers at the French radio in 1948 realized that this invention could be used for musical creation. So they and their composer friends started writing music by manipulating tape. Tape tamperers, I called them. Americans were actually quite late getting started in the tape composition. The business of making anything musical or artistic out of tape is so completely in its infancy that there isn't much you can do except to coo at it. There is a very small repertory and the first time or two anybody makes a tape, of course he does corny things. To make something distinguished with the tape is not impossible, but it's too easy. It's like making sculpture in putty; you can do anything in putty, and the fact that you can makes it impossible to do anything very grand. The Eastern European composers had a great influence in the use of tape. But it was useful only as a way of creating a sound that they're not trying to re-create with orchestras. Now that we have an electronic sound as such, what can we do with it in terms of an orchestra? *To the Victims of Hiroshima,* by Penderecki, takes fifty-two strings and tries to re-create the sound not only of tape but of the bombing of

Hiroshima. The sound of static and electronic reproduction through loud-speakers has become the dominant sound now. Over nine-tenths of the pop-ulation thinks that a hand-played piece is merely a rehearsal for a broadcast or a recording. [Laughter] The stylish manner of orchestration today for the young, far-out composers is to make handmade music sound artificial.

Grandeur requires limitations. It's pretty hard to write something grand, which is inevitably going to be performed through one small loudspeaker about fifteen inches across. That circumstance itself is not exactly the entire Michigan lakefront, mobilized for a Fourth of July. [Laughter] With technol-ogy more and more part of our lives, will there be an avenue for the man-made touch? Everything goes on in duet. Remember that the rise of modern painting through the impressionists is exactly contemporary with the rise of photography; one helped the other out. The expansion of radio and recording was accompanied by an enormous boom in the symphony orchestra. With all the frozen foods around, all the housewives, naturally the busy girls wanting to please their husbands and interest their children, have all learned to cook. Cooking has improved a great deal in spite of the processed foods. I like com-plexity, but I think it needs to be justified either by expression or by an intrinsic interest-holding quality. Setting up a lot of gears together and watching them grind makes coffee grinder music—[it] isn't really that inter-esting. But there is such a thing as intrinsic musical interest, and for that, the more complicated, the better. That's why Bach is fun, because the interest is largely intrinsic rather than expressive. And it is quite complicated.

I'm thinking of Virgil Thomson, from a Protestant Kansas City to a Catholic Paris.

With a Jewish librettist. This is true ecumenism.

Aaron Copland and I were indirectly pupils of Stravinsky, who was fifteen years older. But Aaron Copland and I, of course, were chums, pals, and con-temporaries. So that at the beginning of our careers, we didn't consider our-selves so much in competition as we did as collaborators. Of course, as we get older, we kind of look at each other perhaps a little bit as competition, too, but still we are sort of a Fifth Avenue merchants' association, comparing our commissions. When I was a young composer there weren't any grants, there weren't any foundations giving money to music. We made it with pri-vate help because in those days well-to-do persons very often gave money away to young artists because they weren't paying so much in taxes. And then we put our own savings into organizing our own little series of concerts. We weren't depending on the older people to make successes of us. Nowadays, they always do it through a foundation. My dear sir, money has no odor whatsoever. [Laughter] Any artist who can get himself fed and clothed while doing his work is lucky. If he can get the work also published and/or performed, he is doubly lucky. The United States gives away a great deal of money now to young artists, and to producing agencies for producing young composers and playwrights. Music management boards don't like contemporary music because it costs a performance fee, it's not public domain. And frequently requires extra rehearsals. Also, you can't sell unsold seats on contemporary music because the casual purchaser doesn't know what it is about to be. But if you are completely sold out by subscription you can play all the contemporary music you like, as has long been proved in Boston, for instance. I remember ten or fifteen years ago, when I was still working on the *New York Herald Tribune*, the conductor Dimitri Mitropoulos played a work by Arnold Schoenberg. I think it was the *Five Orchestral Pieces* from 1909, still an advanced work. In order to cushion this, he had put a Rachmaninoff symphony on the program. Of course, it was a mistake because Schoenberg and Rachmaninoff don't appeal to the same people. Mitropoulos played the Schoenberg piece earlier and he was finishing with the Rachmaninoff. During the Schoenberg piece, great numbers of Rachmaninoff lovers walked out. But they walked out ostentatiously. The minute the Rachmaninoff piece began, all the moderns who had come there for Schoenberg walked out. [Laughter] The young, who are music students, go everywhere; they have a vast appetite. They're having to get all those Mozart and Beethoven symphonies under the belt and keep up with the modern world and everything, and they adore it all. They may be a little reactionary, too, because they're wrestling with the difficulties of Brahms, and they find it more interesting to wrestle with those difficulties than to just go through Stravinsky and Schoenberg, which they understand automatically because they are born in these times.

My own taste in music has always been a catholic one, but not comprehensive. I've always paid myself the luxury of disliking certain kinds of music. [Chuckles] And I also love folk music. Very often I take folk songs and use them. If I add an accompaniment, the accompaniment can be however imaginative I wish, but I don't change the tune. If you don't find it in the books or in the background of your memory—the exact tune that you want—then you make something up in the same style. But it's both easier and more satisfactory all around to use the authentic thing which has been molded by some centuries in the human race. Why should any critic have to like something because the audience likes it? You do get fed up after a while. I used to be in the Richard Strauss bag. Now I kind of dig the Beatles, especially the advanced Beatles. The *Revolver*-type Beatles. "Eleanor Rigby" is great, and especially the one that's accompanied by the French horn, and the other one that had sort of that Bartók-y string quartet going on behind it. These are very advanced boys. But of course popular music has been happening for *decades*. What do you think the Strauss waltzes were but popular music? What do you think Victor Herbert was but popular music? Not to speak of, in my own lifetime, Jerome Kern and George Gershwin and Irving Berlin, all great masters. The fact that they were working in direct contact with unbreakable popular traditions, such as the thirty-two-bar chorus, doesn't alter the fact that they were great musical masters. I admire them no end. There've always been those. And don't forget Gilbert and Sullivan operettas and musical comedies. Oh, when I was a child and growing up, I went to all of them! I went to the Chicago ones. You know, there's a whole Chicago school of those they produced here, like *The Prince of Tonight*, with the hit song "I Wonder Who's Kissing Her Now." That's all Chicago, yes, yes.

I'm not looking for any explosion in either music or poetry or painting. They're all quiet these days. The explosions are coming elsewhere, in the reorganization of the world for production, distribution, finances, and the arts of war. Those are going along rapidly. And in a time like that, culture stays quiet and holds on. Get the world a bit steady and then the arts will move.

AARON COPLAND
1961

Like Virgil Thomson, Copland was a disciple of the eminent French music teacher Nadia Boulanger. Both regarded her with reverence. Copland was known not simply for composing American music, but for his arrangements of many of the classics as well.

Nadia Boulanger wasn't that much older than I was when I studied with her—precisely thirteen years older. Yet she had a very young attitude herself.

Her lessons, as I remember them, they were more like discussions than teacher telling the student what to do. She had two very attractive qualities. One was her extraordinary love for music. It was exhilarating, intoxicating just to be near her. Music meant so much to her, and it was so *live* a thing to her that you couldn't help but, if you had similar sentiments, feel stirred up and excited by merely being in her presence. The other thing she had was the quality of giving you confidence in yourself. Some teachers work by tearing down. They tell you that you really are a worm, you don't know from nothing. The composer Paul Hindemith is that kind of man. He tends to tell students they know nothing. Some students love that; they have a feeling, "Well, here's a man who's really honest with me, I don't really know anything, and now I'm really going to begin with him to learn something." Nadia Boulanger wasn't like that. She gave you the feeling that you could do even more than you yourself thought you could do. That was very stimulating. I think it was those two elements in her character that attracted me most in those days. She was very broadly cultured. It was very exciting for me to meet with musicians who understood the very latest things in music. That was in the twenties, when there were a lot of new things happening. She also seemed thoroughly at home with Bach and pre-Bach music, Palestrina, and even before Palestrina, so that you had the feeling her range was terrific. There were no secrets about music for her, so that for any questions you had in your mind, she knew the answers. She was a very fine organist, and she was coming to America to make her debut as an organ soloist with two of our best orchestras — the orchestra that Walter Damrosch conducted, this was in 1925, and also with Serge Koussevitzky and the Boston Symphony. He was having his first winter as regular conductor of that orchestra. They both invited her to play organ solo music with them. She asked me if I wouldn't write her a piece for those two occasions. So I agreed to write an organ symphony, though I didn't know very much about the organ, and I had never heard how any of my own orchestrations sounded. I had orchestrated things, but never heard them. That was very brave of her, don't you think, I mean, to take a chance on a young student? I was twenty-three. I worked very hard. I had come back from Paris by then, and sent her the music. She kept writing me letters: "Hurry up, hurry up. I've got to have time to learn this stuff." I sent her the music and then she came and played it.

I was very interested in jazz in the twenties. Mostly as an easy way, you might say, or an obvious way of using materials which everybody would recognize as being American in origin. In the twenties, several composers, not only myself, had a very strong preoccupation about the writing of a music that everybody could identify with our country. I, after all, was studying in Paris, and I realized that Debussy and Ravel were very typically French, and so one wondered, couldn't we do that same thing in America? Why couldn't we write a serious music that was not jazz, but perhaps related to jazz, which everyone would immediately recognize as American? I think we did. But the fact that we did means the younger people didn't have to do it anymore, so that after the pieces that were written in the twenties, there was a lack of interest in the jazz field. Now, of course, things have changed again.

I was very anxious to evoke a particular atmosphere through the movie music I wrote for *Of Mice and Men* and *Our Town*. One took place on a California ranch; the other took place in a New England town, in New Hampshire. Most film scores in those days, in the early forties, tended to sound alike. It didn't matter whether the movie took place in the time of Henry VIII or whether it was about a couple of today's prizefighters. A kind of late-nineteenth-century, Tchaikovsky-ish, Franck-like score was pasted on whatever the film happened to be about. I think perhaps, in stressing the particular landscape of California and trying to evoke that landscape in musical terms, I had something of an influence on the westerns you hear on television today. In other words, normally you nowadays hear a folk tune, a simple cowboy folk tune, which they'll treat in a more singular way than was customary before. I think *Of Mice and Men* was one of the first scores that would have stressed that idea. When you write music for a film, you live with the film, you live with the actors, for six weeks or more—you react to them. It's very possible that the music could take on the characters, the thing that you look at so often. The most flattering thing that can be said to a film composer is to have someone come up to you and say, "Well, I've gone back to that film and sat there with my eyes closed, just to listen to the music." [Laughs happily] But the use of film music as a concert piece, that's a separate operation. The fact that it might do well for a film doesn't necessarily mean that it will make a successful concert piece. Generally, you would have to rework it so that it would have more flow and connection. Generally musical sequences last over a very brief time, maybe three minutes long. They don't make full movements. You have to rework them. I've done that. I did that for the music I wrote for another Steinbeck film and I made a suite from those pieces—*The Red Pony Suite*.

You said something in a recent Saturday Review *article—you were speaking of the soigné approach, the smooth, slick . . . Would you mind expanding on that a bit?*

That was a notation I made in a musical journal I occasionally keep, a notation that occurred to me when I was sitting in a concert listening to X conduct. I had the feeling that there was too much emphasis being put on just the smooth, beautiful sounds in themselves. And it suddenly occurred to me that really, when composers write music, they're not thinking about smooth, beautiful, round, lovely sounds in and for themselves. They have another idea in mind, and that is the expressive quality of the music. It's like looking at a face that has no lines in it and not too much character. We work in terms of faces that are full of character. You want to see the lines, you want to feel the expressive thing behind the notes, and that's the important thing. Any composer will any day give up a certain smoothness and soigné kind of approach to the performing of this music if he can get in exchange the essence of what he thinks he was putting into that piece in terms of feelings and character and expression. In conducting, I've often had to say to orchestral musicians, "You're playing too beautifully. You're playing the way all your life long you've been trying to play. You study to make the most beautiful tone possible, the most round, the most lovely. That's not what I want. I want a rather harsh sound, but one that has character and which seems to be connected with this particular passage, in this particular piece, and wouldn't belong anyplace else." You need musicians of imagination to give you that.

Composers have very bad reputations as conductors. They're known to be generally inadequate on the podium. It's understandable, because after all, composing and conducting are two very different activities. And a gift in one department doesn't mean you have a gift in another. You might know, and most composers would know, how they want their music to go. But you might not have the technical ability to indicate to an orchestra how that should happen. Most composers make very poor conductors. If you are a composer and begin to conduct, you have that to contend with. On the other hand, people get so surprised if you can conduct at all, with any adequacy, that they possibly exaggerate your qualities. I like to conduct my own things because I have a feeling I know how I want them to go. And I've conducted a sufficient number of orchestras by now so that I feel I'm able to indicate what I want to an orchestra. Koussevitzky used to say to me, even when the composer doesn't technically conduct as well as a professional conductor, he nevertheless gives to the music some quality that no conductor could quite give, and I think there's some truth to that. You have a great advantage as a composer, and that is that the orchestral musician is willing to admit that you really ought to know how this piece should go. Any maestro, aside from a Toscanini or a Bruno Walter conducting Beethoven or Brahms, is subject to doubt in the orchestral musician's mind: "Does this fellow really have the right to be standing up there and telling me how this goes? I played with another conductor who thought it should go differently." You get a great advantage in this instance in being the composer of the piece. And also, if they like the music, they give you something added, a little extra something, in the interpretation, because you are the composer, and here they're playing with you. This opportunity is not going to happen every day of the week. It's not a routine thing. There's something special about the occasion when you play with the composer conducting. So I feel I get the advantage of their extra interest. Naturally, you should have the ability to communicate though gesture and facial expression what it is you want.

*You once referred to opera as "*la forme fatale.*"*

I was thinking of *la femme fatale*, and switching it around to *la forme fatale*. A composer beginning an opera should be a little fatalistic about the whole operation because the end result is *so* unsure, and the amount of work and labor that goes into the writing of a full-length opera is so enormous by comparison with the slight chance of its being a really full-fledged success, that you're really taking a terrific chance. In that sense one feels attracted to it, as one would be attracted to something that's full of danger. One really is quite frightened at the prospect of sitting down to begin an opera. Look how different it is from writing a symphony. After all, in the time that it takes you to write one opera, a three-act opera, you could write three symphonies. Maybe it'll take you two or three years to do it, and in one night, in two and a half hours, everybody decides about it. That's very frightening. If you have a symphony played and it gets bad criticism, it doesn't matter. Six months later somebody else someplace else may take a chance and conduct it. Not an opera. If San Francisco hears that the City Center in New York gave something and it was badly written up, they won't touch it.

Would you mind telling us how you came to write your opera The Second Hurricane?

It was written in the late thirties at a time when there was a lot of interest in something called *Gebrauchsmusik*. That's a large German word that simply means music for youth, it's written for kids. It began, I think, in the minds of certain publishers who thought that here was this large audience, potential audience, of young people who weren't familiar with the contemporary idiom in music, and couldn't composers write music of rather simple, technical requirements which nevertheless would tip them off in the contemporary idiom, which would make it seem natural for them to get started on chords that were a little more complex, and rhythms that were less conventional? With that in mind, a number of composers, Hindemith at the head of them, wrote such works. Kurt Weill wrote one called *The Yes-sayer*, which was very popular in Germany. They wrote works for kids to perform that weren't like Gilbert and Sullivan but that treated contemporary subject matter and used rhythms and melodies and harmonies a little more advanced than the music they were accustomed to. And that was the origin of *The Second Hurricane*. It was shown on TV about a year ago last April, on one of those young people's symphony concerts [Young People's Concerts] with Leonard Bernstein. I wish that TV were more of a musical medium than it is. Actually, it's something you look at, rather than you listen to. And in that sense, I think we composers think of FM stations and regular radio stations as more supportive of our music than we can hope TV to be. But, of course, in special programs, like operas or such things as the Bernstein broadcasts, it's an enormous help because it reaches so many people in so vivid a way. I don't think that they've yet worked out a way of presenting serious music so that it can be interesting to look at the same time as it is to listen to, and I'm not even sure there is such a thing that's possible—it's the very nature of the medium. I say it reluctantly, but I'm afraid that's the truth.

Obviously, the younger generation is always interested in things that interest them, not in things that interest the older generation. In that sense, Nadia Boulanger, who's now over seventy and still teaching young people, would inevitably find some of them not sympathetic to some of her ideas and interested in quite different things, which is what I meant by strange gods. It's very extraordinary, for instance, that the leader of the young French composers nowadays, Pierre Boulez, should be taking so much of his inspiration from German sources. His interest in the music of Anton Webern would never have been able to be predicted by anybody who had studied the scene in the twenties. And yet there it is. So that we, the older generation, can't hope to guess in advance what the young people will be interested in ten years from now. All we know is that it's likely to be something that wouldn't have struck us as being the thing that they would be interested in.

I think that young composers today are living in a rather difficult time. It's because music is in a great state of turmoil, much more of a turmoil than the great public at large knows about. The very basic constructural principles of music are in question now. If we thought that music should have flow, a kind of naturalness of flow, the younger people may think it should be just the opposite, it should be discontinuous—it has too much flow. So that every possible principle that I might name for you, they would give you the very opposite idea as a possibility. Everything seems to be open to question in a way that, oh, I doubt whether it was true in the same way for us thirty years ago. Although we felt that we were living in a very revolutionary period in music then. I think it's more revolutionary now, therefore more difficult, for the young people to find themselves, find their own way, and I don't know exactly what's going to happen. Everything is up for question. And I think you can ascribe this to natural historical development. I mean, our idea of sound, after all, has changed. Think: the way we make sounds, how the word *sonic* is in everybody's mind. That was not true thirty years ago. Breaking sound barriers, using sound to investigate whether ball bearings are working well or not. It's bound to influence music, it must influence music. I think it's a little early to have any feelings about electronic music. Let's try it out. I'm very permissive in my attitudes. Let 'em try it out, give 'em plenty of rope.

[Laughs] Perhaps you read the article by Lukas Foss in the Saturday Review *some time ago called "The Myth of Music's Universality." He says it is a myth that music speaks a universal, international language. We think in terms of cultural exchange, but he seems to deny that this has any effect.*

Yes, I did read that. It's a sort of platitude—everybody says the one universal language is music. Theoretically, it should be, but actually, when I was in Japan, I heard kinds of music that seemed very strange to me, so that when you think about it more specifically, and not in that overall sense, then it's obvious that people do create kinds of music that other people might not understand. I think that's what he was thinking of when he wrote that. As languages go, it has a better chance of being international than most. There are large segments of the world that speak together musically. I realized that when I was in the Soviet Union. There's no trouble at all talking to a Soviet musician about Beethoven's accents and fortes. We think exactly the same in musical terms. So it's easy for artists of different countries with different political systems to get together and completely forget about the political systems during the time that they're talking about art. In that sense, music is universal.

LEONARD BERNSTEIN
1985

In hearing Leonard Bernstein, the maestro, we think of someone whose giftedness and generosity of spirit have enriched us all. He always speaks of delight, wonder, joy in music.

In one of your essays you spoke of a strange time, the twentieth century, in which something is lacking. In the old days, when a new composition was written by a composer, you say there was a sense of anticipation and exhilaration. Today it's more of a "what's this guy gonna do?"

I think I was talking about musical theater in Italy. The advent of a new Puccini opera or a new Verdi opera was a cause for enormous excitement and speculation. And then once it had been premiered, well, it was the talk of every breakfast, lunch, and dinner for the next several weeks. That doesn't happen much anymore. The new works don't seem to cause any anticipation, and very few of them cause any aftermath of excitement. It used to be the same thing in a rather more restricted societal way with the advent of a new Brahms symphony or a new Bruckner symphony or a new Wagner opera. Right up into the twentieth century, into Mahler. But by Mahler's time, I think most people are convinced they have had it. They've had the great ones. Mahler was not considered great in his time at all. It took him fifty years and a very hot PR campaign by me on his one hundredth birthday to sort of get him on the boards. I didn't have to go discover the pieces. They were all there. And most of them had been played by somebody or other. Bruno Walter was his great disciple, and of course he was one of my masters [Leonard Bernstein's debut was as a pinch-hitting conductor of a challenging program of music by Schumann, Rózsa, and Richard Strauss for the New York Philharmonic; Bruno Walter had been scheduled to conduct but suddenly became ill, and the occasion provided an instant celebrity]. But he didn't conduct many. He didn't, for example, conduct the Mahler Ninth until he himself was in his advanced years. He was afraid to. It was so complicated and long, and the audience walked out. Now you can't get a seat.

What do you think explains the change from that anticipation and excitement of some new work to "show me"? There's a slight touch of meanness to that challenge.

It came over into our time, was transferred to Broadway theater—which was sort of our equivalent of what used to be the excitement about a new Mozart opera, or Wagner, or Verdi, or a Brahms symphony. Actually, the symphonic age is more or less over, and that ended with Mahler, Sibelius, Shostakovich. But we did have a phenomenon slightly resembling the Italian opera craze on our own Broadway. There was just as much excitement in the Depression year of 1932 about *Of Thee I Sing* as there was about *La Traviata*, I'm sure. But it was much more commercially oriented, and is. I was at one time so excited about the Broadway musical as an equivalent to a Mozart *singspiel*, and eventually as a kind of American opera that we could develop out of our own roots, namely, our own kind of pop music, and our own know-how. There's a special kind of American take on musical theater that we have taught the world. Nobody else really knew how to do that. It included everything that came out of vaudeville, burlesque, the American musical comedy. I did a TV program on it. We were up to *South Pacific* in those days, that's as far as we had come—and I had traced it from the origins, which went back to something called *The Black Crook*, back in the nineteenth century. That was our first American musical, which was started by accident through a combination of a stranded ballet company and a lousy melodramatic company that got together to save their skins, and formed an American musical. With *South Pacific*, we developed something that was almost operatic. And toward the end of that show, I dared to prophesy a little bit, based on the double monologue from *South Pacific*, which is quite operatic in its tone, and yet completely American and simple and not phony, and doesn't have any sort of mock operatic heroics or anything. I dared to prophesy that something great would come out of this that we could call American opera. I tried to do my bit for it. I did *Candide* that very year, and *West Side Story*. They both came out two years later. Since then I have not been able to touch it. Oh, wow, things have become so commercial that people are afraid to take risks anymore. And God knows *West Side Story* was an enormous risk, as was *Candide*. And don't underrate the book of *West Side Story*. Everybody seems to leave that part out, and I think Arthur Laurents gets a very poor deal in that he wrote one of the really greatest and most succinct, most self-sacrificing, and yet poetic books of any musical I know.

I know that you admire Marc Blitzstein very much.

Deeply. His name comes up not often enough. And in a sense he's one of the fathers of our so-called know-how, as I refer to it. A highly original genius who had several problems. He was a little bit, perhaps, too stuck on the working-class problem, on which you can't be stuck enough, because of the problem and the immensity of it. On the other hand, stylistically and musically, you can get stuck. He had his highest moment with *The Cradle Will Rock* from 1937.

I was in it in Chicago.

You've been *in* it?

I was Editor Daily.

Editor Daily! I would have guessed that. [He sings, "Have you been to Honolulu"; I say the next phrase; Lenny, clapping, joins in, "Where your boredom would be banned . . ."] I know every note and word of *Cradle Will Rock*. In fact, I know every note and word of almost everything he wrote. Now, he never quite made it in the biggest sense of the word. He was always broke, and he always had to be subsidized. As a matter of fact, when he died in Martinique, he was in the course of writing an opera for the Met, which had been commissioned with a lot of push from a whole lot of us. It was about Sacco and Vanzetti and that whole case. I know that the Met was very relieved not to get it, that it never did get finished. There were lots of people on the board of the Met who were more than anxious about the subject matter: "How did we ever get this guy Blitzstein commissioned to do this Communist opera about these two dago reds called Sacco and Vanzetti?" His adaptation of Lillian Hellman's [play, *The Little Foxes*], *Regina,* is a masterpiece, a flawed masterpiece. That is, with flaws that I know I could myself correct if I could only find the time. In fact, when he died, I made an oath that I would. I still haven't found the time to make the version of *Regina* that I know I could make because I followed his progress through the whole backing and filling and changes. And of course, he had a lot of trouble with Lillian, on whose play, *The Little Foxes*, it was based, who disapproved of almost any change he would make. And of course, you have to make changes to make an opera. You have to bring in more things to sing about, more people who can sing.

I'm thinking of the various facets of your career, your life.

How did we get off Marc so fast? I think it's terribly important that people know this name, because I know that I couldn't exist musically as I am if it hadn't been for Marc, and I know the same thing is true of the whole Broadway theater, and I mean the traditional and establishment—the Dick Rodgerses of the world. He had a tremendous influence. Think of the song that opens *The Cradle Will Rock*. Isn't that an amazing way to start it out? Just a little girl, a hooker, standing under a lamppost waiting for a guy to come by. That's one of the most amazing pieces of drab simplicity made into sheer beauty that I can think of. Way, way before the Beatles, it reminded me of some of the Beatles' songs and their drabness—"She's Leaving Home." You know that song, and how awfully drab it is, and how beautiful it is at the same time. That's the essence of Marc: "You can live like hearts and flowers, and every day is a wonderland tour / [Sings] And you can dream and scheme and happily put and take, take and put / But first be sure there's a nickel under your foot. [Speaking] Go step on someone's neck while you take him / Cut into somebody's heart while you put . . ." That's the Brecht line of it. Oh, he was capable of writing ecstatically joyous music, but always music for the layman and the workingman. In fact, *No for an Answer* was all about that. It was a real opera, a hard, stony, severe opera about Greeks who worked in a restaurant who tried to form a union. It was intended to be heard by that kind of audience, too, as well as every other kind. Nobody had ever thought of writing operas for Greek restaurant workers, people who washed dishes and barely spoke the language. He was a genius. I don't mean just these lyrics that we've been quoting, but the harmonies of "A Nickel Under the Foot" have affected American theater music very deeply. And the phrasing, the bar phrasing, phrase lengths. He was very sophisticated musically. He just put it all at the service of the proletarian hearer and viewer, and that was his dedication. And he never lived to complete it in a satisfactory way.

You've often talked about American music, and jazz.

I've been talking about that all my life. There's of course the black pop tradition, which comes from way back, slavery days, chain gangs, blues, and hollers and shouts, and then of course the whole Christian side of it, which is gospel and spirituals, that mixture of primitivism and Christianity which made black music what it was, plus the mixture with European forms and dances and quadrilles and polkas and all the rest of it. Which in the hands of blacks turned into something quite memorable. Way beyond all of that, and even beyond the development of forms such as the blues, which is a truly classical form, I mean, it's not just a style or a mood. A blues is a classical style in iambic pentameter, by the way. That is the only continuing tradition of the black roots of pop music. But it takes you into the great development of this huge tree of popular music, which is now called rock, and which has emerged into one of the highly industrialized enterprises since U.S. Steel—a billion, billion, multibillion-dollar industry. It's almost as big as cocaine, this record business. What I found was not only that there was a new sociological level to the black jazz/rock/pop world, but I recently had a kind of revelation about the nature of the role that blacks have played in our history in every way, and of the great American refusal, or at least reluctance, to deal with it. What would American music or culture be like if there were no black people here? That's a great fantasy. Imagine, what would it have been like? It used to be one of our great racist slogans, and still is in many quarters, I'm afraid: "Well, if you don't like it, why don't you go back where you came from?" Meaning Hungary, Poland, Russia, Italy, Ireland, Africa. There used to be a pop song. Of course, you're too young to remember this, Studs.

I top you by ten years, but go ahead.

There was a highly patriotic pop song. I wish there were a piano here, 'cause I'd sing it for you at the piano. It was called "Don't Bite the Hand That's Feeding You." It went: "If you don't like your Uncle Sammy / Then go back to your home o'er the sea." How do you like that lyric? "To the land from whence you came." Another solipsism. [He semisings] "Whatever be its name / But don't be unfaithful to me." Uncle Sammy speaking. "If you don't like the stars in Old Glory / If you don't like the red, white, and blue / Then don't be like the cur in the story / Don't bite the hand that's feeding you . . . ta-da-da da da! If you don't like your Uncle Sammy . . ." It was exactly in the George M. Cohan style. If you don't like your Uncle Sammy, then get the hell out of here. Who needs you? But the whole point was that this was a country to which you could come and be free not to like your Uncle Sammy and criticize him while at the same time you loved your country. All these millions of immigrants who came here came out of love for this country. I know my father did, my mother. My father came at the age of sixteen—cleaned fish under the Brooklyn Bridge for a buck a week. My mother came at the age of six and worked in the cotton mills in Lawrence, Mass., where I was born. Bread and Roses [a labor song that came out of the Lawrence strike]. And it's still number Z on the list of acceptable cities in this country, by the way. It's the lowest, still to this day. They did a wonderful thing on my sixty-fifth birthday, which was only two birthdays ago. They turned it into a celebration in the city of Lawrence. I turned down every city in the world, the ones that wanted to have grand things, and grand philharmonics, and opera companies, and stuff. I went to this little town with my mother, and millions of people turned out. We turned it into a day for peace and nuclear disarmament.

This was out of context for a "celebrity" celebration.

What we've lost is that drive. You've left out a couple significant things, like dope, instant gratification. These things go with television. You push the button, instant gratification. That is a form of infantilism, which you well know about. Dope satisfies the same thing. And living in a world where everybody born since 1945 is born into a world where they automatically accept the minute-to-minute possibility of planetary destruction has turned out a couple of generations since then that are completely different from any generation that ever lived, especially in this country. Why bother? Why knock your brains out if in five minutes the whole thing can blow? Push the button. Get your instant gratification on television. If you don't like what they're showing, push another button and you see something else.

I don't think anybody will disagree with the fact that music is one of our basic and deepest levels of communication. You and I could talk for hours using words, and maybe spurt a few metaphors, and we could suddenly be talking on another level, which would be poetry. But we could never communicate on so deep a level as if we sang to each other, even if it's "The Nickel Under the Foot" or "If you don't like your Uncle Sammy." Musical communication occurs on a very profound level. Therefore, why isn't it of necessity included as a language that can be read, just as every other communicated language is taught? When I went to elementary school, I was taught to read music. I guess I was especially attracted to it because I was musical. But it seems to me everybody could do it. And we did some fine things. It wasn't a very special elementary school—it was just the William Lloyd Garrison School in Roxbury, Massachusetts, public school. Of course, the minute I got into the great school, my high school, the Boston Latin School, they wouldn't hear of music. It was compulsory Latin and Greek and high intellectuality.

I think we have a new little hope, I mean, if we can manage to survive at all—which is up for grabs, your bet against mine—if we survive at all, I think we have an interesting period coming up, a whole new bunch of young, serious composers, who are serious to the extent that they can write pop music and nonpop music, whatever that is. I call it all serious music, and I abhor the term *classical,* and I won't use that. *Porgy and Bess* is a classical opera, and certain Beatles songs are classics. So I cannot make this phony distinction between classical and pop music. But there is a generation of people coming up whose works you can trace back to Marc Blitzstein and before that. Again bringing our conversation around: if we can live through this present ghastliness, if we can find some kind of road to disarmament and some end to the madness of an arms race, I think we're going to have a very interesting kind of blend of music. But this depends largely on education, as does everything, as you know. You know, *West Side Story* is a highly critical piece [about] America. The Russians perform it all the time. Of course I never get a nickel from it because they pirate it, they steal it. [Laughter] They translate it into their own language and change the lyrics, ad lib, and make it much more critical of America. In fact, they make it critical of America from their point of view. I can't control this at all. But what they don't understand is that the great value of a piece like *West Side Story* is that we live in a country where we can do that. And that's what we've got to preserve, and we can do that only by education. We have to make education the keynote again, just as it was with Jefferson, the key to everything.

∾ Impresario (1) ∾

SOL HUROK

1971

He was considered the most successful, and certainly the most colorful, of all the impresarios in the world of classical music and dance. Among his clients were Feodor Chaliapin, Isadora Duncan, Nellie Melba, and Anna Pavlova.

What was your first impression of the singer Feodor Chaliapin, since you were his American impresario?

My first impression of Chaliapin—this was in 1906, when I arrived in the United States. He was at that time singing at the Metropolitan Opera. The first time I heard him was in Boito's *Mefistofele* and as Don Basilio in *The Barber of Seville*. He didn't stay long; he left in the middle of the season because the critics said that he was too vulgar, too undressed, half nude in the middle of *Mefistofele*. I brought him back in 1920. I was always crazy about

Chaliapin; I communicated with Chaliapin for years and years and he never answered anything. Suddenly, I get a cable: I should come to meet him in Paris at the Grand Hotel. When I arrived in Paris, he wasn't there. He said he'd be back at five o'clock, and in Russian I talked to him: "I'm here because I got your cable, now we'll be ready to come to the States." He said, "What? I should come to the United States? I don't like it, the critics didn't like me, and I don't like them, and I don't care." "So why did you ask me to come here to see you—to talk?" "Because I wanted to see the man who writes me for three, four years letters and cables. I wanted to see how he looks." He saw that I felt pretty bad, I had expenses and everything else. He said, "Oh, don't worry about expenses." Then he got quite moved. He said, "What are you doing tonight?" And at that time I already managed Nellie Melba and the violinist Eugène Ysaÿe. I said, "I have dinner with Melba and Ysaÿe." So he says, "Wait a minute. We all go to dinner tonight." Jules Massenet had composed the opera *Don Quixote* and dedicated it to Chaliapin in 1912 or 1913. So he called up Massenet, he said, "My American manager is here, I would like you to invite him for dinner tonight." Here he is calling me his American manager, I'm quite enthusiastic. He calls up Nellie Melba and Eugène Ysaÿe. We all went to dinner at Massenet's home. We got there about nine o'clock and we stayed until about four. Chaliapin sang with Melba together, and Massenet was at the piano. At four o'clock, I said, "Mr. Chaliapin, what are we going to do about it?" He said, "Oh, we had a wonderful time, but the States, I'm not doing it." I left Paris without a contract. It took so many years, revolutions, and wars to bring him back.

He was a man of impulse . . . ?

Every great artist has the characteristics of the character they play. That's the problem with most artists. You see an artist singing, you see the singer, but you don't see the character. Chaliapin used to sing the character; he portrayed the character. You didn't see Chaliapin there, you saw the character portrayed. When he sang *Boris Godunov*, that was Godunov. Great artist. You know, Anna Pavlova I managed. Anna Pavlova had in her ballet those certain characters. You didn't see Pavlova, you saw that character she portrayed as she danced. The trouble with a lot of our young artists or young singers, or young dancers, they don't know how to hold their hands, and they don't portray the character.

The critic Claudia Cassidy [Chicago's influential music and drama critic] was saying of you: "Temperament is caviar to Hurok. Very expensive and very trying, but there is no art without it."

People say, "How the hell in the world can you manage these people who have so much temperament?" My answer is, if they wouldn't have no temperament, I wouldn't manage them. You wouldn't go to listen to them. You would come out of the theater saying, "Oh, very cold. It didn't lift me up at all." They have to have temperament. People are stupid when they talk about temperament. If anybody had no temperament, he is nowhere. A man gets sick, a woman gets sick, and they cannot talk anymore, they call them vegetables. So I call people without temperament vegetables.

Cassidy said that you once heard the Russian writer Maxim Gorky speak.

In 1904 I heard Gorky in Russia. I was a young boy. My father used to take me into places where he used to buy one thing, steal everything else. A lady said to my father, "I'll take your son to an important gathering." He didn't know what it was. She brought me to a great factory. Suddenly I see ten thousand people in that plant. One speaker speaks, an old man. I was amazed to hear him speak. The next morning, she said, "Do you know who you heard speak there? That was Maxim Gorky." He was arrested. That's the first time I heard Maxim Gorky and the next time I heard him was in America, 1906. Between 1906 and 1915 and 1920, there was, I would say, an American renaissance. The very greatest artists of the world were here.

What led you to become interested in the arts and performing artists? Was it hearing Gorky?

My people, my parents, had some plantations as well as businesses. I used to watch the girls and boys go to work and sing on rowboats and sing with the balalaika, with accordions to accompany them. The seeds were planted in my heart, the sentiment, the songs and the dance movements that leapt in there. When I arrived in Moscow at the age of fourteen, fifteen, already I wanted to go to concerts, music. My dream was how I could get into this business.

Chaliapin, I suppose, represented the earthiness as well as the loftiness of the artist.

Chaliapin was not only Russian, he was international. He was the greatest singing actor in the world. I managed Chaliapin, Pavlova, Luisa Tetrazzini. I managed Ysaÿe, I managed the violinist Mischa Elman, Artur Rubinstein. I brought Isadora Duncan and the Isadora School over from Russia.

Here came a revolutionary artist.

Well, I forgive Isadora Duncan. She made a lot of trouble and everything else, but she had greatness, her personality, her charm, her philosophy of life. And what she did for dance in the United States and in the world, I forgive her. All the trouble she has given me, I forgive her. She once wrote me a note to the Continental Hotel in Paris. She said, "Forgive me for the troubles I've given you. I would like to see you." I went to see her because she was not the same anymore. We went out for supper in Paris. I was with a lady friend, and we had one drink of champagne. There begin to be suddenly ten or twelve young men around Isadora Duncan. My friend says, "You better go, because it's going to be unlimited here." Isadora says, "Let her go, you stay here." The next day, these two gendarmes and the managers of that restaurant, they come over. I say, "What is the trouble?" "There is this bill here. She sent the bill to American impresario Sol Hurok at the Continental Hotel." We had to settle it. Instead of seventy-five thousand francs, they settled for thirty-five thousand, for half of it. But I forgive her everything.

You also brought over the Ballet Russe and the Bolshoi.

The Kirov, too. And the Georgian and the Ukrainian dancers. And the Stuttgart Ballet—one of the greatest ballets, tremendous. Nobody should miss it. It's coming to your city, Chicago, for a week. That is a dramatic ballet company. They unfold the dance, you don't need any dialogue—dramatic expression and the interpretation of that music or that particular ballet. Should not miss it.

You've done remarkable work in the world of diplomacy as well, through the arts, helping span the gap between the Soviet Union and the U.S.

I've done this before even in Russia, the cultural exchange. I did it on my own, I brought artists from all over the world. I brought from Japan, from India, from Italy, from France. I was the first one to bring the Comédie Française, nobody had seen them before. The Peking Opera. Richard Strauss, I brought to America. There isn't anything outstanding that I didn't manage.

You also brought [the dancer] Uday Shankar. You introduced a wholly new culture which Americans had never known before.

I've introduced music for the masses, which is very seldom done in the United States.

You said culture for the masses. You have a faith that if the artist is great enough he can reach out to more than the elite?

I always maintain and say that. When the people talk about acoustics, oh, the acoustics are bad, I say there are no good acoustics for bad artists, but there are no bad acoustics for great artists. You must hammer music to the masses, in particular to the youth. This should be a part of the program of the educational committee in every city, in every town. Music should be a part of elementary education. Then you have a better world to live in and better youth to go on with it. Everything I brought in. I haven't got the time to sit and tell you all this. I have to catch a plane, and you have a hell of a goddamn long walk over there till you get to the plane. You have to have a bi-cycle to get there.

~ Part Two ~

∽ **Jazz** ∽

LIL ARMSTRONG
1957

The second wife of Louis Armstrong, she came into the studio one day during the last years of her performing life—she was a pianist, composer, and singer—and sat down at the piano and started playing and talking. Somehow it's hard to separate her from the very beginnings of Louis Armstrong's career. Probably her greatest contribution was acquainting Louis with the nature of urban life. There's no doubt that she helped his career to speed along. His knowledge of behavior both musical and otherwise in the big city came from her.

I guess I was destined to be a musician because we had an old organ at our house when I was a kid. And they could never keep me away from it. I'd have my cousin do the pedaling and I would do the playing. Finally, my mother decided that maybe I should have music lessons. So one of the schoolteachers taught me music on the side. And side it was. [Laughs] Because, technique,

I never heard of technique. She only taught me to read the notes. But as far as the proper use of my fingers and things, I didn't get proper technique until I went to Fisk University many years afterwards. I was a music major there. After about two years of home lessons, I was the organist for the Sunday school at our church in Memphis. I might have known I was going to end up in jazz—oh my God, my mother was so disappointed when I finally got into jazz—because I used to play "Onward Christian Soldiers" with such a de-cided rhythm that the kids would be marching like little soldiers. Reverend Petty, he used to look over his spectacles at me and wonder what I was doing. But the kids enjoyed it. Later I played the marches at school. I always had that rhythm, that bounce, that definite beat. [Laughs]

Our family moved to Chicago. Oh, Chicago, that was heaven. I strolled all over this town, so much happening. It was during vacation time that I went walking along State Street one day and I passed a music store. I just stopped to look at all the sheet music in the window and, oh, I just wished I had some of it. So I finally decided to go in and buy just one number. They had a man there demonstrating the music. He played several numbers for me, and I didn't like the way he played them. So I said, "Would you mind letting me try?" He said, "Not at all, not at all." So I played them. He said, "Oh, boy, you can play! Do you want a job?" I said, "Oh, I don't know." He said, "I'm not the boss. She'll be in at three o'clock. You come back and I'm sure she'll hire you." So I went home, but I didn't tell my mother about the job. I thought I'd wait and see how everything was going to be with the lady at the store. When I came back at three o'clock, the lady looked at me and said, "Oh, Frank, she's nothing but a child." Frank says—his name was Frank Clemmons—"I don't care, she can play." He said, "Play something for her." So she went to the counter and brought out several pieces and I played them over for her. She said, "Oh, yeah! Well, honey, if you want work, I'll give you $3 a week." I said, "Oh, yes ma'am, yes ma'am." I went home and told my mother, "I have a job playing music." She said, "A job?" I said, "Yes, playing music at the music store for $3 a week." She said, "No, indeed! $3 a week? No, I won't think of it." I said, "I don't care about the $3, I just want a chance to learn all the mu-sic." She said, "Oh, that's all right, then. You can go." So I used to go every day at twelve o'clock and I'd be off at five o'clock. Oh, I got busy learning everything on the counter. In two days, I had memorized everything.

Up to that time, I hadn't heard jazz. I played sheet music, popular songs— "I'm Forever Blowing Bubbles," "Alexander's Ragtime Band." This music store was also a booking agency. All the musicians and entertainers, as they called themselves, used to hang out there and look for jobs. They had jam sessions every day. Different piano players would come in and play and have cutting sessions, as they used to call it. Competition. I took charge of all the piano players that came in, until one day Jelly Roll Morton came in. Oh, boy, he sat down at the piano and his long skinny fingers were hitting those keys and he was beating out a double rhythm and the people were just going wild. I was going wild, too! Jelly Roll is the first pianist that influenced my playing. He played very hard. You could always hear every note I played, 'cause I put all eighty-five pounds to work. [Laughs] He was passing through Chicago from New Orleans on his way to New York. He played all originals, his own pieces. I learned "The Pearls" right off the bat. I've always played that as a tribute to Jelly Roll. It's still a little difficult for me.

While I was at the music store, this New Orleans Creole band came to town. And they didn't have a pianist. Mrs. Jones booked them at a Chinese restaurant on the West Side. They had three girl entertainers there—that's what they called themselves, not singers. So naturally, they had to add a piano to the band. They tried out all the available men around and none of them suited. So just for fun one night, she decided to send me over. Oh-h-h, I was so thrilled. I was gonna play with a band! So I sat down at the piano and I said, "Where's the music?" And they said, "Music? We haven't got any music. We don't use any." I said, "Well, what key are you going to play in?" They didn't know what I was talking about, what key! The leader said, "When you hear two knocks, you just start playing." So he said, "Boom, boom." I didn't know what key they were in, so I just hit the piano real hard. I didn't hit any particular chord, I just hit it, and whatever key they were in, I'd be in it too. So after a few seconds, I could feel the chord changes they were making, and, oh, in no time I'm definitely set with the band. They said, "Don't you go back to the music store. We're going to keep you." They called up Mrs. Jones and made arrangements for me to work with them. They only stayed in this restaurant two weeks after I joined them. We came to the South Side and did the New Deluxe Cafe at Thirty-fifth and State. This was 1919. And Izzy Shaw was the boss there. Mind you, my mother didn't know I was at the cabaret. I told her that I was playing at a music studio where they taught dancing. That was a very common thing then, you know, the dance studios. All went well until one day a neighbor told my mother, "I saw your little girl at the cabaret the other night." [Laughs] My mother tensed up. "My little girl? You must be mistaken." "No," said the neighbor, "I definitely saw her pounding away at the piano." My mother corners me and she says [imperiously], "Lillian, what were you doing at the cabaret?" I said, "Oh, the school gave an exhibition." She accepted that and everything went well until another lady came by. "I saw your little girl at the cabaret." I said, "Uh-oh." My mother was indignant. "Uh-oh, nothin'. I don't want any more of that. What *are* you doing at the cabaret?" I started crying. [Laughs] "I was afraid you'd make me quit and if I quit, I'll have to pay the union $100 fine." She said, "The very *idea*, as hard as I've worked to make a lady out of you, you're playing at a filthy cabaret. Nothing but vulgar music!" I said, "I don't do anything but sit up there and play." She said, "I'll send Mr. Miller to look that place over tonight." Oh my, *she'd* never go there herself to that bad place. Mr. Miller was my stepfather. She let me work that one night, on account of the $100 fine. I made that up, of course. I had to tell her something. Mr. Miller came back and told her it was a horrible place, that people were doing *everything*. So my mother put on her clothes and came up there with fire in her eyes. I already told Mr. Shaw that my mother was on the way and determined to make me quit. When she walked in the door, he greeted her as though she were the Queen of Sheba. "Oh, so you are Lillian's mother. Oh, she is such a *nice* little girl, you should be so proud of her." He went on and on in this smooth way. I could see my mother's chest swelling. He said, "In no time at all, she'll have the world at her feet. When she finishes playing, just listen at the applause she gets." Of course, he had already passed the word that everybody should clap loud. As a rule, they didn't applaud after a dance number. When we got through, you should have heard the thunderous ovation I got. My mother said, "Well, now that you're in this terrible thing, I guess there's nothing I can do. But I will certainly be here every night when you finish, madam." So every night, I'd be the hot Miss Lil till one o'clock. And there she was, like clockwork, standing at the door to take me home.

My mother accepted the inevitable, but she never really forgave me, because I never got back to Fisk University. I was now deep into jazz. I loved that band. After the Deluxe, we went across the street and worked at the Dreamland, 3520 South State. During that time, Joe Oliver heard of me in New Orleans. The fellows of the other bands were almost all from New Orleans. They were telling him of this little ol' girl. We were such a sensation in Chicago that all the places that had dancing wanted a New Orleans band. So the woman who ran the Royal Gardens on Thirty-first Street sent for Joe

Oliver to come and form a band for her. When Joe Oliver heard me at the Dreamland, he asked me to join him. That was the last of 1920. He brought the New Orleans boys with him: Honore Dutrey, trombone, and Johnny Dodds, clarinet, and Minor Hall, Tubby's brother, at the drums. In 1921, we went to San Francisco, played for six months on Market Street. That's when Baby Dodds, Johnny's brother, joined us on drums. Minor Hall had left. I came back to Chicago when King Oliver quit and stayed out a whole year. In 1922, he came back to the Royal Gardens, but he brought another woman piano player with him—Bertha Gonzales from Frisco. She didn't stay long, so I rejoined the band. In the meantime, he had sent for Louis, who was still in New Orleans. That was in the beginning of 1923. I was supposed to play chords and only support the band. Whenever I'd get to feeling good and run up and down the piano and want to make some runs or something like that, they'd say, "Just a minute, lady, we have a clarinet in the band." So I'd have to go right back to chording again. Whenever we wanted to learn new songs, I would get the music and learn it and play it for them, then they'd learn it by ear. We had nothing written. King Oliver sent for Louis to join him in Chicago. That was July 1922. He gave him a nickname, Dippermouth. That was our first record, "Dippermouth Blues," May 1923. We had to go all the way to Richmond, Virginia, to cut it. Louis had learned to read some with Faith Marable's band on the riverboat running from New Orleans to St. Louis. But when he came to Chicago and Oliver, we used no music. So it wasn't necessary for him to read at the time. But *I* knew there would come a time when it *would* be necessary to read music, and I was ambitious for him. I wanted him to be the best cornet player in Chicago. I had no idea he was going to make it as the best in the world. I influenced him to quit the band because I figured as long as he worked for King Oliver he would never do much for himself. Oliver was his idol. Louis wanted to play like him, be like him, everything. He was trying to play like Oliver so bad. But it just wasn't his style.

As soon as we got we married I told him I definitely didn't want to be married to a second-trumpet player. "You've got to play first." He left Oliver and walked around Chicago for a few weeks and got a job at Dreamland, just a couple of blocks away, where I had played with the Creole Jazz Band. That was the first job he got for himself. While he was there, Fletcher Henderson heard about him and sent for Louis to join his band in New York. I remained in Chicago. I don't remember how long he stayed with Fletcher, but I didn't like the idea of us being separated. I was ambitious for Louis and Fletcher Henderson never put anybody's name in the advertising but his own. I wanted Louis' name to be made. So I got the band in Dreamland and I told the boss I wanted my husband to get $75 a week. Fletcher was paying him $55. And I said his name out front. So they advertised him as the world's greatest cornet player. [Laughs] Everybody thought I was crazy. Louis said, "Girl, you're crazy." I made up my mind now that Louis was on his way, and it didn't matter whether I played jazz or not; I went back to school. In 1928, I gave my first public recital. I had studied academic work, counterpoint, composition, conducting at the Chicago Musical College. I was destined to be a jazz pianist, because immediately after all that studying, giving this recital, I cut my finger and couldn't play piano at all for about nine months. Until today, I don't use this fourth finger on my right hand too well. I cut a ligament on it. So after that, I didn't even bother with classical. [A long pause.] I said, "Well, if I go back to school again, take some classes, I'll probably get both hands cut off." [Again, that soft laugh.] I went to school and took up tailoring. I sewed for a year and gave a style show. People came to the show and after they saw all those gowns, they always said, "Now play us a piece." After all that sewing and work, they still wanted to hear me. So jazz it is. I went back to working as a singer. In the meantime, I did have a sixteen-piece girls' band. Oh, yeah, I tried everything. For the last ten, fifteen years now, I've been working a single. [She tears into "Lil's Boogie," whooping at one point and finishing with a flourish.] This was a favorite in Europe. I was there four years, forty-five towns in France, fifteen towns in Switzerland. Berlin, Frankfurt, Copenhagen, Amsterdam, London. Those people really know jazz, everything you're playing, the history. They're catching up to modern, too. Bebop is big there now. I like it. I like everything.

LOUIS ARMSTRONG
1962

It was around midnight and we were in the dressing room of a Chicago
nightclub. It wasn't one attended by jazz aficionados. Its patrons were
usually visiting firemen, merchants, gathered at conventions. They were
more accustomed to another sort of entertainment: exotic dancers and go-
go girls. Armstrong would do; he had become an international icon, but
mostly it was that interpretation of "Blueberry Hill" and his grin and
white teeth were much to their liking. Why his agent had booked him
there for a weekly gig in the late years of his life was something of a mys-
tery. Why they had persuaded him to agree to an interview astonished me.
I was self-conscious and slightly embarrassed. His towel was draped
around his neck; several of his white handkerchiefs were on the table,
moist with perspiration. His upper lip was swollen, having for more than
half a century been pressed against the embouchure of his horn. He was
obviously dead tired, and I suggested that perhaps we should postpone our
conversation. He said, "No, let's do it. I'm okay."

Some six years ago, 1956, you performed in Accra, Ghana.

That was a great feeling. I never saw so many people gathered at one time before. And the way they reacted to our music and everything. I thought it was
great. We were all over Africa, but Ghana was the first. It was just like America to me, the way they appreciated the jazz. At the time, our vocalist, Velma
Middleton, she made that leap in the air and they went wild. Broke it up.

The highlife music of Ghana, did it stem from the jazz of America?

No, we copied it from them. The beat. Tom-toms and drumbeats. I realized
when I went down there that it was copied from them. When the slaves
came, they brought the music with them and they've still got it. It brought me
back to generations, my ancestors in Africa, in New Orleans . . . I could see
so many things that was brought from Africa. It brought back memories.
They used to do their dances for us. Every time we got in a country, there was

always a tribe there, and they'd do their dance and play. I'd sit in with them. Even in the Congo, Leopoldville, there wasn't no fighting the four days we were there. How could they fight with that music goin' on?

It don't matter what the song is, a pop tune or a blues. In the olden days, that's the way we delivered songs. You have to feel the song. It's the same with the horn. I used to sing in a quartet when I was a kid, not even thirteen. I used to sing in church. That's where you get your feelings of songs, in church. Let's say you sing a spiritual. It still has that feeling of reverence, even though it has a different jazz feeling. In *Shadrack,* the album, nothing but spirituals. A lot of people wondered how I could jump from jazz to spirituals. You take an album like *Louis and the Good Book*, and you sing all the spirituals. I'd say, "Whatever song I'm singing, I'm in a spiritual feeling in the song," because in church we did the same thing. At a funeral, a wake, we'd do all the same. In New Orleans, when I was a little kid, we'd go into the cemetery. You'd see those cards in front, and the notes are there and everything. It's up to you to express yourself as you play. "Just a Closer Walk with Thee." It's two feelings you have there. You learn how to read the notes, but you don't learn how to express yourself. The notes is good for you to learn the tune. But it's up to you to phrase it right. There's something beyond the notes, 'cause you're feeling it in your heart. We did the same thing when we were singing in the quartet. All four of us. Pass the hat. I'll go anywhere, go anyplace. Just a day's work. You know, I went to Europe in 1932. Played the Palladium in London. Big ovation, and the people at the stations, airports. People were so excited in Copenhagen that they gave me a trumpet of flowers. They got so excited the trumpet crumpled up, all the flowers, and I run back to the train. I said, "They ain't gonna break my arm." Too excited, you know.

We used to scat sing in the early days, you know, like instruments in the quartet. And so I just went in there and reached back and pulled one out of the bag, and just go on up there and did it. So they kept the record, and called it scat singing. First time I heard the word *heebie-jeebies.* I dropped the music and I looked in the control booth and he kept saying, "Go ahead, keep singing." I didn't see any words, so I made up all the words. Scat. [The band was the Hot Five, with Lil Armstrong at the piano, Jimmy and Baby Dodds at the clarinet and drums, Kid Ory at the trombone.] I know a lot of musicians can sing their parts, but they're not singers. Like, a guy wants to hum your part to you, in the early days, he'd sing the whole thing. But you put him out there to sing by himself he'd probably shiver in his boots. [Chuckles] The instrument then was like his voice. You make the same notes, you know, like his horn. That's why we could scat and do things like that. I always would sing. I was singing before I played the horn, see. So, quite naturally, I could sing the same notes I make on the horn. In the early days, a lot of the boys didn't read music, but they had a good mind—we called it a good ear—and they'd go and put the parts to the lead. Somebody would buy a piano part. Somebody in the band that could read, like the clarinet player, and they had some that could read and they couldn't play as good as the musicians that didn't read. [Laughs] 'Cause they just stuck right to the notes all the time. All we wanted to know was how it sound. After a second chorus, we'd put that piano part down and never look at it again. Good memory. Wasn't nothing written down. Long as somebody could decipher that tune, then everybody would get their parts. When I played second trumpet to Joe Oliver I didn't need no music. I just wanted to know what he was playing. I was so close to Joe that every note he would make, I could put a second to. He'd make the break while the tune was going on, and we'd get to that break. I done put a second to it. And there's never been a team like that since. That's why I think so much of Joe Oliver. I always will. He was the first to use the mute. He had a little flat metal mute. And it's hard to blow in them things, but it got a tune out of it. That mute made it sound more like a human voice. Couldn't nobody else. He put the mute in and put his hand over the barrel with that mute, and he could talk it like a baby or anything. Cry like a woman. He could do anything with that horn. I never tried to do what Joe did on the mute, 'cause nobody could.

In Chicago, 1922, they had plenty of nightclubs. I think they had more nightclubs than they have now. The South Side was loaded with clubs. They had more nightclubs here than they had in New York at that time. [A long pause. Mournful.] Oh, there ain't no excitement now like there was in those days. It ain't like it was in the twenties. I mean the Roaring Twenties was something in Chicago. They had after-hours places that started at midnight.

There's also Armstrong the actor.

We call that our hustle, you know. [Chuckles] When you get a chance, you can ham it up. That's about what I do when I ever put the horn down, just singing and being assured. Blessed assurance. [Laughs]

I'm doing everything I like to do. Everything is all right. A man my age ain't looking for things like that, for no new world. Just get somewhere and live a beautiful life, you know, relax. Because after sixty-two years, you don't have too many more, you know. Just relax. [He sighs.] Very few bands stand up under them one-nighters like we do. We just came from Europe, and we had one day off, and flew down to Chile for the State Department recently. And we had three days off, played one in New Jersey, and then come here for two weeks. So you see, we're kind of busy. Hey, you go to bed day after day, right after a concert. We play a two-and-a-half-hour concert, probably catch the plane the next morning. It wears you down. Get so I can't do it no more. I had a good career, fifty years. Pretty nice.

EARL HINES
1976

"When I met Louis he was playing the same style that I wanted to play on the cornet. And when I was playing on piano we'd sit there and play and we used to use each others' ideas and say thank you for it."

Earl "Fatha" Hines is described by critics as a man who could play the piano as though it were a horn. He blew into it, he breathed into it. He was one of the early pioneers exploring new avenues in the use of this instrument.

"Hines additionally earned immortality as both pianist and band leader. In the years of his early record partnership with Louis Armstrong, he became known as 'the trumpet style pianist,' because of the incisive use of single note lines in his right hand and the dynamic use of octaves that gave his solos a bright, brassy quality. His performances were, by the standards of those days, endowed with a phenomenal beat. Another of his characteristics was the use of the tremolo much in the manner of a trumpet vibrato. Hines' style was the inspiration of many jazz pianists in the early '30s." (Leonard Feather's Encyclopedia of Jazz)

I was listening recently to a recording of "Deep Forest," the theme song of your days as bandleader at Chicago's Grand Terrace Cafe.

That takes me back. I remember the happiness that everybody had during those days. The big bands were very popular. We didn't realize it at the time.

One day a boy named Leonard Reed, who had made some arrangements for me, told me we were a smash in Philadelphia and New York because of our radio program. That started us on our way. I'm talking about 1934, 1935. Our manager and owner of the Grand Terrace, Ed Fox, didn't know what good musicians meant to a band. All he knew was how to run a nightclub. We had just left the Sunset Cafe at Thirty-fifth and Calumet. Across the street was the Plantation, where King Oliver was playing. Somehow the street had died out and there was a lull on the South Side. Everybody said, "This man's losing his mind, gonna open a club in the Black Belt!" Actually, it was a theater with a sloping of the aisles. So he made terraces out of them. That's how it got the name. It was only half completed, no rugs on the floor, an upright piano. The first thing he said, "I'm gonna run it with $100,000, and you'll get your money every week, whether there's anybody in here or not." He was right. For the first three months, we didn't have anybody in the place. Some of the musicians would come in there with their girlfriends and buy this big sandwich or something like that. Any number of nights Fox would sit down on ringside with his family, two boys, and we had to do the show as if the place was full. For three months we didn't get nothing but musicians. They used to come in there and eat steak sandwiches and that was all. He always paid us off. It went on this way until our first broadcast on a station owned by a Cadillac car dealer, Emil Denemark. Our club manager had to fill in as announcer. He didn't know what to talk about. All he could say was so and so just come in and was wearing such and such. Then he said to us, "You're on" and left the stage. It was from that small station people began to learn about the Grand Terrace. After awhile, we were getting people coming from the Gold Coast, the upper crust. That's when the major radio stations became interested and we switched to the big time, the networks. And that's when the boys got interested. The mob saw all those Cadillacs out there with the chauffeurs and what have you and people were hollering over the radio and having so much fun. Al Capone told me long ago—yes, I knew him very well, as well as I'm talking to you. He says, "I've got to have a playground." That's all he wanted it for, just a place to bring some of his people and have fun. He only took 25 percent. He said to Ed Fox, "You need protection." Fox said, "No, I don't. I've been going two years and don't need protection." So Al says, "There's a couple of nice young boys there you like, your two sons." Fox says, "Oh, you wouldn't do that." Al says, "No, we're just trying to protect you." So they had one guy at the cash register, two on the front floor, and one walking around the house. The police never did come in. They come by the door but never inside. Oh yeah, they'd come through the kitchen to have dinner—in the kitchen. If anything rough happened in the house, the gangsters threw them out in the street. The police would pick it up from there. There was law and order in the place. There were some nights when Al would come in and say, "Here's $2,000, Mr. Fox. Close up the place." He wanted it just for his friends and maybe some business associates. We'd put on a show just for them. Then he'd say, "Come on down," and we'd all join the party. This was 1928, when we opened the Grand Terrace and were there for close to twenty years. I had worked at the Apex with Jimmy Noone [jazz clarinetist] in '27, I think, and for a while at the Sunset with Louis. On a number like "Weather Bird," I was the rhythm section as well as playing the piano's harmony parts. I was playing in that style before I met Louis. When we met, we used to knock each other out, because I was doing the same thing he was doing, only I was at the piano.

It started back in my hometown, Pittsburgh, after I had studied classical piano. That posed a big problem when I started doing solos with a jazz band. With my classical piano fingering, I could hardly be heard because we had no amplification then. The singers used megaphones. There was nothing for the instruments. So I had to cut through the band in some kind of way. I started using octaves and playing as though it were a trumpet. They heard me then. That's when the other pianists said I had a trumpet style. That's where it came from. Piano playing is like anything else. I've never tried to play anything the same. When I sit down at the piano, it's always a challenge with me. I'm always exploring. Every time I sit down, I'm looking for chord changes, new ideas. And sometimes I do get tied up in a knot. [Laughs] When you see me smiling up there, I'm lost, trying to find a way to get out. I used to amaze a lot of musicians, especially the rhythm section. They don't know where I'm going. When they finally come in and get back with me, they just smile. That's how one of my big hits, "Boogie Woogie on St. Louis Blues," came about. We were at the Oriental Theater in Chicago. The crowd kept applauding for my piano numbers. I didn't know what in the world to play next. So I just started to play boogie with my left hand. I had a drummer that would catch anything I did, so he started playing the same thing. I said, "Oh, well, everybody knows 'St. Louis Blues.'" So I put in the familiar song and kept the boogie-woogie going, told the brass section to give me a riff, and then I said, "Reed, you give me an organ chord, because I'm going to hold that note up here." "Remember, the end!" Walter Fuller, the trumpet man hollered. "We'll play till 1951." This was 1938. Everybody laughed because none of us thought we'd live that long. It's more fun when you're fishing around. You don't know what you're gonna catch.

What I tried to do was to stay within the range of the chord structures and within the range of the melody, although we'd leave the melody any number of times. But always we came back to the melody. Louis was the same way. Some of the musicians couldn't figure out how I could reach the notes. The story went around that I had my hands operated on to lengthen my span. The boss of a young guy said, "Why can't you get the Earl Hines style?" He says, "I'm not gonna have an operation done on *me*. Hines had all the webs of his hands cut so he could stretch the tenths." [Laughs] I had a long time talking that down. A number of times, they'd come up to me and say, "Let me see your hands."

Oh, Chicago was really jumping in those days, after that temporary lull. I remember one time there were thirty-two bands in town. It was a dancing town. Dancing is what caused the bands to be as large as they were. Promoters were always trying to get bigger places for the bands to play. I remember when we went south, we played in tobacco warehouses where they'd have ten thousand people. That's what caused the bands to increase from three trumpets and two trombones to five trumpets and four trombones. To be heard because the halls were so large. Before they got decent amplification. We were traveling and playing a lot of one-nighters. No concerts, they were dance music. The band jumped. They danced all over America. It was then that some of the younger musicians and arrangers were trying to seek new territories and bring out something new in jazz. They went into what was called modern music. They forgot that there was such a thing as beat, such a thing as melody. It got out of hand as far as the average layman was concerned because they didn't understand those modern terms. People stopped dancing and became spectators. When we were playing jazz we used to get them from eight to eighty on that floor. The kids were dancing as well as the grandfathers. Everybody was on the floor. Some of the ballrooms had a great big screen in the center of the floor. They'd cut the lights down and put the lyrics of all the songs on that screen while the band played it. America was more romantic then. Then, after the war, they were more show bands than dance bands.

Bebop started in my band, yeah. Dizzy Gillespie, Charlie Parker, they were my men. Dizzy used to go to Charlie's dressing room and play out of his exercise book. Charlie would do the same. Play a lot of passages. They had photographic minds and they used to insert some of these passages in the things we were playing. But they were doing it in such an advanced way, especially the original tunes, that the average musician didn't know what it was all about. They had to get some sort of name for it. I remember at Minton's, the club where they used to meet and have jam sessions, playing all those long passages. They end in a sort of bebop sound. That's how it got the name. I always used to like to see guys go as far as they possibly could. They might come up with something exciting that makes sense. But it didn't make sense when they got to the place where they lost the melody and lost the beat. I like the exploring, but I couldn't go all the way with them. I wasn't going to change my band around. Count Basie's another one, never did change. Neither did Duke. I always thought jazz was like the trunk of a tree. After the tree has grown, many branches have spread out. They're all with different leaves and they all look beautiful. But at the end of the season, they fold back up and it's still that tree trunk.

DIZZY GILLESPIE
1982

Dizzy Gillespie was always exploring new sounds. John Birks Gillespie was irrepressible from the word go—the youngest of nine kids, the most irrepressible. At fourteen he joined the school band, the trombone his first instrument. He taught himself the rudiments of this one. But it was the trumpet that Dizzy wanted most to master. His idol was a trumpet player. Each week it was a ritual to listen to the broadcast from the New York Savoy Ballroom. Roy Eldridge's trumpet was featured with the band of Teddy Hill. Young Gillespie listened intently to the solos of Eldridge. This man had his own special style, an amazing range of rich colors and sharp bite. Little Jazz, as Eldridge was called, had gone beyond the New Orleans trumpet style as perfected by Armstrong. He discovered in the trumpet a new dimension.

It is impossible to talk about Charlie Parker without talking about me because we were equally impressed by one another. You could tell by the records that we made before we met. We knocked one another out. Before Charlie Parker came on the scene, there was a resurgence of music in New York City, especially Monk, Kenny Clarke, Charlie Christian. We were looking into new forms, chord progressions. We'd make a standard of regular chords. Where one chord was, sometimes we'd put four chords there. When we put those four chords there, you had to have a new melody because that old melody wouldn't fit those changes. We were doing things with rhythm, with chord changes, progressions, before Charlie Parker came. When he came, he identified our music with a style. So everybody said, "Hey, look! That's the way it's supposed to go." I don't think it was that earthshaking because there were some trumpet players before, and they did things with trumpets that were innovative—guys like Jabbo Smith, Red Allen. Our phrasing was actually different from the phrases of the generation before, which was Roy Eldridge. I would be very downhearted if someone hears me play for a long time and don't hear something new. That would really crush me. If Charlie Parker were alive today, he'd be right in the middle of the jazz scene, I'm quite sure, because he was always in the forefront in composition and as a soloist. As a matter of fact, he's still on the scene because every saxophone player I hear is so widely influenced by Charlie Parker. They just can't get away from him. The same thing happened to Charlie Christian. He was such a prime force in the development of the guitar. Of all of the good guitar players, there was only one that didn't sound like Charlie Christian.

My trips abroad were some of my most important, I feel. Once we were coming from, I think, Karachi in West Pakistan—we were under the auspices of the State Department and the United States Information Agency. They sent us a telegram and said, "It's pretty rough here in Athens. They threw rocks in the window of the United States Information Agency in Greece and broke a lot of furniture. I don't know whether it would be proper for Dizzy to come now." So we sent them back a wire that said, "Believe it or not, here we come." We didn't have too much time; everything was set up. So we got into Athens and we played. It was packed, packed, absolutely packed. At the same time, the Russian ballet was in town. We invited them to our performance and they invited us to theirs. In the middle of our performance—we were playing "A Night in Tunisia"—I do something, an arpeggio or something, and in the middle do a Russian musical phrase. It was a spur-of-the-moment thing. I wanted to make them feel at home, so I played that. We had a good time. But this afternoon, the same kids that were throwing rocks into the Information Agency, we invited all of them, lower grades in school and the college students, to our concert. Those must have been the same students that were throwing rocks. When I came out through the theater, as soon as I hit the sidewalk, these Greek kids grabbed me up and had me up in the air, see. I thought they were going to dash me to the pavement with the anti-American feeling around. But it was the best audience I think that we had overseas. I heard a couple of them say, "Bravo, bravo." I said, well, that's not too bad. And the policeman had to get me down. They wouldn't even let me down. Oh, you would be surprised at the impact music has anywhere in the world. Forget the politicians, send the musicians—jazz, classical, anything. I was thinking that if the government would send us again now, I would like to take my quintet and my music and augment it with the musicians in the country where you are. Instead of playing for them, you'd be playing with them. Being close to another musician, it's one thing when you're on the stage and they're looking up at you, but it's another thing altogether when they're sitting down right beside you and playing with you.

We wanted to play standards that had been written before. We wanted to put new life in them, so we started writing these things. A lot of our numbers are based on the chords of standard tunes. If you take some water and you're gonna make a new drink, and you put in a lot of these other ingredients, the water has got to be the basic thing to work with. I think that rhythm is the basic thing that you have to work with in jazz. When you lose sight of your rhythm, you've lost sight of the whole thing. I remember a piece we played in the forties. Charlie Parker played a two-bar break and he only played one chorus. When people say, "I don't understand your music," I say, "Don't try to understand it, just try to *feel* it. If you get a feeling about it, it's not too necessary to understand it." I hate people that sit down and try to pick music apart. Why do you want to sit down to music to be a surgeon and pick out this little thing that you don't like? Just sit and try to enjoy it. I listen to other people but mostly to myself when I'm playing. I listen to it with that ear because I'm very, very self-critical. I hardly ever listen to my records anyway. When I go to somebody's house and oh, they got a stack of Gillespie records and they put 'em on, I go someplace else. It's already done. Almost everything I play, I say, "Oh, man, I could have played that better, I could have used better taste." Because it's just a matter of taste anyway after you get to a certain point in your development. It's gotta be changing, because your taste is supposed to get better, allegedly.

Latin music rhythmically was so different from our music that its impact just came to me recently. I can understand it now. We'd take three drums on these long country rides, on the bus we'd sit back in the back. You'd think we were in Africa because Chano Dominguez [Spanish pianist] would show me a rhythm, show Al another rhythm, and he'd take another rhythm and then he'd sing. Oh, it was quite something. I became interested in Cuban music when I was with Cab Calloway, but I didn't do anything about it. Cab had a Cuban trumpet player, Mario Bauza. He used to play with Chick Webb, the first trumpet player with Chick. He liked me, and I used to follow him around. Chick used to let me sit in. I was the only one that he'd let sit in. Oh, man, New York was full of trumpet players that wanted to sit in with Chick Webb. Finally, when I got this big band, I told Mario, "I want to get one of those drums those guys play." I know absolutely nothing about it, maybe two bars, something like that. I went to see Chano and he couldn't even speak English. I think my makeup, musically, is sort of on the Latin side because most of the tunes that I write have a Latin influence. They have some kind of a rhythm, something to it. You know, "Night in Tunisia," all these different things, they have the Latin thing. I don't mean to go into this, but it's like the melody that I have in my mind always lends itself to a Latin beat.

I hate drunken people listening to music and trying to make you think that they're enjoying it, and they're only enjoying the whiskey. I've had some experience playing with nonalcoholic audiences before, such as in college concerts. You can't play under the influence of stimulants. Your blood pressure goes up and your mind doesn't work as fast. Playing under the influence of a stimulant is like if as soon as you wake up in the morning somebody gives you a horn and says, "Here, play . . ." Cobwebs, all over your mind. Some young musicians think because they're under the stimulant of one sort or another, it sounds better. Whoo-ooo, but they got a *rude* awakening coming. [Laughs] If someone were to put a tape recorder on you when you're under the influence, you really notice just how you sound, because it sounds good to you. I'm not speaking against whiskey because it has its medicinal values. Your reflexes slow up, therefore you're a little behind. You have hallucinations. You think you're fine.

I expect to settle in West Africa. I want to start a little school down there because they have contributed so much to us and they've gotten so little in return. Maybe Ghana, maybe Nigeria. It doesn't matter what country, because I have such a strong feeling for the whole of Africa that any part of it would be just like being in my living room. I have a school, but I'd have a name for the school. It wouldn't be a *conservatoire*, it would be a coat puller. Musicians would be saying, if someone pulls your coat, they're giving you information about something. Say a musician would walk out of this building here and it's real cold outside and he doesn't know it. So he walks out in a shirt and another musician had just come in and knows it's cold out there. So this musician walks out in his shirtsleeves, he asks the other musician, "Why didn't you pull my coat?" I'd like to take the kids because, boy, there's a wealth of talent down there and I figure I could [teach them] something. With the experience I've had from people who pulled my coat, this is dedicated to them. I remember one time in Detroit with Cab Calloway. I used to always hold my horn down into the stand and play. This symphony trumpet player was in the pit at the Fox Theater in Detroit, he told me, "Gillespie, you're all right, but hold your horn up so we can hear the parts. Your part is lost." I say, "Well, I'm reading the music." He said, "You gotta learn how to look over." He sat down in that pit and every time my horn would go down this way, he'd bring his hand up. "Come on, bring it up." And that got me in the habit of holding my horn up. So my school in Africa would be a coat puller. Do you know how I'd like to be remembered? A student of humanity!

BETTY CARTER
1989

*I shall never forget the first time I heard Betty at a Chicago nightclub.
Her musicians, three or four at the time, were all her disciples, her students. I discovered toward the end of the evening that, as Betty said to me,
"These kids were so nervous and scared when I first met them. I said to
them, 'The last thing you must be is scared. It isn't your purpose to say, "I
must please this audience, I must make them think I'm good." No, no.
You must make yourself think you're good. I want you to be free. Because
that's the basis of jazz: improvisation. To improvise. If you feel something
right at a certain moment, when ordinarily it should be the end, and you
feel, know there's something else, do that something else.'" And it's that
aspect of Betty Carter I most remember. Her capacity—not simply as a
teacher, as a leader, as a performer—but as someone who made you feel
free. I'm referring not simply to the young members of her group, but we
in the audience as well felt free. If there's one contribution of Betty
Carter aside from her imagination and giftedness as a composer and as a
performer, it was her capacity to free people to improvise and to be satisfied with themselves.*

*Who is Betty Carter? How you came to sing as you do? We heard scat
singing and we associate that with early Louis Armstrong and the Hot
Five. Years later, you come out of Detroit. A young girl. It's at the end of
World War II. Something is happening in jazz. It's called bebop.*

It was a bunch of young black musicians coming from all different parts of
the country. We had a silent leader. His name was Charlie Parker. Everybody
tried to simulate Charlie Parker. He was carrying the torch of changing the
music. What it involved was lots of energy. The chord changes had changed.
The standards—the musicians were taking old tunes and putting new lines on
them. It was faster, it was quicker, it was a risk-taking music. I was involved
because Charlie Parker made frequent visits to Detroit, and also Dizzy Gillespie. We supported that much more than Chicago. In Detroit, we'd see Charlie Parker with open arms, no matter what his condition was. We just wanted

to hear him play. Dizzy brought the young big band to a club called El Cino, which was in the heart of the black community. Life is full of taking risks. I'd go to the club and they'd say, "Do you want to sing?" My God, I was like in heaven. There was a connection between Charlie Parker and me that was really very, very real. I didn't realize how real it was until I'm in a club last week in New York City, and a friend came and he said, "I was sitting in the audience one time in Detroit, with Mr. Parker, and watching you sing. The look on his face was really wonderful. And when you finished singing, he got up and left." I never knew that happened. I don't even remember that happening, but I felt so wonderful.

You were using your voice as Charlie Parker used his alto sax. Your voice was an instrument that you were exploring, as he was.

I think he knew that I didn't want to be just an improviser. In my early records, you can see the influence of the horn players more than you can hear the influence of them now because I try not to simulate horns and their licks. I couldn't absorb someone else's music that long and not get over there into their world. I butt out and lay back and don't listen to a lot of instruments. My mind is fresh, because I haven't absorbed a whole lot of them. That's one thing—musicians don't really like scat singers because they do the same thing musicians do. I remain in my sphere. [Laughs] They say: "Don't riff like I do!"

Your jazz is something more than just something invented. It's a part of a continuity. You mentioned Parker, and Parker would mention, perhaps, Lester Young, and Young would mention Coleman Hawkins, perhaps. At the same time, there has to be this new development of that person, Betty Carter. To see you in person, to see you reacting with your young colleagues, is to see a teacher as well as colleague. You once worked with Lionel Hampton.

I didn't realize the value of that experience until I got much older. You look back and say, "Doggone it, if I had not been with the Lionel Hampton band . . ." I was always working, mostly with the young. There's still an interest in jazz. But the movers and the shakers, they don't believe in it. They don't have any idea that they could market this music into a new peak. They're satisfied with their 1 percent, and they don't want to carry it any further than that. You can't shake them into realizing that these kids really would like to hear some interesting music, along with whatever they got.

Carmen McRae and I sang with each other in New York at the Blue Note. I go to see her if she's working a job, and she calls me on the stage and we sing together. It was born out of something that happened like that, a very spontaneous thing. The album is also spontaneous. We do it live. We set up a harmony thing here, just to get the story across, to show that we could do something with two-part harmony. I have always surrounded myself with young musicians. Something I seek is energy. They're not going to be watching their watches, thinking, "When is she going to come off the stage?" [Laughs] I do have long shows. My shows tend to run about an hour and a half, sometimes longer. I also want to feature these young guys, give them a chance to perform, so they'll know what it's all about. They've got to start somewhere. I want young people to play this music and I want young people to see me, at my age, and the young people coming together. That's very important, when young people see that I have a young group and we're coming together as one. It's not four contemporaries or four old people doing this music. It's not just "old folks' music." I want them to see their peers taking the chances along with the old girl here, and we're making music. We're not faking; we're making real, honest-to-God music. They know nothing about the music that I'm doing. A lot of them weren't even born when some of the standards were coming out. I'm giving them a chance to learn these melodies and play the melodies. So when they fool around at sound checks and play standards that they don't know and they play the melody wrong, I'm there to tell them that they're playing the melody wrong. My ears are to inform them that they just played the wrong note in that melody, and first let's learn that melody before you do anything else. That's education all in itself, just learning the melody. I know the melodies. Kids don't know anything about dynamics. It's all crash, bang, bang, bang, crash, bang, bang. So I have to put them in a position where they know when to come down, when to work softly, know the texture of their instruments. I say to my guys, "I want you guys to play the spot that you have, make it difficult for me to get on the stage after you. I mean, command your instrument, attack it. Make sure that the audience is going to listen to you. Make sure that you get their attention." That's what they have to learn, how to get on and off the stage. I came up in a period when theater was involved. You had to learn how to get on the stage, you had to follow different acts, and you had to stop the show. You learn all that stuff by trial and error and that's what I had the opportunity to do. These young kids don't have that opportunity. It's energy and fun at the same time. And all the time, discipline.

It disturbs me that your audience is college kids a lot, primarily white kids, and very few black kids.

But it's turning around. Wynton Marsalis has had a lot to do with it. I think he's inspired a lot of young players. There was a time when blacks did support the same musicians who are now making more money in the white colleges than they did before, because of B.B. King and John Lee Hooker and all those guys I worked with before in the Apollo Theater and the Howard Theater, all these venues that provided work for black musicians. Black music is what white musicians should learn how to deal with. They must go to the authentic musicians to do this, and that's what they've done. Most of our black colleges are land-grant and church-owned colleges, and the church thinks that the music from the street is necessarily bad. Why should we perpetuate it in our schools for our young? I tried to get them to understand what was happening twenty years ago, in 1964, but I didn't get anywhere. In the past, there's been the separation of religious sacred music and what is called sinful music. It was called race music, and the sin and the decadence of it. We've come a long way since then.

HENRY THREADGILL
1988

Henry Threadgill, aside from being a remarkable alto saxophone player, is one of the most imaginative of jazz composers today. "He seems to be deliberately challenging the audience: My lyricism and mastery come complete with thorns and spikes, and I promise to yank the props out from under you," quoted John Litweiler, longtime Down Beat *jazz critic, in an article he wrote for the* Chicago Sun-Times. *Threadgill was one of the founding members of the Association for the Advancement of Creative Musicians, a Chicago group that was free-form, you might say, in its philosophy and approach. Not long ago Peter Watrous of the* New York Times *described Threadgill as "perhaps the most important jazz composer of his generation." Recent concerts in Chicago have led the local critics to speak of him as a revolutionary figure, altering the manner in which jazz itself is going. Said Howard Reich, jazz critic of the* Chicago Tribune, *"It would be difficult to overestimate Henry Threadgill's role in perpetually altering the meaning of jazz. . . . He has changed our underlying assumptions of what jazz can and should be."*

In Chicago in the sixties, what the clubs wanted was traditional standard music. But it seemed just to be a climate for artists to create their own ideas; it seemed just to be the day for creating their own ideas, and that's what the AACM [Association for the Advancement of Creative Musicians] started with—people who were going to write their own music, invent their own instruments, and kind of determine their own future. We know how much grew out of the sixties. So much got questioned in terms of ethics, morality, and institutions. The AACM was just a natural product that grew out of the sixties. You had groups coming together. Ours was a group of musicians coming together as a collective, the same way you were getting groups formed like SNCC—people coming together to form groups to protest things involving the environment, to protest war. But this was an American music group coming together for the same reason: to protect and establish their freedom in this new marketplace.

My aunt was a singer. I remember as a kid her going off to school to study voice. When she came back, she had gotten married to a bassist. So I had that immediate musical attachment near me. I used to stay with them off and on when I was a kid, and he'd be playing the bass. It brought me real close to the music on a physical plane. I was brought up around music, listening to it on the radio, in the environment. But to have it right around you, somebody playing it right around you, made a big difference. I remember hearing Charlie Parker. I was really a kid, and I was listening to all kinds of music. You're a Chicagoan, you know that you could hear all kinds of music on the radio before it got controlled, before the programming got so predictable. You could hear Polish music, Mexican music, rhythm and blues, jazz, classical. There was just a whole cross section of music on the radio. You could get educated on the radio and in the community. When I heard Charlie Parker, I didn't know what it was about, but I loved it, I was just crazy about it. And by the time I became fourteen, fifteen years old, after hearing Charlie Parker, I knew I had to play saxophone. I heard Lester Young. I loved all these people. But there was something about the reality of what he was playing, in terms of the time I was living in. I could feel an association in terms of social events. He came down as a virtuoso. We had come out of the swing era, which was large ensembles, the big band era. The bebop era contracted everything down to these small, virtuoso ensembles. Not with just fantastic virtuosos, but they extended the concept of the musical language from the rhythmic and harmonic points of view. Very much from the rhythmic point of view, because most of the time, change is much more significant, and everything just follows from the rhythm point of view, then harmony, et cetera, follows. You can't really have a significant change in most traditional music without a rhythmic change. Parker explored new ways of using the instrument. When he took it out of the larger context and put it in a smaller context, he magnified it, he looked at it much more critically because it didn't play a part, it wasn't a part of a chorus anymore. It had to stand alone. See, we made Charlie Parker a museum piece and made him a stylistic end. He didn't finish. You can't hardly pick up a book written on Charlie Parker and even see where they mention his interest in the music of Edgard Varèse. That's where he was moving next. But you don't see that in books on Charlie Parker. You got him classified in some little stylistic museum category. But he was a man in evolution; he was evolving.

An artist can't live on an island. Sometimes this information is not translated to people. We can't stay in these little small worlds. What I do in music is exactly what should go on in our natural life. I can't just listen to American music; Americans are not the only people in the world. We're not the only people that have something to say. I can't *just* listen to music. I have to see what's going on in dance. They might take the direction further, they might open me up to a greater sensibility. Opera, film might open me up. Music will only show me so much. I have to look at the accompanying arts and see what they have to say.

Before I moved from Chicago, some of the only work I was getting through the summer was playing in marching bands, parade bands all over the city of Chicago. In the Polish community, the Mexican community, Serbian community, everything! As a kid, the first jobs I had were playing with the VFW and the Shriners. Most of these guys, they weren't from World War II, they were from World War I. I learned a lot of music playing with these people, and learned a lot about music, and about the world. Chicago probably has more street parades than any city in the country. All I did was play in the street. I came out of this type of an environment. It's part of where my materials come from.

I did a lot of studying here in Chicago. I studied the longest at the American Conservatory of Music with very fine people like Stella Roberts, who I'll always be grateful to for the things she told me and showed me about music. I spent a little time at Governor's State. Then I was in Kansas at the Manhattan School out there. And then I was in Cambridge, at the Longy School of Music. I've done a little bit in different places all around. Then I studied a lot with people like Muhal Richard Abrams, who's been very important in my musical life—he's a fantastic leader, teacher, composer, musician. You can never trap him. You go after him, he goes out another door on you. He's like a rabbit—he's got a bunch of exits. Finally, after institutionalized learning, I got down to people on a one-to-one basis. I knew that a lot of people were objecting to the type of music we were playing. But look at the objections in the world to everything. I couldn't play the music that I had been thinking about before, not in this new world where people were saying God is dead, and we're involved in a war that nobody understands. There's a new reality, it's a brand-new day. The music had to reflect the brand-new day. That's what bebop reflected. It was like a change in the social situation and a change in consciousness. The time demanded it. It's like a type of aesthetic, spiritual demand that comes from the artist.

KEITH JARRETT
1995

Keith Jarrett is a unique artist who spans two worlds. He's not a crossover artist—he's an artist who happens to be highly respected in two worlds, the world of jazz and that of classical music. He has become something of a controversial figure, yet his giftedness is taken for granted.

I think and feel that my essence is in improvisation rather than in being conditioned to interpret a certain way. And if someone has that essence, when they improvise, it can sound like a lot of things. But in Bach and Mozart, for example, many people would think that I would be free with this music, but I'm not. I see that as respecting those pieces. All we have left of these people is the notes on the page. I do much less adding than a lot of players do. And I also think that the earliest jazz had less of what they call improvisation. People were playing with what they had but they didn't add much. But what jazz signifies to me now is the freedom to be yourself, which is what the listener wants for you.

When I was a child, I was in the world of classical music; I wasn't in the improvising world at all at that time. I had perfect pitch and my parents recognized that when I was three, and they found a teacher who was either amazing enough or silly enough to take a three-year-old, but it worked out. All I remember of my teacher is the gate at the top of her stairs so that kids wouldn't fall down the steps. I was one of those kids. [Laughs] I think my intuitions even when I was a kid were correct, but I didn't know why I was doing the things I did. But when you're going to go into a situation that starts to put names and categories on things, it can be the wrong thing to do, even if it's the right teacher. I think that's what I felt. I didn't want to analyze what was going on, and I realized it as soon as I got the actual chance to study. I don't mind people making categories, but what that does is make everyone comfortable as long as they're inside them. So that's a problem. If we had a society that looked at these words as mere pointing-towards-something, that would be different. I do everything, but I keep things all in their own time frames. In other words, I never mix them. Sometimes people wonder if I could do half a concert with classical music and half with jazz, and my system goes, *no way.* I think that's one of the problems with how people perceive. Supposedly there is such a thing as a crossover artist, but it's really not true. But there are people who constantly walk across the street and do something for a few minutes and go back across the street and do the other thing. I would say that those are, in a funny way, crossover artists. But what they've done is crossed out both things. [Laughs] If I'm preparing for Mozart, which I recently did, to play some of his concertos, all other channels are off. I listen to music that I like, but if I'm working on that project I don't play jazz, I don't improvise for whatever amount of months that project is.

What was it mostly you learned from working with Miles Davis?

That's a hard one because I think one thing I learned from him is that conceptions of public people from the outside can be completely wrong. In other words, what you and I see are figures we can't ever talk to or be with, we can't ever know those people very well. We come up with conclusions about what they are or who they are. A lot of what he really was like was the opposite of what the perception was. I think he was trying sometimes to keep the two things apart by some of his actions on stage. It sounds ridiculous, but at least when I was with him there was never a time when you were playing that he wasn't the best listener, whether he was playing or not. If the band was playing, I could know for sure he was listening. That's a very unusual thing. It sounds like it's normal, but in music this is not normal.

You can hang on to a note far more than would usually be the case because there's a richness in that to be explored.

You're the first person that's let me not have to try to say this myself. On the *Bye-Bye Blackbird* CD I understood something about how Miles played. But I'm a pianist, so no one was listening for that one thing you just mentioned. If I play simply on piano, it suddenly is not pianistic, it isn't virtuosoistic. So everyone is saying, "Well, when's he going to get into it?" But I'm already into it. [Laughs] There's another thing that Miles is important to me for, and that is that whatever direction he took, even if all the people that used to like him suddenly didn't like him, he always took these directions mainly because he never had explored this particular place before. That's important because if you're an improviser, the whole idea is to erase, or at least ignore, what you did before. So in a solo concert, if I don't come onstage with anything in my mind, then there's a problem. I start by sitting on the piano bench looking at the keys. I don't start from an idea. That's hard for people to grasp, especially other pianists. On rare occasions when something was in my mind that was possible to be molded further, I would allow it to be there and I might use it. But that may be one out of a hundred times or something.

Did Bach improvise Bach?

Oh yeah, he was known to be a great improviser, which we have no record of, of course. Maybe that's good. I think that would blow so many theories. All the people who say improvising is shallow and composition is deep might have to leave the room if they had heard his improvising. So many people see Bach as densely cerebral or highly intelligent, over-the-edge-Olympian, kind of. But even in the most complex thing, the lines he writes are all melodic. Math is one thing, but math won't create melody, so the part of your brain that creates melody is not the part that makes this math come together. So I'm seeing Bach as just an incredible improviser because when you're writing music, although it's much slower than improvising, it's improvising. No one is telling you what notes to put there. [Laughs] He certainly is lyrical. We don't talk about the great lyricists of music, including Bach, that often. Somehow or other everyone puts him in this closet and closes the door and that's where he lives.

You had a short period of playing electronic stuff with Davis.

Well, I'm very well known for saying electronic music doesn't exist, and things like that. But if I wanted to play with Miles, at that time that's what I had to be playing. Other than that I haven't done anything electronic. But there are so many different keyboard instruments of the past that no one's really investigated properly. The thing about clavichords is that you can bend the notes. You can't do that on any other authentic keyboard instrument that I know of. The harder you press, the more you change the pitch. And you can have vibrato.

In the past, in the case of keyboard instruments, each change was asked for by the players. In other words, you were a player and you thought, gee, I want to put more of myself into this, I want to use more of my physical nature. So over those many years we ended up with the modern piano. Everything since the piano has been dictated more by market forces, audience size, and also the desire of the players to do less with their physical body. Now you can get a keyboard that will print out the music when you have a good idea. So you can sit all day and everyone can probably imagine that if they fooled around with a keyboard long enough they might come up with something interesting. But where would it be coming from? It wouldn't be coming from them, it would be coming from accident. So they spend twenty-four hours at the keyboard, and suddenly they say, "Print," they push the print button and it prints out the thing they liked. Some composers—for example, Samuel Barber—wrote great piano music, but he couldn't play piano. His imagination had to be incredibly strong and his knowledge of piano actually had to be even better than a pianist's, because in everything he wrote, he had to know if it was possible. So in those days, even if the composer or musician couldn't play every instrument that he was writing for, he needed imagination. But now you can ask the machine to tell you, Can a violin play this? Yes or no? [Laughs] Picasso, late in his life, said: "Computers are useless because all they give you are answers."

In a funny way, Western music in general, if we could say that there is such a thing—through composed music and the world of interpreting that music—has played a trick on us by having [as] one of its priorities to distract us from time. In other words, I see these architectural creations sometimes as being bigger structures than they're worth. Whereas something that Ravi Shankar might play is so much smaller in reality than its meaning, in the same way that I feel film has in a way poisoned a lot of us to the size of things. You go to a bad film and it's a bigger experience. It's out of ratio to the meaning. In improvising, in thinking of music as a flow, you start to realize that the things that are important, that make the meaning, are very small, and you have to be patient, and you have to be wise about how to find them and intelligent about how to use them, and I have worked forty years to try to figure out how to play a key. Those kinds of things, those are being lost in this fast, fast age.

∾ Impresario (2) ∾

JOHN HAMMOND SR.
1975, 1987

When we think of jazz, certain names come to mind, of course: Armstrong, Ellington, Parker, Coltrane. There is another who is perhaps the best non-musician friend jazz ever had: John Hammond. From the thirties until his death in 1987, his life had been the discovery of gifted jazz artists who might otherwise have remained anonymous. More than any aficionado, he's been critic, collector, scout, and A&R (artists and repertoire) man, as well as a key figure in breaking the big taboo, the color line.

You are of an affluent, WASP family, Hotchkiss Preparatory School, from another part of town. What is it that drew you to this other life, this other world?

Getting to know the people, I guess. I'd known a couple of black people who lived near us up in Mount Kisco, two schoolteachers, Miss Green and Miss

Cameron, I'll never forget—they were West Indians, wonderful people. But I had never known any of these people socially. We're talking about the World War I years. My father drew the wrath of the neighbors by renting the cottage to these two wonderful black women.

When Hotchkiss let me out to take lessons in New York and play in a string quartet, I didn't realize that my fiddle teacher lived on the edge of Harlem. I took that trolley across 125th Street. I looked to my right and there it said: "This week in person: the Empress of the Blues, Bessie Smith." It changed my life. I started going to hear some of these great black artists. I may have been the only white person there. I guess they thought I was nuts. I was this kid. I didn't smoke, I didn't drink, I didn't lust. [Laughs] I lusted for music. That was really the only thing. The music was gorgeous, the music was free; it was improvised, it wasn't the same every time. The first record that got me was James P. Johnson's "Worried and Lonesome Blues," which I heard when I was twelve. That changed my musical life. Then I found out there was something called race records. That got me up to Harlem. I couldn't buy those records downtown; they didn't sell them. This was long before Bluebird. There was Vocalion, and there was Okeh. These were records that were put out by Negroes for Negroes. We called them race records in those days.

I recorded Bessie in 1933, her last session. I finally got Brunswick to agree to give her a 5 percent royalty cut. We got her up to New York, and she did a concert on a Sunday afternoon at the Onyx Club, with the Hot Jazz society. I really think this was the first time that Bessie ever performed before a white audience in New York, because she had only played ghetto theaters. It was a turkey of a show, but Bessie was just marvelous. Bessie was on her way to join the Silas Green show in 1937. This was a minstrel show, which kept a lot of black artists working. The exploitation of black artists was quite overwhelming, and they played the TOBA circuit, freely interpreted as "tough on black artists." Bessie, on this trip down to Silas Green's show, was involved in an accident, the car overturned, and Bessie's arm was nearly severed. I got the story from the owner of the Silas Green show because just a couple weeks after this happened I was in Huntsville, Alabama. Suddenly, the man told me, "You know what happened to Bessie Smith? She was killed in an automobile accident. She bled to death because two ambulances passed her by and wouldn't pick her up. When she was finally taken to a hospital, she was refused, and she died between one hospital and the other." That was the story I believed and I wrote about it at the time. Since, it has been pretty well established that it was not the complete story. The doctor has been found who did attend Bessie at the Clarksdale Hospital in Mississippi. By that time, she was so far gone from loss of blood that she couldn't have lived.

I sort of stumbled onto Billie Holiday in 1933. It was in a speakeasy in Harlem during Prohibition. Monette Moore was opening a little after-hours joint. I was hoping to hear Monette on opening night, but she was so busy greeting Clifton Webb and Carl Van Vechten and other celebrities from downtown. Instead, this young girl, seventeen maybe, was going around the tables singing. Every time she sang, she was singing the same thing, but differently. I realized here was another of those extraordinary improvisers. She had an innate musicianship and genius. I never heard the likes of her before or after. She would make it her own absolutely. She was singing a tune I'd never heard before: "Big Red Apple." She was singing it differently at every table. I found out she was Clarence Holiday's daughter. He was Fletcher Henderson's guitar player. I got her in a studio in '33, with Benny Goodman [Hammond's brother-in-law]. The first record she ever made. And then all those Teddy Wilson–Billie Holiday records came out of that in '35 and '36. Billie had an innate musicality. She didn't read music. Teddy Wilson would play over the melody or something. They'd work in the corner. They didn't even rehearse before they got to the studio. The whole thing would explode there. Thelonius Monk, Lester Young, her favorite jazz colleague, and the Basie rhythm section [Jo Jones, drums; Walter Page, bass; and Freddie Green, guitar; with Basie at the piano] backed her on that one. This song was junk, but she does *something* with it. And makes it far better than it deserves. "Strange Fruit" was, of course, her most celebrated song, dealing with lynching. It was a poem by Lewis Allen [pseudonym of Abel Meeropol, who adopted the two sons of Julius and Ethel Rosenberg]. She became self-conscious and a little uncertain when she was first requested to sing it. Barney Josephson, who owned Cafe Society, persuaded her to sing it at his club. It was the first place in downtown New York catering to an integrated audience. I'll never forget the night Josh White was singing it at Cafe Society. Art Tatum was on the bill and shook his head. He said: "He should never sing that song in front of white folks." [Laughs] But it did make Billie a big favorite. I booked all the jazz performers at Cafe Society and we broke the color line. When Count Basie played at the Famous Door in '38, I was very concerned about the hot summer. I put in air-conditioning equipment in return for which management promised not to discriminate against blacks. [Laughs]

Among my favorite creative, inventive, natural jazz musicians, there are two that stand out. One is Charlie Christian, the guitarist; the other, Lester Young at the tenor sax. Charlie's concept of ensemble playing, his dedication to making other people play beyond their capacities, was unique. Mary Lou Williams told me about Charlie. I flew to Oklahoma City to hear him in '39. I got him with Benny Goodman the next week, even though I had to break up the band Charlie was with; a tragedy—nobody would ever have heard of him. There was Buck Clayton and Jo Jones and Walter Page and Teddy Wilson at the piano. You'd hear Benny at the clarinet, a little confused because he had to follow Lester. It was pretty tough. Nineteen thirty-seven. Variations on a theme. We got absolutely the core of the melody all the time. I knew it was history. I'd never known anything like it before. I was in the control room at the time.

I first saw Benny Goodman when he was with Russ Columbo's lousy band [Columbo, popular singer of the time, was a contemporary of Bing Crosby, though he lacked the other's sense of jazz]. But it did have Gene Krupa playing brushes, and it did have Joe Sullivan on second piano. Benny was playing maybe four bars at the most, eight bars occasionally. It was a commercial band. I got to know Benny best when he was in the pit of a Gershwin show, *Lady, Be Good!* He and Jack Teagarden and Gene Krupa were all in that band. That was in '29, I think.

I also heard about a pianist named Teddy Wilson. It's sort of a wonderful juxtaposition of the strange things in my life. In 1933 I met a marvelous man in Chicago called Lloyd Lewis. He was the drama critic for the *Chicago Daily News*. I produced a play that he wrote with Sinclair Lewis in 1934. In 1933, when I first knew Lloyd, I used to listen to WMAQ quite often because Earl Hines was broadcasting from the Grand Terrace. I was listening one night and I heard a different band. I heard this fantastic piano player. It wasn't Earl, 'cause he was on tour. So I called my friend Lloyd Lewis, and I said, "Can you find out who the piano player was in this band on WMAQ?" The *Chicago Daily News* owned the station. Bill Basie had made a fantastic record with Benny Moten back in 1931 or '32 in Kansas City. Basie proved that he was a stride piano player easily the rival of Fats Waller, because they both stem from James P. Johnson. When Coleman Hawkins left Fletcher Henderson to join the BBC in London, Fletcher told me that he was out in Kansas City, and he heard a saxophone player called Lester Young, who was in Bill Basie's band. We brought him to New York and I went up to a rehearsal at the Cotton

Club—I hate to use that name even [though the Cotton Club featured great jazz artists, no black people were allowed in the audience]—and I thought it was the greatest tenor sax I'd ever heard in my life, but the band hated it because it wasn't big and throaty and full like Hawkins. It sounded more like a C melody or an alto. To me the musicianship was impeccable. He didn't last too long with Fletcher, but Fletcher told me, "John, if I had a chance, I'd fire everybody in my band and I'd put this man in."

When Billie Holiday and Lester Young got together, this was made in heaven. He was an extraordinary musician. He was from New Orleans originally. He had come under the influence of a saxophone player who didn't like blacks at all, Frankie Trumbauer. He was hung up on race. Him and Red Nichols, those were the two. Trumbauer played with Bix Beiderbecke, but Beiderbecke never dared to record with a black man. Never. I wish he had 'cause I used to hear him in Harlem. He felt right at home there. I was out in Chicago with Benny Goodman in 1935 and 1936, and I'd get a little sick of hearing Benny's band every night. One night I went out at one o'clock in the morning and I turned my automobile radio all the way over to the right. I caught some music from a station in Kansas City. By God, it was the Count Basie Band from the Reno Club. Again my life was changed, because this was completely free, completely improvised.

I first heard Mildred Bailey when she was with Paul Whiteman's band. She could sing a popular as well as anybody. She loved jazz, but she wasn't commercial, and she was self-conscious about her size. Somehow in 1935 I conned Mildred into making some records because she loved Bessie Smith, though she didn't love Billie Holiday.

There was a sort of a rivalry there?

Oh, and how. I said, "Why don't we make records sort of the way Bessie used to make them in the twenties, with just a trumpet and a saxophone player, no drums, bass and piano." She said, "If you say so, John." I said, "They'll probably never be heard in America 'cause they're being made for a little label in England called Parlophone. I don't think it'll do you any harm." So I got Bunny Berrigan on trumpet, Johnny Hodges, the great alto man with Ellington, but I added a bass player, Grachan Moncur, and Teddy Wilson on piano. But let me not forget Fletcher Henderson. He had the most sophisticated band in history, and the loosest. It was Fletcher Henderson who really made Benny Goodman. What an arranger he was! He took pop tunes and made musical masterpieces. He also believed in giving soloists their head.

In 1938 I organized a concert at Carnegie Hall called "Spirituals to Swing." I had wanted to do something for years and years. I became a complete nut on breaking down racial barriers. It was tough. Middle-class black organizations looked down on country blues and looked down on jazz as something demeaning. I had this idea of bringing the greatest rural and urban black artists together in a concert in New York. I went, first of all, to the NAACP—I was on the executive board at the time. Walter White was sympathetic, but the others shook their heads. "John, our audience won't take anything like this." Then I went to the ILGWU, the International Ladies' Garment Workers' Union, which had done *Pins and Needles* [a hit revue sponsored by the ILGWU, with performers who were actually factory workers]. Finally, the little business manager of the *New Masses* came to me, Eric Bernays. He said, "John, I think we can get an audience for you." This scared me because the *New Masses* was a Communist Party organ, though a lot of non-Party people wrote for it. I said, "All right, I'll let it happen just as long as no communist literature is hawked out front and there's no obvious propaganda on the stage or anything." They said fine. I brought in Big Bill Broonzy from the South. Sonny Terry at the harmonica. The boogie-woogie pianists from Chicago—Albert Ammons and Meade Lux Lewis—as well as Pete Johnson from Kansas City. James P. Johnson and Sidney Bechet. The Goodman Band and Basie combos. Oh, everybody. Big Joe Turner had come in from Kansas City. He recently told somebody, "John was paying me out of his own pocket. I felt I just couldn't do it any longer, so I went back." He'd been performing at Cafe Society, too. And during that 1938 concert I introduced Mitchell's Christian Singers. This was the first time a New York, cosmopolitan, mostly white audience of about 3,000 people ever heard non-jive gospel. There was no guitar, there was no hand-clapping. The Golden Gate Quartet did that the next year and they were wonderful too. But Mitchell's Christian Singers were the pure ones. They were all laborers in Kinston, North Carolina. I went to the house of one of them—no plumbing, no electricity, a candle. We heard them sing one night. Tears streaming down our faces. I've never heard anything so moving in my life. Most of the stuff was straight out of the Baptist hymnal. The audience didn't know what to make of it because there was no showmanship. These were amateurs, these were people singing from the heart. They didn't know how to *bow*. These were people who sang in country churches on Sunday. That's the only time they got together.

I would say less than 10 percent of the audience for the 1938 concert was black, alas. It was a jazz audience. Some were obviously politically aware folk. To have any black people downstairs in Carnegie Hall was a political gesture in itself. My very own conservative Republican family was up in a box loving it. The *New York Times* had given it a fantastic send-off; so had the *Herald Tribune*. The fact that the *New Masses* sponsored it didn't seem to bother anybody. It was standing room only. We had four hundred people on the stage. If there were one exhilarating moment in my life, this was it.

～ Part Three ～

Spirituals, Blues,
∾ Folk, Rock ∾

THOMAS A. DORSEY
1961

Undoubtedly the most respected and certainly most prolific of gospel songwriters is Thomas A. Dorsey. In his younger days he was known as Georgia Tom, the accompanist of the blues singer Ma Rainey, until he was "saved," after his wife died. Since then he has written hundreds of songs. Among the most celebrated is "Precious Lord Take My Hand," Martin Luther King Jr.'s favorite, which he requested moments before being assassinated in Memphis, and the one that acquainted him with Mahalia Jackson, who was his favorite gospel singer. Perhaps the words gospel and spirituals should be differentiated. Spirituals are the songs that originated in the slavery days, the original liberation songs, with double meaning. In "Swing Low Sweet Chariot," the chariot was not the River Jordan but the swampland separating free from slave country. There were hundreds of the double-entendre slavery songs known as spirituals. Gospel songs are known, as Mahalia would put it, as the "good

news" songs. Gospel songs came out of the North and were written by specific people, whereas we don't know who wrote the slavery songs, which
are folk in the truest sense. Gospel and spiritual are often fused. Mahalia
was the master of both. Dorsey wrote scores of songs especially for Mahalia. The one I first heard her sing was "Move On Up a Little Higher" on
some old tinny little record. I heard that in every black home I visited.
One day while on assignment, covering the birth of a black child for a
documentary, I was talking to the doctor and nurse, and heard "Move On
Up a Little Higher" from the room where the mother was giving birth to
her child. The song was everywhere.

You were once known, before you were saved, as Georgia Tom, the accompanist of Ma Rainey, the "mother of the blues."

Oh, yes, I accompanied Ma Rainey for several seasons. I wrote and played
more than two hundred blues songs back in that period. I don't know if they
all were published, but there's over four hundred. They were called jubilee
records in the early days. Jubilee was a word used for most of the songs that
were sung back then by my people. They had that patting rhythm of hands
and feet and a jubilant spirit. They felt that they came out of an age that
was depressing and they wanted more of a happy, jubilant spirit. The spirituals that came along, say, after 1900 were mostly called jubilee songs. After
the earthly trials were finished, then the people were looking forward to a
happy day, to a time to shout, to be happy, to be joyful, to be jubilant. And if
they got there, they said they'd shout all over God's heaven. [Laughs] To my
knowledge, the Fisk Jubilee Singers was the first group of singers that went
through the United States and to Europe and other places that carried these
jubilee and gospel songs. Notwithstanding that, the minstrels did some of the
spirituals also back in the early days, as far back as 1870. But the Fisk Jubilee
Singers were known for introducing these spirituals to the world. I can remember when the old minstrels would come to town and they would do several spirituals also. They would put on a humorous program, but the
spirituals would be done seriously. Oh yes, yes.

Eleven years later, the Fisk Quartet with "Walk All over God's Heaven."
Something rather interesting takes place, aside from the mechanical improvement. Professor Dorsey, there is what seems to be barbershop harmony.

Yes, the harmony's getting closer there. I don't know if these jubilee singers had anything to do with that. What we mean by the barbershop harmony, the boys used to get together and hang around barbershops and little joints where the fellas hang out, and they would harmonize. And brother, in the afternoons or the evenings sometime, you could hear some of the best harmony and melody getting together that you'd never heard before. That was quite close harmony. We feel that the people had forgotten about the old spiritual "Walk All over God's Heaven": "I'm going to shout all over God's heaven." We dressed it up, gave it a beat. You hear that in the bass. We put some embellishments and variations there, where the musicians could stand out and be heard. We tried to keep in the deep feeling, the spiritual meaning of the song. We picked a really great artist to do it: Mahalia Jackson. Mahalia sang just as she felt. The Fisk Quartet were trained singers and they tried to polish it. They tried to stick to the letter, which was good, for they had to sell them to an audience who would expect such, white people. Mahalia just threw it out from her soul to everybody, says, "Take it or leave it." [Chuckles] I've tried to be authentic and discover some innovations for myself. I'm not a great pianist performing, but I do have some little things that the greater fellas can't get [that] I keep for myself. I used to do an act where I would play the hammers in the old upright piano, take the top out and play it all on the hammers.

Years ago in Atlanta, Georgia, the Reverend J.M. Gates, preaching before going into "Amazing Grace," once said, "People, you know we're living in a time now where Atlanta gets her style from New York, and New York is getting her style from Paris, and Paris is getting her style from hell. If we don't sing more of these old familiar hymns, we'll find ourselves in the same city. I want you to open your mouth and sing." I knew the Reverend Gates back in those days there. "Amazing Grace" is one of the old hymns of the church there, one of the songs that we call the old Dr. Watts numbers, back in that early period of hymns. You will find them in the study of hymnology, such hymns as that. The Reverend Gates, you won't find a minister like the Reverend Gates who'll preach like that now in this day, but at that time, back in the rural districts where they didn't have a preacher for every Sunday—one preacher, sometimes he would have three churches, maybe four churches, one for each Sunday—these records were very popular. They ministered to the people back in these backwoods who could get ahold to one of those portable phonographs. Now, a good choirmaster doesn't go in to his service unless he knows what is the text of his pastor—the subject of his text. Then he selects the songs to fit the text.

Some audiences, I've heard them, chant. [He sings] "Lord, I want to pray, Lord I want to pray, all night long. Pray for me, pray for me all night long." The minister is continually preaching. Those things spur the minister up, gets him warm, gets him hotter. [Chuckles] There's no separation of the sermon from the congregation. We know they are one. Call and response in jazz, and we know it's in church music. You'll hear the minister call out, "Do you hear me?" And they say, *"Yes!"* "Do you hear me?" *"Yes!"* "Do you hear me?" *"Yes!"* Then they'll start out a chant altogether. He'll say something and they answer. I mean, even in music, in a musical tone. It is a thing that is typical with us, and I think that should be preserved. There's the use of the symbol, the train, or the arch, or the chariot. Always upwards. Everything looks up so far as the Christian is concerned. You have the song: the old arches are moving. The arch is supposed to be moving toward God, moving upward. You have a song about the gospel train coming. They're going to get on board and they're going to be taken away to a land where it's better living, where there's more joy. [Sings] "The gospel train is coming, it's coming around the curve. Spending her speed and power and straining every nerve. But get on board. The gospel train is coming, don't you want to go?" I used to hear my mother sing that when I was a boy. "I know you want to go." There were a time when you got the folk together. We didn't have gathering places, meeting places. You just got a few of the neighbors together. They said, "Tell the folk tonight." And they'd come out in the yard, if it was a nice lovely summer night, with various types of music. Every nationality has its folk songs. But I think folk songs belong to everybody, all peoples. They're all folk.

Spirituals were not written, the music was not put down when the spirituals were really born. They were just spontaneous outbursts of how the individual felt inside, and they opened the mouth, and they [pulled] out what was inside. In the days of slavery, the gospel song—gospel is good news—is a name that was given to the songs when they had those great gospel campaigns. The Great Awakenings. Gospel is a song of good news, a song of good tidings. The name has served well, and I think the name holds well. I am a writer of gospel songs. I have written some spirituals, too. New-day spirituals. Spirituals go back to slavery days, unwritten, come from the lives, whereas a gospel song is written by a specific person.

There's the "how long, how long" refrain that is in so many songs, whether it be blues or religious music.

"How long, how long" is a great question there. How long, how long will it be before happiness comes? How long, how long will I have to endure this? Or how long, how long before I'll become rich? Or how long, how long will I be poor? How long is justice? It fits in everywhere. There's the other train. There's the sorrow train, death's black train is coming. That depicts the darker side of life or the darker side of death, the darker side of an individual who passes. All the sad trains I've ever seen were black, especially those that burn coal. But maybe this train was blacker. [Chuckles]

I was born about thirty miles out of Atlanta. I grew up there. I played for the dances and all of the parties, rent parties. I helped open the roof garden in the Odd Fellows building in 1914. I was one of the piano players there. They called me Dorsey. But I hadn't yet gotten famous as Georgia Tom. [Laughs] Street singing became part of these men who sang spirituals and the blues. There was never a greater street singer than Connie Rosemont, who used to sit on the street, on the corner, with a little folding organ, and he sang these spirituals and all of these religious songs. I've seen him have crowds around him there. And the people would be weeping. I think he had one of the most marvelous tenor voices that I've heard in my life. Right here in Chicago. Connie Rosemont. I think he's dead now, I'm not sure. He was a product of Memphis, Tennessee. He would pass the hat and they would take up dollars, plenty dollars for him. I remember when they used to have church on the street in years past. They'd have quite a crowd. That sort of thing doesn't work out very well now.

I knew Reverend A.W. Nix, who preached here in Chicago. I remember his recording of "Black Diamond Express to Hell." It dealt with the good-timers, the whiskey drinkers, and the card players. The train was supposed to be a good-looking train, a pretty train. The people were deceived. It was going the wrong way. "Black Diamond is sitting on a fresh supply of brimstone and now she's ready to pull out for hell. Sin is the engineer, pleasure is the head-light, and the devil is the conductor. Next station is dancing town. I have a large crowd of church members to get on down there. Some of you think you can sing in the choir on Sunday and Charleston on the ballroom floor Monday, but you're going to go to hell on the Black Diamond train. The Black

Diamond's pulling off now for hell. Next station is Gamblers' Town. And then all the gamblers get on board. Have a big crowd of gamblers and crapshooters and card players and bootleggers that will ride the Black Diamond train to hell. Y'all gets on the Black Diamond train, gets on board for hell now. She's almost in hell. Next station is Stealing Town. Straight to hell, and then all the church please get on board. I have a big crowd of members in the church always been stealing. I'm always begging money for the church and never turn it in, always giving church suppers, and then stealing half the money. *All* you church thieves, you got to go to hell on the Black Diamond train." [Chuckles] He was a great preacher.

Some of the spirituals are what we call recited. And some are recited to music, and they're very beautiful like that, very impressive. I have a song that I wrote, "Walking on the King's Highway": "I'm always contented as I journey on and travel through the sunshine and the rain." That's my song. Rosa Belle Brooks of St. Louis and I wrote that back in 1932. I had one verse there: "I'm always contented as I journey on / And travel through the sunshine and the rain / The winds may beat and play / The storms may find a way / But I keep on traveling just the same / Traveling on / I'm traveling up the king's highway." I'm the first one that made the market for gospel songs. I went to the churches and sang my songs at the end of the service to those who would let me. I had to make a market for them. But all of the singers who came after have a part of Thomas A. Dorsey in their songs.

There are Holiness churches. You have Methodist, Baptist, and the Presbyterian. Then there's the Holiness, the Church of God in Christ, and so forth. They are a spirited and a lively group of singers. Some of them have dancing with their singing. They get out in the middle of the floor there sometimes and they enjoy a nice crowd too, with the way they carry on this dancing and this music.

Is it that the Holiness people feel that grace can be captured all at once, rather than growing to it through the years?

I won't say yes and I won't say no. That depends upon the individual. So far as I'm concerned, you don't get all the grace at once. But I feel that after you get a start, you get a taste of it, it ought to grow on you, you ought to grow in it. No baby is born a full-grown man or woman to start with. So I think it is expedient that we grow in grace.

Which church do you belong to?

I belong to all of them. [Laughs]

Isn't the fact that the Negroes were traveling so much, seeking new means of living, and using the train so much, the Jim Crow train . . . ?

Between the years of 1912 through to about 1918 is when the great exodus from the South started, to the North, of my people. Anything that moved seemed to have a bearing on them. They couldn't say very much about automobiles, for they didn't have them. In that time, I wrote a skit about the folk from the backwoods who took the straight line, straight to Chicago from the cotton fields, from the turpentine fields, from the lumber camps. They hit the straight line, and came straight to Chicago, where they felt that money grew on trees, eggs was made in a factory, and a man could scratch his bread out of the concrete. They felt that it afforded opportunities just that way. The working facilities were so much greater, the pay was so much better. They just felt that they had greater opportunities, that's all. That's why I'm here! I wouldn't have been what I am if I hadn't'a come up, got on the straight line, and come up to Chicago. [Laughter]

So we come to Mahalia. Again, she too is traveling. "Move On Up a Little Higher."

Move on up! [Chuckles] I knew Mahalia back in the late twenties. I was Mahalia's pianist and her promoter for seven years. The first time Mahalia made an appearance in New York, I took her. I told Mahalia back in those days, "I'm not able to do the things for you that I would like to do, or the things that you deserve, but you have a voice that no other singer has, and someday someone will discover you and you will be a great singer." I want to say that the gentleman talking to me here, Mr. Studs Terkel, is one of the men who discovered Mahalia Jackson, put her on the air for the first time. Blessings to you.

This is a sad commentary. I probably was the first white man to introduce Mahalia to radio on white radio. Mahalia had filled ballparks before, but the audience was all black. This is the tragic thing. We use the word dis-covery, that is someone is not discovered until a white discovers him.

This, to me, is one of the tragedies in our culture. She filled ballparks, with Negroes, whether it was in Memphis or in Atlanta. But I happened to be a disc jockey at the time, who liked this particular record. It's not a matter of modesty; it's a matter of correcting the record.

I don't think there's anything sacrilegious about it. If jazz musicians feel like they can serve in the church, I don't think it's going to desecrate any part of the church to let them come in and do something. Right here in Chicago, right out in my neighborhood here, here at Drexel Boulevard, they had a jazz class, a band there that taught them to keep the fellas out of the street, to keep them from running here and there. They organized a band, they taught them to play jazz there in the church. We have an orchestra in my church and they play more gospel songs, they're not all hymns. We take some secular numbers.

Mahalia says, "I don't care if the devil plays a good song, so long as it's played."

So long as he plays it good.

MAHALIA JACKSON

Adapted from Studs Terkel's *Talking to Myself*, 1973

It is a harsh, wintry day in Chicago, 1947. At a record shop, George Hoefer, a critic for *Down Beat* and a friend of jazzmen, works behind the counter. He insists I hear something that has just come in. It is on the Apollo label. He plays it. It is gospel. "Move On Up a Little Higher." It builds and builds and builds for six minutes. I am floored and lifted. Who is she? George tells me she lives on the South Side and sings in a lot of black churches. I am caught.

As a disc jockey on a weekly radio program, I play Ellington, Caruso, Armstrong, Chaliapin, Leadbelly, Lotte Lehmann, and those others of the God-possessed. Now I add Mahalia. I'm flying high. (I play the Goodman Sextet, too.) It is an exhilarating time for me. And, I hope, for some of the listeners.

On Sunday mornings, I visit the Greater Salem Baptist church. It is on the city's West Side. There are intimations of rubble around and about.

Urban renewal is just getting under way. Here are parishioners, bone-weary after a week of unsung work, for a wage not worth singing about; here they are, listening to song, such as I, whose work is so much easier and whose wage is so much better, have never heard. It is at such time and circumstance that I become aware of my own arrogance. For a stupid moment, I had thought *I* discovered Mahalia Jackson. On occasion, I run into somebody who obtusely insists it is so. Most disheartening are those quite gifted singers of gospel music in this city, who, God help us all, attribute Mahalia's "success" to me. It is cause for tears as well as laughter. The people of Greater Salem know better.

Consider this. A single voice. A piano and an organ. A record label little known. Consider this. More than two million people, way more, have put out hard-gotten cash for "Move On Up a Little Higher." In scores of thousands of homes, among the devout and God-fearing, oh yeah, and in taverns and pool parlors, too, lowly spirits are lifted by a soaring, winged voice. Again and again and again, this record is played on phonographs and jukeboxes. The grooves are worn deep and the needles are dulled, but they keep on listening, through scratch and static, to this voice. And hardly a white has heard of her.

It is the story of Bessie Smith all over again. They say, a couple of generations ago, when a Bessie record came out, people would line up for blocks. Many who could not afford coal would derive warmth enough from the glow of "Backwater Blues" or "Baby Doll" or "Nobody Knows You When You're Down and Out."

I kid Mahalia about this. "If you took up the blues, you'd sound like Bessie Smith. If Bessie had ever sung spirituals, she'd've sounded like Mahalia Jackson." She laughs. She gets a kick out of it. Funny or not, it's true.

We're seated in her Prairie Avenue flat, oh, shall we say about twenty-five years ago? It is just before she moves into that ranch house, one of the first blacks in a white neighborhood; a few broken windows and a few phoned threats. She stares out the window, toward the setting sun, miles away and centuries ago. "Mahalia, she was a girl in the slave days. She was dreaming of Jubilee all the time. Of better days to come. My people gave me her name."

Her hands are clasped on the kitchen table. They are delicate, graceful hands. Not dainty, not soft. The calluses are eloquently there. She had scrubbed floors of other people's kitchens and finery. She had nursed other people's children. A bitter reflection some years later: "I nursed little Jimmy like he was my own. Do you think he was in that mob that threw rocks at Dr. King?"

I stare at her hands. She opens them and lays them on the table. "You got to work with your hands. How can you sing of Amazing Grace, how can you sing prayerfully of heaven and earth and all God's wonders without using your hands? My hands demonstrate what I feel inside. My hands, my feet, I throw my whole body to say all that is within me. The mind and the voice by themselves are not sufficient."

She was part of an early migration to Chicago from the Deep South. Her people wanted her to have a better chance than she'd have in Louisiana. Perhaps beauty culture. She tried. She didn't make it. She worked as a factory hand and as a domestic. Come Sunday, she found respite and exhilaration. She sang open-voiced and freely at Greater Salem. For that matter, she sang at any church you could name on the South Side, on the West Side, wherever black working people gathered to find a one-out-of-seven-day solace.

"When did I first begin to sing?" She laughs. "When did I first begin to walk and talk? When did I first begin to breathe? I remember singing as I scrubbed floors. It would make the work go easier. When the old people wasn't home, I'd turn on a Bessie Smith record and play it over and over. 'Careless Love,' that was the blues she sang."

"'Careless Love,' Mahalia?" I act out horror.

Her eyes suggest a twinkle. "That was before I was saved. I don't sing the blues now. The blues are wonderful, but I just don't sing 'em. When I imitated Bessie Smith, I was just a little girl, remember that." Significantly, she repeats, "Before I was saved."

Uh-oh, I know what's coming. And she knows I know. "An' I'm gonna save you, too, Studs." It isn't the first time she offers this challenge; nor is it the last. It is to become our Chautauqua debate: believer versus atheist. The studio audience at her radio programs, during the warm-ups, have come to delight in this theological dispute, knowing quite well who will come off the laughing winner. I always lose. Don't misunderstand. I have never in my life thrown a match of this nature. I am, in this instance, pitifully overmatched. All my Bob Ingersoll arguments are demolished by her soaring song. And her humor.

Will she ever sing the blues? She laughs. I know she loves the blues, but there isn't a ghost of a chance. Big Bill Broonzy, who sings a country blues like nobody ever, before or since, understands: "It ain't right for Mahalia to be asked to sing the blues. They all respect her because she sticks to her beliefs. I feel funny when they put me on the same platform with her. It don't seem right. 'Course, you know Mahalia. She don't complain about it, 'cause that's the way she is. I guess it's all right, though, if we're on two separate parts of the pro-gram. Like that time in Oxford, England. Those Englishmen liked the both of us. Just between you an' me, I don't think they knew the difference. But they were very nice just the same. No, Mahalia shouldn't be made to sing the blues. They should just let her sing only what she believes and feels inside. Without feelin', there's nothin'. That goes for all kinds of music."

Mahalia is equally fond of Bill. One day, as she lies in the hospital bed, gaunt and emaciated, she talks of Bill. As if by magic, she feels better. She is wildly comical doing Broonzy. She recounts their joint triumph at London's Albert Hall. "I'm scared. I never sang for those British people before. Bill, he says, 'Just sing, baby, they won't know the difference.'" As she captures his voice, his inflection, his throwaway manner, her visitors laugh uproariously. She's getting a great kick, too. She no longer looks gaunt and emaciated. Only the clergyman, at her bedside, is not amused. He is praying. Mahalia, though, is Here rather than There. And not about to die.

Under other circumstances, Mahalia might have become an outrageously wondrous comedienne. She could do Moms Mabley and then some. Her gift in mimicry; her sense of the absurd; her nimbleness in repartee. Oh yeah, easy. Were it not for her voice. And something else.

"I don't know what it was all the time. All I know is it would grip me. Bessie's singing gave me the same feeling as when I'd hear men singing out-side as they worked, laying the ties for the railroad, working on the docks. . . ."

Her reminiscences are always interrupted by friends and strangers. The doorbell rings; it is always ringing. And the telephone is always the hot line. A blind bass and four women singers enter. They are a gospel group from Washington, just passing through. They've dropped in to rehearse. Mahalia's piano is available.

Mildred Falls comes by. She is Mahalia's accompanist. She knows every breath the singer takes. What Paul Ulanowsky is to Lotte Lehmann, what Gerald Moore is to Dietrich Fischer-Dieskau, Mildred is to Mahalia. And more. In their early travels, they suffered humiliation together. And glory. It is in every chord, in every song.

She belongs to the people on the street. How often in my stumbling along with her has she been stopped by the old lady with the absurdly heavy shopping bag, who effusively greets "Mahalie." And the waiter, the garage mechanic, the young schoolteacher, the pretty girl who makes sandwiches at the mostly black drive-in. They'd heard her at such and such a church; she's a friend of an aunt or a cousin or a neighbor; they'd worn out "In the Upper Room" or "Even Me" or "Didn't It Rain."

And yet, Mahalia is discontented. There is a plaintive note to her voice as she calls late at night. What's the trouble? She can't put her finger on it. Something about not being "successful." I kid her because I think she's kidding. She's not. There are Carnegie Hall triumphs, Columbia albums on more than a few coffee tables, college professors paying her tribute, an appearance at the White House, an honorary degree—what is it? She can't explain, she, who is usually so deft with the telling phrase, so quick at getting to the heart of the matter. It is something she is reaching out for that may not be there. But it is. And it appears quite suddenly.

Is it 1955? 1956? Another call in the dead of night. Her voice has an unaccustomed ring. She says something about a phone call from Alabama. A young Reverend Abernathy has called on behalf of another young reverend, a Martin Luther King. Something about a Montgomery bus boycott. They'd like her to sing at one of the church rallies. What's her fee?

I know what's coming and I delight in it. She's having a high time.

"You ever hear of these people?" she asks.

She knows very well I've heard of these people.

"Don't you think the colored are pushin' too fast?"

I am rolling off the bed.

"Why they lookin' for trouble all the time?"

When I laugh uncontrollably, it sounds like a cackle. I am cackling.

She is doing Moms Mabley now.

"Mmm, chile, you laugh at crazy things. 'At's why you get in trouble all the time you'self."

"I can't help it, Mahalia, I don't look for it. It just seeks me out. What did you decide?" As though I didn't know.

She lets out a long sigh. "What do *you* think I should do?"

"When are you goin'?"

"Day after tomorrow. Reverend Abernathy asks how much I'll charge." She laughs.

"What'd you tell him?" As though I didn't know.

"I said, 'Reverend Abernathy, I don't charge the walkin' people.'"

Mahalia has found what she was looking for.

Time passes, cataclysmically. The walking people of Montgomery set hearts on fire. So does song as well as the word. Martin Luther King knows what he's about in calling on Mahalia Jackson. He has found a way; so has she.

How green is the memory of 1963 and the March on Washington. The Lincoln Memorial is the backdrop. The reflecting pool is ahead. As the assembled thousands await Dr. King's memorable plea for mankind, the heavy woman, wearing a new multiflowered hat, celebrates life. She is singing "Precious Lord, Take My Hand." It is Dr. King's favorite hymn. She has never sung this one better.

As she goes into "I'm Going to Live the Life I Sing About," an airplane—or is it a helicopter?—for some unaccountable reason, is impiously flying overhead. We all look up, slightly distressed. Mahalia looks up, too, without missing a beat. She outsings the flying machine, as it vanishes into the blue. Even now, I see those scores of white handkerchiefs waving as banners of triumph. . . .

BIG BILL BROONZY
1958

Big Bill sat all by himself in the enormous room. The most gregarious of men, he was this night a man alone. The size of Universal's jumbo studio accentuated the singer's solitude. He didn't say, but I'm sure it was the way he wanted it.

Three of us were in the control room: the engineer; Bill Randle, the Cleveland disc jockey, who subsidized the session; and I. There was nothing for us to say. More than window glass was between the singer and us. We were strangers, friendly strangers, but strangers nonetheless. Big Bill was miles away, dirt roads and turnpikes of miles away. And how many, many years away? But it was *now* that counted. He was wasting no time.

"Machine goin'?"

I nodded. The impersonal spool of tape was rotating. He murmured to the mike: "I'm gonna sing some blues of other guys. Friends of mine, they're all gone. That's why I'm gonna sing 'em. If I don't who will?"

A soft introduction for each song and each man.

Leroy Carr. A faint smile played around his mouth. "Once I remember me an' some other guys, we went over to his house an' woked him up in the middle of the night, got 'im outa bed an' made him sing this blues." *In the evenin', in the evenin' / Mama, when the sun go down . . .*

So many times had I heard Bill sing this one. At schools, clubs, house parties. That time on the Near North Side at Jimmy Yancey's memorial with Mama Yancey in the audience rocking, keening, moaning softly, "Sing it, baby, sing it." Eyes closed, he was shouting for the widow. For all widows. Even the cool, dead-eyed young hangers-on who patronized the pseudo-Bohemian tavern stopped their playacting at the bar. *Yes, it's so lonesome, it's so lonesome / I declare, when the one you love is not around / When the sun go down.* But this night at the studio, Bill was singing for keeps. The vibrating "yeah-ay-ay-ay-ay ooohh-ooohh" was more than just lamentation for a woman gone off. It was for life itself. *So goodbye, old sweethearts and pals / Yes, I declare I'm goin' away / I may be back to see you again, little girl / Some old rainy day . . .* When he finished this one, he said to the mike, "He's gone."

A pause.

About Richard M. Jones, "the man who wrote this next song." About the girl, Georgia White, whose big hit it was. Good-looking, friendly, all the fellows liked her. Her husband watched her every move, he was her valet, dresser, he looked after her every need. *I'm troubled in mind, baby, I'm so blue / But I won't be blue always / You know the sun, sun gonna shine / In my back door someday . . .* When he finished this one, he said to the mike: "He's gone." And so it went with Jim Jackson and his blues. Big Maceo—Maceo Merriweather—and "Worried Life Blues." After each song, the wistful coda: "He's gone." Leadbelly. "He was foreman, what we call straw boss of the work gang. 'At's how he got the name Leadbelly. Him an' Sleepy John Estes. He'd sit under the tree while the other guys did the work. His hips was gettin' full of lead." *Take this hammer, take it to the captain / Tell 'im I'm gone, tell 'im I'm gone . . .* Sung not in the manner of Leadbelly nor of the Weavers nor of Odetta. Sung Bill's way. A different tempo, a different feel, yet truly a work song. Were the spirit of Huddie around and about that night, there'd have been a great to-do. A banter back and forth. A Leadbelly reply to Bill's "libel." Though even Lead himself (I recall a night in Chicago when Big Bill was the prime subject of his conversation) would have been the first to admit that Bill was a rough man to top in the matter of riposte. *If he asks you was I laughing, tell 'im I was cryin'* . . . Song ended, the murmur: "He's gone."

Time out. Time out for all of us. The purpose of this recording was an attempt to capture on tape as much of Big Bill Broonzy as possible. His songs, others' songs, remembrance of things past, goodness, badness, and indifference. Randle had in mind a project similar to Jelly Roll Morton's Library of Congress sessions with Alan Lomax. Perhaps it worked out that way. I don't know. One thing I know. There was a singular difference. While Jelly Roll made himself the hero (and justifiably, how else could it be?), Bill made the blues the overwhelmingly personal hero of his story—a disturbing, impish, terrible, wondrous hero, a creature of so much ambivalence, both demon and comforter at one and the same time. Wasn't it Leadbelly who sang it so? *Woke up this mornin' / Blues was round my bed / Ate my breakfast / Blues was in my bread.* Guy Kelly, was it not, who on some Decca 78 sang of the blues and the rabbit? *Blues jumped the rabbit / Run 'im a solid mile / Poor fellow lay down / An' cried like a natural chile.* Not humans alone does the blues devil.

This was Saturday. Bill was going under the knife the following Monday. He had a feeling; it would be a long time before he'd ever sing again. It wasn't so much the ailment that worried him. It was the knife. Would they cut his throat? No, the doctors told him, it was a matter of the lung. But the knife . . . In describing how he writes a blues, how he formulates the idea (Bill has written 360, give or take a dozen; he's lost count of the scores he gave to other singers, Lil Green, Memphis Slim, Brownie McGhee, Sonny Terry, Tampa Red—"if it fits somebody else better than me, why shouldn't I give it to 'im? Don't do any good layin' around, it's all wrote"), he chose the knife as the sample object. "Now take a knife. How many things can you do with a knife? You can cut fish, you can cut your toenails, I seen guys shave with it, you can eat beans with it, you can kill a man. There. You name five things you can do with a knife, you got five verses. You got yourself a blues." Apply this to a woman, a job, another man. *I wonder when I will get to be called a man / Or do I have to wait till I'm ninety-three?*

He wrote that one in 1928. You may remember his comments in his autobiography, *Big Bill Blues: William Broonzy's Story*. "There was a man I knew, when I was ten years old, that the white people called a boy. He was about thirty then. When I went to the army and came back in 1919, well he was an old man then and the white people was calling him Uncle Mackray. So he never got to be called a man, from 'boy' to 'Uncle Mackray.' And so it still is today. They call all Negro men 'boys' and some of them is old enough to be their father. In fact I do not know that some old men is glad to be called boys, but they call you so until you get to be fifty, and at the time you would appreciate being called a boy they start calling you 'uncle.' That's the time when I would like to be called a boy, when I get to be fifty or older. It's all right for my sister's kids to call me 'uncle,' but not by a man or woman eighty years old."

Again, Bill faced the mike. Which of the hundreds of blues, his own, others', friends', strangers', came to his thoughts, to his tongue? What place? A dot on the map called Scott? William Lee Broonzy, place of birth, Scott, Mississippi. Was it his boyhood of which he was thinking? He stared silently at the mike. Where was he? On a Mississippi field, helping his tenant-farmer father, pushing a "single sweep" at the age of eight and quickly graduating to the "double shovel"? Or was the scene Arkansas, just outside Little Rock, where a young, strong, way-better-than-six-foot plow hand was turning up the loam? London? Paris? Amsterdam? Marseilles? Where an American singer of the "undressed" blues shouted his life, while his guitar dotted the i's and crossed the t's? Senegal, and an overwhelming spiritual experience? "I look at those people an' I felt I must've been here before, my people I mean. All my family is tall. And I looked at all these seven-footers, I felt like a midget. I run into a family named Broonzie. They spelt it -*ie* instead of -*y* but it was the same name. Yeah, I think my ancestors came from there."

(Senegal. The time Bill had returned from a European-African tour, he recounted experiences, some sober, many humorous, always with his razor-keen wit and deft turn of irony. The Senegalese, though, he viewed with awe. "In this nightclub, I see this beautiful girl. I'm goin' over to her, but a man says no, no, she belongs to somebody else. He points to a Senegalese. That didn't bother me. I had a few drinks anyway. Just then somebody comes in askin' for help. His car is stuck in a hole outside. The Senegalese, he goes outside all by himself, he lifts the whole back of that car and sets it straight. I didn't go near that girl. Suppose me an' him had a fight, what do you think would've happened? Bill put his hand to his cheek and shook back and forth, chuckling and moaning.)

Was his first appearance at Carnegie Hall on his mind? "The Spirituals to Swing" concert instituted by John Hammond? Alan Lomax recalls the disturbance and discomfort of New Yorkers at the naked rawness of his songs—disturbing yet unforgettable.

Where was Bill? Randle was talking to him from the control room. "Anything, Bill. Anything you want to say or sing, whatever comes to mind, feel free. It's all yours." Bill's fingers played lightly over the guitar. "This is a song I know I like. They been playin' the melody since I was a boy. My uncle used to play it on a five-string banjo. That's how I learn it, listening to him. All I did was put new words to it." "Keys to the Highway," . . . *I'm gonna leave here runnin' / Because walkin' is much too slow / So long, goodbye / Ye-e-e-e-s, I hate to say goodbye / Because I'm gonna walk this old highway / Till the day I die.* "That was Jerry Belcher, my uncle, he was my mother's brother. Him and Stonewall Jackson, they was buddies, used to run around together. They didn't exactly call what they was playin' blues in them days. Negro reels. There was two kinds, one Negro, the other white. White reels is what we call square dances today. Negro reels is what we call the blues. My uncle and Stonewall and See See Rider—there was a real man named See See Rider, the song's about him, he'd ride everywhere for free—they said these reels were sung in slavery days. My uncle, my mother and father was all born in slavery. My mom wasn't freed till she was twenty."

Bill smiled. A new thought. "My uncle would get in trouble with my mother over this song. 'Mindin' My Own Business.' It had spiritual-like words, church songs we called 'em in them days." *Good Book tell you you got to reap just what you sow / An' I declare you got to reap it / I don't care where you go . . .* "She run him outta the house when he had gambling words to it."

What would this devout mother have thought of the lyrics added by her son? Perhaps this comes as close to the essence of Broonzyan philosophy as anything he has ever written. *Takes six months to tend to my own business / And six to leave other people's alone / By the time I do that / I declare all twelve months is gone.* No questioning of others' moral values. Never. When young hipsters have walked out on his work blues, mouths slightly opened, bored stiff, scraping a chair on the way out, Bill may have been hurt, but not a word. "They're right. When I sing about my mule bein' sick and those crops getting' rotten, they don't know what I'm singing' about. They never had no mule get sick. Don't mean nothin' to them. People in Europe cryin' about the bomb fallin' on 'em. What do we know about it? We never had no bomb hit us. Same thing. I don't blame 'em for walkin' out. But I gotta sing it. That's what I know." So with the church people. "I got respect for Christian people. I'd never sing the blues to Mahalia when I come to see her in her dressin' room.

Because those people got just as much right to their way of thinkin' as I do. Take the mixin' up of spirituals and jazz on the jukebox today. They don't know what they're doing'. They like the music, the young people, but they don't like to hear the words. They say that's the horse-an'-buggy days, that's the past. We don't want to be reminded."

Elvis Presley? "I like what he's doin'. He's rockin' the blues, that's all he's doin'. They don't listen to me but they listen to him when he plays it. That's good. Makes it easier for me. They been rockin' the blues since the world began. Rock an' roll is here to stay because it comes from natural people. Rock an' roll is a natural steal from the blues, an' the blues'll never die. The blues can't die because it's a natural steal from the spirituals. I sung spirituals before I sung the blues." *Ananias, Ananias, tell me what kind a man Jesus is / Spoke to the wind, wind stopped still . . . / Spoke to the sea, sea got ca'm / Spoke to the sick, sick got well . . . / Spoke to the dead, dead did rise / . . . Spoke to the sick, sick got well . . . Tell me what kind a man Jesus is.* "Younger people say you're cryin' when you sing like that. Who wants to cry? Back in them days people had nothin' else to do but cry. Today, they do nothin' but talk. Got lawyers."

Softly, Bill went into "Swing Low, Sweet Chariot." Not the way it was heard in school. Not the way the Fisk Jubilee Singers did it. Not the way Paul Robeson or Marian Anderson did it. Bill's way. A man was calling . . . *I-I-I-I look to Jerden, now what did I see / Comin' fer to carry me home / A-A-A-A-A band of angels, comin' to me / Comin' fer to carry me home / I-I-I-I-f you get there before I do / Pl-e-e-ease tel-l-l them all that I'm coming too / Comin' fer to carry me home.* "Home" sounding ever soft after the imploring call. Journey's end. Another version. A gentle rolling of the chariots, a swinging of the carriers of all the hopeful ones. (James Agee would have loved this, so much comfort and tenderness to it. *A Death in the Family.* The little boy hearing his father sing of the chariots, or "cherryits," and the all-encompassing warmth it provided. So Bill affected us.)

What else to remember of the lone man in the studio? His singing of "Backwater Blues" and how Bessie came to write it. There was a contest. Who is it can write the best blues memorializing the flood of that year, the terrible flood? There were a number of entries. Bessie's was chosen. Songs of women he had known and known about. Willie Mae . . . Louise . . . Alberta . . . Crow Jane. Never bitter, always with affection—for their frailties as well as their strengths.

"Crawdad" as a whimsical lullaby. A lullaby when softly sung by the mothers, but oh, what a wake-up song when the men come home, genial, drunk, and boisterous! Never in all of his performances of this ditty has Bill failed to evoke the broad-beamed grin even from those for whom it was a world they never knew. Yes, he sang "Black, Brown, and White," too. Worth pulpitfuls of sermons. And how many sanctimonious celebrants of Brotherhood Week will ever dig it? Guitar solos. Electric? His fingers. Nothing plugged in the wall. He was heard. "I didn't play guitar till I came to Chicago. Before that, it was the four-string fiddle, which I picked up in hearing a man play it in Arkansas. I didn't learn guitar till after I got out of the army. Started in 1921, didn't get good at it till 1923. I must have been around thirty."

He never brought the guitar into his mother's house. It was sinful. Always parked it outside the door whenever he visited her in Little Rock. Once she heard him play. "First time I was booked in Arkansas, Little Rock, in 1940, she stood there at the door, she didn't come in, just stood there. When they found out who she was, they didn't charge her nothing." A wizened, ninety-year-old woman listening, listening to her son. What was it she heard? How well did she hear his voice, his songs? Born in slavery, this old, old lady. At 103, died in freedom—or whatever portion of it Little Rock allotted her.

The difference between New Orleans blues and the stuff from Mississippi: "They play more chords, we play more blue notes. We push the strings more." He demonstrates. One is more restrained, the other more wild. One is more musical, the other a harsh cry. "Fellow should sing the way he feels. They're right an' we're right. Their life is different from us. What do they know about raisin' potatoes an' peas and pickin' cotton? Only cotton they ever see is in bales. They ain't farmers in New Orleans, we're farmers. 'Course they do different kinds of work. I don't mean a man has to live what he writes about. But it helps. He don't have to guess." *Plough Hand's been my name / Lord, for forty years or more . . .*

Cryin' Joe Turner. This is the one. If ever there was a hush in the control room, the edge-of-the-chair anticipation, it is now. Bill is retuning his guitar. This one calls for extra-special tuning. "You guys can go for a drink while I'm doin' this." Now he's ready. We hear a guitar, but it's like no guitar we ever heard before. It's a human voice, not one but a whole ramshackle town. Now Bill is talking, simple narrative about a terrible flood, people losing homes, crops, everything. And Joe Turner comes along, he's two men—a white and a black—and he helps out. "And they would start cryin' and singing' this song." And now that chord—*whang*—only it isn't that—it's crying, everybody crying— a cry of salvation.

Let Charles Edward Smith tell it: "Some of the best blues guitar ever recorded and certainly this is one of the great blues of all time, expressing in ingenuous symbolism the human tragedy of the slave society—the black man on the mule going down the road we all must go, to the rich heartland of a common sharings of hopes and hungers. The singing and talking are folk eloquence at its best. It is definitely 19th-century and the melody, like the legend, probably goes back to slavery days. And what an amazing real life characterization for a legend—the black-man-white-man concept—the tragedy of a slave society and the hope in a common humanity!" *They tell me Joe Turner been here and gone / Lord, they tell me Joe Turner been here and gone / They tell me Joe Turner been here and gone . . .*

Toward the butt end of the night, two friends drop in. Brownie McGhee and Sonny Terry. There is banter, byplay, an exchange of songs. A rich vein of humor is tapped. Bill is the interlocutor, the mover and the shaker. Each takes a whack at a blues. They all do.

The night is over. Bill's story is on tape. Not all he had to tell, not all he had to sing. But enough to give you an idea of the man, the artist.

Postscript: Something unsaid, yet implicit in the bracketing of two songs. "I remember fellows they called 'man-catchers'—or 'snatchers,' they sometimes called 'em. Like employment agency men. He sees guys workin' on the road, he says, 'Come with me, I'll get you a dollar a day. Oh, makin' stave bolts or cuttin' lead bolts.' He gets 'em in a wagon, has 'em feelin' good, next thing they're fifteen miles from home. Cuttin' cordwood for the gins or big homes. Supposed to get paid, didn't get paid. Only way to get back home was to walk. An' they'd sing this song." *Goin' down the road feeling' bad / Ain't gonna be treated this-a way . . .* As though it were an answer-back song, Bill tells of the other. "Guys who worked railroad gangs, levee gangs—one guy gets away to Little Rock where he gets $1.25 a day instead of 75 cents. Maybe thirty, forty, fifty guys workin', singin'. Every one takes a verse. But one guy is givin' the signal. He's gettin' away. I been on gangs like that. Same melody was sung in slavery times. The mean driver—or overseer, as they was called—he didn't know what the song meant, but everybody else did." Shall we play on a phrase and say one song is "call" and the other "response"? *If I could feel in the mornin' / Baby, like I feel today / Ye-e-e-e-s, I'm gonna pack up / An' make my getaway.* A long-drawn-out, shouted, affirmative *yes.* So often Bill has said a man doesn't sing the blues because he thinks things are going to be the same. Of course, he hopes they'll be better. Otherwise, he wouldn't be singing at all.

A second postscript: "Big Bill died 5:30 A.M.—rainy morning, August 15, 1958. On way to hospital—Chicago. Somewhere between 61 and 64. Twin sister says he's 61. Let it go at that. —Studs."

EMANUEL DUNN
1963

Like Kaspar Hauser, the legendary nineteenth-century wild boy raised in solitude, Emanuel Dunn, from the Deep South, grew up under mysterious circumstances. The folklorist Harry Oster, of Louisiana State University, said of him, "Here is the natural. He doesn't know where he's from, no one does. He doesn't know his childhood, father, mother. This white couple took him in and adopted him. That's all he knows. But he does know the music, and the mystery is where and how he learned these songs, and understood them, and came to talk as he does."

You were from Liberty, Mississippi.

About fifteen mile outta Liberty, Mississippi. I sure don't remember my early years with my mother and father. I just only know that I had a white mother and a white father, but he was crueler on me. Because I guess that I was dark and Mister was white. Because they was brighter than I were they had to be white. And from little on up. Because I was ten years old when I knew that's who I was staying with, those white people. Them the only two that I know. I don't remember my real father and real mother because I don't guess I never had them. I sure don't know when it was I first came to these people. I wasn't named nobody. Just Boy. That's all, just called Boy. No name. The name

Emanuel Dunn was imbued in me later, after the years passed and I got married. Well, I got me a family of my own. Well, I named my own self.

Mister was cruel to me more than he was anyone else. Which, he was cruel to all of us, but he was crueler on me more than he was the rest of them. My brothers were good to me, oh, indeed, they were. There was nothing too good for them to give me, and there was nothing too good I had to give them, which I didn't have nuthin' to give them, but just this one asked me to give him a piece of bread. Well, I'd give him that, you know. Well, my father would look at 'em. You know, we would always sit to the table. He would look at them, three boys all on one side, and wife, would be over next to one of the boys, I'd be between him and his two boys. 'Cause all three were supposed to sit together.

Oh, you'd eat together with him. Has the idea occurred to you that he might have maybe been your real father and you had a black mother?

He couldn't have been, because if he had, he wouldn't have been that cruel on me, I don't believe.

Or else you might have been maybe your mother's son. It's hard to tell. You don't know what it was that made this man so cruel to you?

Well, I sure don't.

When I was seven and a half years old he went and bought a mule, and he told me, he said, "Boy, I want you to plow this mule; and this mule die, I'm gonna buy another one, and if you die, I'm gonna hire another." Well, I didn't know nothing about no plow, no mule, nuthin' like that. So he carried me to the field and showed me how he wanted the ground plowed, which he made a few rounds with the plow and the mule. Well, by him being a man and I was a child, I couldn't handle that mule like he could. He told me, he says, "Now, you take the plow." Well, I did. Well, by eleven-thirty, the mule brought me to the house. So he's sitting on the porch, he looks and says, "Yeah, you done come out before twelve o'clock, huh?" I told him I couldn't help it, the mule brought me out, me, plow and all. He went back into the house, looked up on the rack, and got a rawhide whip and laid it across his shoulders, and said, "Well, I'm gonna take you and the mule back to the field." He said, "Me and you gonna plow it." I was wondering how me and him were going to plow it, you know? So when I got down to that field I *learnt*. He'd taken them harness offa that mule and put 'em on *me,* and told me, he said, "Now, we gonna plow around." Which I did. He put the line just across my shoulders and my back. With that he flayed the whip and told me, "Let's go!" His wife was standing up there and she said, "You shouldn't do that child like that." He told her, he said, "You better go back to the house." She started crying and I was crying. So, instead, when he had to go to Liberty, she had one dollar and a dime, she said, "Boy, I want you to take this dollar and a dime, and you run off." So my two little white brothers, they says, "Well, Mother dear, reckon will we ever see our little colored brother again?" She says, "Some day, you all might, I hope." And then I started me off a song. (He strums . . . "Lord, lordy me, man. lord, he's treating me so bad, meanest old man . . .") When she told me to run off, I left there running. I went through swamp, and rivers, and valleys. . . . I stayed in the woods about three weeks. Whenever you hear a person say they can't do without eating nothing but steak . . . If you get in the woods, especially if someone puts something for you and they fed 'em, they can live longer than just three weeks without eating. I lived offa water. And then I came to another town, it was in Louisiana, which I didn't know it was in Louisiana when I got in it, until I got to talking with a girl, the girl I married, and her knowed what the name of that town was, Eastwood, Louisiana. So I stayed there and got me a job at a sawmill, and that's where we got married. I knew her when I was seven and a half years old. And then I grew up, me and her together.

You and music, how did you take to the guitar?

My first guitar—I took a five gallon bucket, I cut me some rubber out of an inner tube, small rubber, I slipped them across that bucket, and it would make a little noise [he strums gently for a moment] . . . and from then on I started playing with the guitar. I got me a little ol' guitar and I started rapping on it, playing, from then on. When I was a boy there was a song, "Lost John," and played with a mouth harp. Well, now "Lost John," it actually came from a buzzard. A buzzard was sitting on a snag one day, and he was moaning, just moaning and moaning. And they had another one come sit on the same snag where he was at, and they both started moaning. Well, the way they was moaning, "the old cow dead, never left nothing but the roots and the head." Well, long years back, people used to burn up the cow what died, horses, all what died, well, they used to burn it up. Well, the poor buzzards couldn't get nothing to eat, 'cause there wasn't much for them to eat. You couldn't eat them bones because the meat was all burned off it. So he was moaning, and his moan, the way I come to say in this song, it was Lost John. The old cow dead, never left nothing but the roots and the head, the poor buzzard have to go back to get him something to eat. That was "Lost John," discovered from a buzzard, and I made that music go the way he was moaning was Lost John. Because, otherwise he'd have been a lost bird if he had stayed over there, because if he couldn't get nothing to eat he was gonna die. It could be as myself. Because places I crossed, ain't no telling what kind of animals was in those woods or swamp.

Well, the way it do, all of the songs I just makes it up and it just comes out. If I blow it, it just comes out. The way all this accumulates in my brain, I guess. You know as I make it up, it just comes out. I started playing about eight years old and I was sitting out at the gruel house there, and my mind kept on just humming, just humming, and that's why I started to making all this kind of good music. That's why I made a harmonica. With rubber, take me a can, I stretched me the rubber across the top of it, I bent the can in the middle, and I taken me a nail and driven a hole through it. And as I would do, run it across my mouth like that way, and it would make a little music. But it would change it as I moved my mouth and the sound was coming through the hole. That's how I learned how to blow a harmonica.

I worked at a sawmill. I made a song about the sawmill, and that song, you know, it just runs through in my mind. The way I started, you know in the sawmill, when you crank them big old diesel engines up, you know, they go loud. When they start, they're sort of turning, and they go . . . [he hums, strums louder] Well, you know, when they roll a log on the carrier, it hits that carrier . . . [He sings] Oh, this . . . roll one away . . . never gonna fly . . . Now what I mean by never gonna fly . . . [Sings] on an airplane, baby . . . Now that's a song and I made it up myself just by the hum of that mill running and the saws that was cutting the logs. In other words, they'd be cutting boards out, and that hmm-ching, the way it would hit the end of the log. And the song was they're never gonna fly. They have airplanes that haul the lumber from city to city. Well, by sailing, they have ships made to carry it overseas to build places over there. And about motoring, they loads it on trucks, and while the truck drivers standing close to danger, if he breaks a limb it's going straight through that cab, and there ain't no way he can be saved. That limb is gonna kill him. And if he don't die, well, he gonna wish he would, 'cause he's gonna be in such a bad shape.

When you married your wife you had no name. What did she call you?

Well, Boy. I just wasn't named nobody. And she says, "Why you want to pick out Emanuel?" I said, "Well, that suits me more better." She said, "Why you couldn't be named Jack, or Billy, or something like that?" I said, "I don't like them kind." So, she agreed with me, she said, "Well, okay." I said, "Well, we grew up together my name Emanuel Dunn, so that's the way it is."

You make up everything about your life because you started as nobody. Your own life you make up in your songs.

That's right.

The Titanic, *the great disaster on the sea, how did you hear of it?*

Well, I heard a guy, he was saying that the *Titanic*— Well, you know, he stand by me and that's the word he was saying, and he said, "You know the *Titanic*, I don't know if she was sinking down. An iceberg came over and hit her in the side." And that's, when he said the side, I slid over, and I said, "On the side? A song could be made out of that." And the song come into my mind. So then I started singing, I said . . . [He sings] On the great ocean, the *Titanic* was sinking down . . . it's a blues talking/singing song. Well, the people, I don't even know whether they were on the *Titanic* or not. I just prayed to God. The captain went down and he said before he let all of them, let other people go down, he's going down, too, and they had crippled and blind, and they couldn't walk, couldn't talk. Before he'd see all of them going down, he's going down with the *Titanic*.

Now trains, you do trains on the mouth harp. Now, you've seen many trains passing.

I done saw some of them. They had one, they called it the Smokey Joe. The older trains, they had steam trains. They didn't have trains like they got now. They had a lotta smoke would be coming out of it. It would go up and down the track. Well, that's Smokey Joe. [Harmonica for a bit] A lot of y'all may not use that word, but actually the train, from its operation to me it'd be saying, catch the nigger, black and dirty. That's the way, you know. [He plays] When Old Black Joe is getting on down the track, you can tell the operation is getting faster and faster with the music of the harmonica. [He plays faster and faster] It's like a song. [He sings softly.] I'm going home on the morning train [then full out] I'm going home on the morning train [and sings *a cappella* on through the song].

Did you go to church much?

Well, I never did go too much to no church until a good while after I was married. I went to church, Baptist church, so I started to praying myself, you know, and it got into me. It came into my mind, you know, that by the people who's praying, you know, the song what came to me, I said, I sung it too, about a motherless child, there were hard times and the mother was gone. I started to moan that song. [He moans into the words, "Oh, motherless child, has a hard time, mother is gone . . ." sings *a cappella*, taps beat on guitar wood.] See, that song started the men, everybody was in the church, you know, and they was singing it too, you know. And they wondered where he done stole that kind of song at. So the preacher asked me, "Where did you stole that?" I said, "Well, it just come into my mind." See, I was only moaning and that song just come to me.

Motherless child is so much your life, isn't it?

Well, that's right because I don't have me one.

BOB DYLAN
1963

Bob Dylan was a young folk poet at the time I spoke with him, one of the most exciting singers of songs around—rumpled trousers, curly hair, wearing a skipper's cap, twenty-two years old. He can't be pigeonholed. Bob Shelton of the New York Times *writes: "His lyrics mix a sermon out of Woody Guthrie's conversational folksay with a dash of Rimbaud's demonic imagery and even a bit of Yevtushenko's social criticism. Whether his verse is free or rhymed, whether the mood is somber, crusading, satiric, subject to the fanciful, Mr. Dylan's words and melodies sparkle with the light of an inspired poet." He is an American original.*

Where did you come from, Cotton-Eyed Joe?

The beginning was there in Minnesota. But that was the beginning before the beginning. I don't know how I come to songs, you know. It's not up to me to explain—I don't really go into myself that deep, I just go ahead and do it. I'm just sort of trying to find a place to pound my nails.

Woody Guthrie, is he a factor in your life?

Oh yeah. Woody's a big factor. I feel lucky just to know Woody. I'd heard of Woody, I knew of Woody. I saw Woody once, a long, long time ago in Burbank, California, when I was just a little boy. I don't even remember seeing him, but I heard him play. I must have been about ten. My uncle took me.

What was it that stuck in your mind?

It stuck in my mind that he was Woody, and everybody else I could see around me was just everybody else.

If I may venture an opinion, that could apply to you, too, Bob. Unique. It's hard to separate you from the songs you sing. You write most of the songs you sing, don't you?

Yeah, I write all my songs now.

There's one song, the only way I can describe it is as a great tapestry—"A Hard Rain's A-Gonna Fall."

I'll tell you how I come to write that. Every line in that really is another song. Could be used as a whole song, every single line. I wrote that when I didn't know how many other songs I could write. That was during October of last year and I remember sitting up all night with a bunch of people someplace. I wanted to get the most down that I knew about into one song, so I wrote that. It was during the Cuba trouble, that blockade, I guess is the word. I was a little worried, maybe that's the word.

You're right. Each one of the lines, each one of the images could be a song in itself. You know why I asked you to sing that live? I have this letter from a kid who's about your age, he's twenty-one. He was wondering what this new generation is really thinking of. We hear so much. At the very end he says, "America's heard the story of the bright, straight-A student, the fraternity-leading good guy Charlie. But there's a quiet group that remains. One that has no overwhelming crusade that is outwardly on the make, but one that is uneasily discontented. Thoughtfully or restless, young people of this sort may eventually determine future directions. . . . Outwardly we seem to be cool, but there's a rage inside us."

I've got a friend who wrote a book called *One Hundred Dollar Misunderstanding*. I don't know if it's around Chicago. It's about this straight-A college kid, you know, fraternity guy, and a fourteen-year old Negro prostitute. And it's got two dialogues in the same book. A dialogue is one chapter and the other chapter follows with just exactly what he's thinking and what he does. The next chapter is her view of him. The whole book goes like that. This guy Robert Gover wrote it. That would explain a lot too. That's one of the hippest things nowadays, I guess. I mean, it actually comes out and states something that's actually true, that everybody thinks about. I don't know if this fellow who wrote the letter was thinking crusades. This guy who wrote it, you can't label him. That's the word. You understand what I mean?

I follow you, I think. Back in the 1930s there were young people feeling passionately under one label or another. They were pigeonholed. What you stand for, it seems to me, and the fellow who wrote this letter and the guy who wrote that book, they belong to nobody but themselves. But we know something is there. Outwardly cool . . . I suppose you have to be that because the chips on the table are so blue.

Maybe it's just the time, now is the time maybe you have to belong to yourself. I think maybe in 1930, from talking with Woody and Pete Seeger and some other people I know, it seems like everything back then was good and bad and black and white and whatever, you only had one or two. When you stand on one side and you know people are either for you or against you, with you or behind you or whatever you have. Nowadays it's just—I don't know how it got that way but it doesn't seem so simple. There are more than two sides, it's not black and white anymore.

"A Hard Rain's A-Gonna Fall"—I think it will be a classic. Even though it may have come out of your feelings about atomic rain. . . .

No, no, it wasn't atomic rain. Somebody else thought that too. It's not atomic rain, it's just a hard rain. It's not the fallout rain, it isn't that at all. I just mean some sort of end that's just gotta happen which is very easy to see but everybody doesn't really think about overlooking it. It's bound to happen. Although I'm not talking about that hard rain meaning atomic rain, it seems to me like the bomb is a god in some sort of a way, more of a god and people will worship it actually. You have to be nice to it, you know. You have to be careful what you say about it. People work on it, they go six days a week and work on it, you have people designing it, you know, it's a whole new show.

These are all pretty good people too, in everyday life.

Yeah, I don't believe they're bad people. Just like the guy that killed this fella hitchhiking through Alabama. The guy that killed him, I forget his name.

It might have been the storekeeper. We don't know if he did it, but this is the fellow—

Yeah, who might have killed him. Even if it's not him, if it's somebody else that actually shot the bullet. There's nothing more awful, I mean, shot right in the back. I seen so many people before I got to New York, that are good people, that maybe are poor, and there are other people telling them why they're poor, and who made it so that they are poor. To take their minds off of that they are poor, they have to pick a scapegoat—

But you do believe, Bob, in good and evil. There is a basic good—

Oh, I'm sure.

Obviously you do from the songs you write. One of the lines of the song that got me . . . earlier you said things are not quite as simple as they were. "The executioner's face is always well hidden." That's on the button.

Yeah, oh golly. All over the place it's hidden.

It's so impersonal today. You said it's gonna happen. What's gonna happen?

What's gonna happen, there's got to be an explosion of some kind. The hard rain that's gonna fall. In the last verse when I say, "When the pellets of poison are flooding the waters," that means all the lies, you know, all the lies that people get told on their radios and in their newspapers. All you have to do is think for a minute. They're trying to take people's brains away. Which maybe has been done already. I hate to think it's been done. All the lies I consider poison.

I'll be fifty-one soon. My generation has had it. I'm talking about you now and your friends, nineteen, twenty, twenty-one. How many feel as you do?

Oh, there's an awful lot of them. Well, I don't know, you said my friends—

I don't mean just your circle, 'cause you've traveled a good deal.

I can tell you something about my friends, I can tell you about people I growed up with, that I knowed since I been four and five. These same kind of people I knew when I was ten and twelve. Little small-town people. This was in Hibbing, Minnesota, and some other places I lived before I finally split for good. These people were my friends, I went to school with them, I lived with them, I played with them, I ate with them. We did good things, bad things, we went through all kinds of things together. As I stand here right now, the last time I saw any of them was maybe two or three years ago, and you know, either me or them has changed.

What's happened to them?

They still seem to be the same old way. Like when they seen me, they heard I was in New York and they have words like—I can just tell by their whole conversation it's not a free feeling that they have. They still have a feeling that's tied up, where it's tied up in the town, in their parents, in the newspapers that they read which go out to maybe five thousand people. They don't have to go out of town, their world's very small. You don't have to, really. If you leave one town into another town it's the same thing. I'm not putting them down. It's just my road and theirs, it's different. Like a lot of them are married, maybe some are going to school. Some are working, you know, just working. They're still there. They're not thinking about the same things I'm thinking about.

They're not thinking what you're thinking. You spoke of those poison pellets on the water. Maybe it hit them too . . . ?

Oh, yeah. It hit me, too. I just got out of it. I just got out of it, that's all.

You were ten years old when you saw Woody, and it was about five years ago that you took to the guitar and singing.

No, about five years ago I just sort of never really did go back home. I've been in New York City for the past almost two years. Before that I was just all around the country, to the southlands, and I was in Mexico for a while.

You've been influenced not only by people like Woody but by blues singers as well.

Oh yeah. Big Joe Williams, I think you might know him. He lives here, I guess.

Yeah, he does. I know him.

He's an old friend of mine.

You also take traditional songs and make them your own.

Not anymore. [Laughs]

You did "Man of Constant Sorrow," the white spiritual. You took that and made it something wholly different. But not anymore, you say?

Two or three years ago I was singing folk songs that I'd learned. Now I don't sing any of them anymore.

Has it occurred to you that your own songs might be considered folk songs? We always have this big argument: what is a folk song? I think "Hard Rain" certainly will be one, if time is the test.

Yeah, yeah, time will be the test.

It seems you can write about any subject under the sun.

Anything worth thinking about is worth singing.

Any subject. A love song, let's say, like "Boots of Spanish Leather." There we have a song of a lover's farewell. This is far, far removed from the June-moon-spoon-theme way of writing. I suppose it's difficult for you to answer, Bob: what led you to the idea of writing these songs? Was it always with you?

Yeah, it's always been with me. I can't really say what led me to them. I'm one of these people that think everybody has certain gifts, you know, when they're born, and you got enough trouble just trying to find out what it is. I used to play the guitar when I was ten, you know. So I figured maybe my thing is playing the guitar, maybe that's my little gift. Like somebody can make a cake, or somebody else can saw a tree down, and other people write. Nobody's really got the right to say that any one of these gifts are any better than any other body's. That's just the way they're distributed out. I had seen that this is exactly what my gift is. Maybe I got a better gift. But as of right now, I haven't found out what it is. I don't call it a gift, it's only my way of trying to explain something that is very hard to explain.

There's a piece you wrote called "My Life in a Stolen Moment." You say, "I wrote my first song for my mother and I titled it 'Mother.' I wrote that in fifth grade and my teacher gave me a B+. I sat in a science class and flunked out for refusing to watch a rabbit die."

That's my college days. I only was there for about four months. But I really did get to see it. If I talk about college I ain't talking about 'em just from anything people have told me. I was actually there. I seen what goes on. I started smoking at eleven years old, I stopped once to catch my breath. I don't remember my parents singing too much, at least I don't remember swapping any songs with them. I just write. I've been writing for a long time.

Some will say: listen to Bob Dylan, he's talking street mountain talk now, though he's a literate man, see.

[Laughs] I don't think I am.

How do you answer that when they say it?

I got no answer. If they want to think I'm literate, it's okay by me.

Probably it's just easier for you to express your feelings this way. I suppose the influence of a great many singers—

Woody.

Woody, the fact that Woody, more than college, was the big influence on you. Did Woody hear you sing some of these songs?

Every time I go sing these songs I wrote for Woody, he always wants to hear "A Song for Woody." Even when he was in the hospital. [Laughs] He always wants to hear that.

The tribute of a young folk poet to an older one who has meant so much to him. Do you remember the words to that one?

Yeah, but I never sing it. Only to Woody.

I'm thinking of the Irish antiwar song "Johnny I Hardly Knew You." You're saying the same thing in your own way.

Somebody's come to the end of one road and actually knows it's the end of one road and knows there's another road there, but doesn't exactly know where it is, and knows he can't go back on this one road.

He knows there's something else.

He's got all kinds of stuff which just doesn't add up, you know, all kinds of thoughts in the head, all about teachers and school, and all about hitchhikers around the country, all about— These are friends of mine, too, you know, college kids going to college. These are all people that I knew. Every one of them is sort of a symbol, I guess, for all kinds of people like that. In New York it's a different world, you know, especially 'cause I never been to New York before and I'm still carrying their small-town memories with me, so I decided I oughta write it all down. The road is very hard to find now. Maybe sometimes I wish this was 19-something else.

Nineteen thirties?

Before that. You know like I was talking about pounding a nail in a board: it seems like there's a board there and all the nails are pounded in all over the place, you know, and every new person that comes to pound in a nail finds that there's one less space, you know. I hope we haven't got to the end of the space yet.

You're looking for a fresh piece of wood.

No, I'm content with the same old piece of wood, I just want to find another place to pound in a nail.

Isn't that what most of them are looking for? A place to pound a nail.

Yeah. Some of the people are the nails.

You mean they're being pounded. [Laughs]

Yeah.

Your new album has "Oxford Town" on it. That deals with the James Meredith case. Was he one of the nails?

Yeah, it deals with the Meredith case [James Meredith was denied entrance to the University of Mississippi], but then again it doesn't. Music, my writing, is something special, not sacred. Like this guitar, I don't consider sacred. This guitar could bust and break, it's pretty old now. I could still get another one. It's a tool for me, that's all it is. It's like anybody else has a tool. Some people saw the tree down, you know, or some people spit tacks. When I go to saw the tree down, I cut myself on the saw. When I spit tacks, I swallow the tacks. I've just sort of got this here tool and that's all I use it as, as a tool. My life is the street where I walk. That's my life. Music, guitar, that's my tool, you know.

WOODY GUTHRIE
Adapted from Studs Terkel's foreword to Ed Cray's *Ramblin' Man:
The Life and Times of Woody Guthrie*

Woody Guthrie was, is, America's balladeer. During the epoch of our deepest despair, the Great Depression, his were the songs that lifted the lowly spirits of the "ordinary," the millions of the dispossessed. They may have lacked for bread, but he offered them something else: self-esteem, hope, and a laugh or two along the way. Who was this bard?

Woody Guthrie, a tough, skinny, wind-blown, freckled, curly-headed Huck Finn. A little piece of leather. A dirt-road, hard-pavement, dank-box-car, cold-city, hot-desert gamin. Coast-to-coast poet and minstrel. Plus shoe shine boy, spittoon washer, hoer of fields, picker of mustang grapes, carpenter's helper, well-digger's assistant, sign painter, merchant mariner, fortune-teller, radio entertainer, street singer. The only thing I'm sure he hadn't been was a lawyer. I guess he'd never been a banker, either.

In 1912, the *Titanic* sank. In 1912, Woodrow Wilson was elected president. In 1912, Woodrow Wilson Guthrie was born. Fate sings its own kind of poetry. The day was July 14, Bastille Day in Paris, France; Woody's day in Okemah, Oklahoma. On that day, the French "ordinary" sang their anthem, "La Marseillaise." In America, we sing ours, "This Land Is Your Land." It has nothing to do with bombs bursting in air, nor with sanctimonious blessing. It has to do with what this country is all about.

> *This land is your land, this land is my land,*
> *From California to the New York Island,*
> *From the redwood forest to the Gulf Stream waters,*
> *This land was made for you and me.*

Nobody knows the exact number of songs written by Woody. Take a thousand, a good, round, conservative figure. The odds are better than even that there are more, many more, written on the spot, any old spot: the wayside inn, the gas station, the greasy spoon, the ma and pa tavern, the hamburger heaven, the subway bench, the jungle camp, the friendly davenport; been-here-and-gone pieces. How many of these were lost, bartered for a bologna sandwich or a pint of muscatel, or casually slipped away—not even Woody had the slightest idea.

I remember the summer of '41. Woody and three singing colleagues were in transit and spent a few days and nights in our jam-packed Chicago flat. [One was Pete Seeger, a skinny, gangly kid of nineteen with a bobbing Adam's apple; another was Lee Hays, a mountain man from Arkansas; the third was Millard Lampell, a writer.] At four in the morning, my dream was interrupted by the click, click of my portable typewriter, my Royal. It was Woody, who had just ambled home, touch-typing like crazy. I turned over and slept dreamlessly. A few hours later as Woody snored softly, innocently in the adjoining room, I was picking sheets of paper from out of the wastebasket. There must have been at least thirty pages, single-spaced. Verse, prose, fragments of songs, impressions, wild, vivid images of his night at a South Side tavern. They danced off the pages. It was Joycean, poetic and crazy and wild. It was sort of "Ulysses in Nighttown," with interior thoughts and everything.

The remembered words of barflies, their lost-in-the-fog look, and the cock-eyed, tangential wisdom poured forth from the mumbo-jumbo of beer, the whiskey shot, the false-bottom glass, and the wino's muscatel. "I cannot help but learn the most from you who count yourself least," wrote the bantam bard on another occasion. "But I feel my best with you that need me most. I never did exactly know why this is, but that's just the way we're built."

Dust bowl songs, hobo songs, children's songs, work songs, loafing songs, union songs, lonesome turtledove songs; songs infinite in their variety, celebrating the wonder of man. For what is man to Woody? "Just a hoping machine, a working machine. The human race will sing this way as long as there is a human race. The human race is a pretty old place."

The men of the Bonneville Power Administration sensed the strength and poetry of Woody's ways. They commissioned him in 1941 to write songs celebrating the building of the Coulee and Bonneville Dams, of the Columbia River Project that was changing the whole face of our Northwest. With pencil stub, pen, battered portable, or whatever he could lay his hands on, he wrote twenty-six such ballads in thirty days. The impact of these rolling, sweeping songs on all who hears was inestimable. A Washington State senator said that any one of these Woody songs was worth a dozen legislative speeches in getting things done. Getting things done. Affecting people. Touching them where they live, moving them up a little higher. This was Woody.

PETE SEEGER
2002

Whenever you see a young folksinger, banjo chest-high, Adam's apple bobbing, you know that Pete Seeger—the legendary folksinger and song-writer—has, like Kilroy, been here. (Kilroy was the name left as graffiti on walls by all GIs in World War II as they moved through foreign lands.) I know of no singer who has influenced more young people singing or at least attempting to sing folk music.

My great-great-grandfather, Karl Ludwig Zaiger, was fourteen years old when he read the Declaration of Independence. He lived in Stuttgart, which was then a small town. The Duke of Wurtenburg needed a veterinarian for his horses. He gave my great great-grandfather a free education. The subversive document, the American Declaration of Independence, circulated through Europe and inflamed the heads of all sorts of young people. Ten years later, my great-great-grandfather graduated from the gymnasium. One of his class-mates was Friedrich Schiller, the poet, writer of *William Tell*. He set out to this country, probably hitched a ride on a riverboat going up the Necker River to join the Rhine, and down the Rhine River to Amsterdam, where he some-how got a boat for the USA. He wrote a note to the duke: "I want to be a doc-tor of people, not a doctor of horses." Over here, he ended up marrying into old New England. My father knew that in his ancestors were doctors and businessmen and some preachers. One was a preacher in Salem, Massachu-setts, during the witchcraft trials. I read that he tried to save the life of one of the witches but did not succeed.

My mother's grandfather came over from France. He landed in New York a hundred and fifty years ago or more. He put an advertisement in the paper saying: "If you want your son to go into the diplomatic service, he should know French. Very exactly. Come send him to Professor Charlier." My great-grandfather was the son of a Huguenot minister. Pretty soon he was hiring other people and getting a big brownstone house. Now the Park Lane Hotel is there. My mother took me around to see it in the 1920s, before they tore down the old building. From the letters I've read, I remember that Professor Charlier's daughter married a conservative, a quiet doctor, whose father had run a business in Troy making steam boilers. He married an Irish girl who was supposed to have sixth sense, they called it in those days. One morning she said, "Darling, please don't go to work, I dreamed that something terrible was going to happen at the factory." He said, "Well, I can't not go to work just because you had a bad dream. There's things that have to be done there." In the middle of the morning, there was a loud boom. An hour or two later work-men brought his hand to his wife, with the wedding ring on it. He was test-ing a steam boiler and it blew up. My grandfather was about six years old at the time. He became a doctor. His uncle was mayor of New York back when the Brooklyn Bridge was built, back in the 1880s, and should go down in his-tory because he made the kind of speech that should be made. It was the shortest speech of the day. There had been one speech after another, and the crowd was getting restless. Edson was my mother's maiden name. Mayor Ed-son was my grandfather's uncle. He got up and said, "It seems to me that everything that needs to be said has been said. Congratulations to everybody!" And he sat down. You can bet he got a large applause for making his speech so short.

They were of very different opinions. My mother's father was descended from a well-known Tory up in Massachusetts, Deacon Edson, a deacon in the church. When George Washington won the Revolution, a mob came to his house and said, "Why don't you go back to Canada, or go back to England if you love your king so much. We don't want you around here." But he said, "No, I've lived here all my life and I'll live here the rest of my life if the Lord allows me to." And they weren't up to lynching him, so they grumbled and went away. You have to hand it to him. My grandfather was still conservative. One of his papers said: "What a shame England and America couldn't have settled their quarrel amicably. Together, we could have shown the world true civilization." [Chuckles] My grandmother, who married Edson, the doctor, sent my mother to the Ethical Culture School just so she would not have to hear the word *God* every day. She died at age ninety-four, still a cheerful agnostic. In her later years, she joined the American Labor Party and voted for Mayor LaGuardia, all four times.

My father was completely into music. He didn't think anything else in the world was worth thinking about. At a very young age he was appointed head of the music department in Berkeley, University of California. Some fellow professors took him out to the San Joaquin Valley. This was about 1911. My father was horrified by what he saw. He came back and gave a speech somewhere in San Francisco. "It's disgraceful that such things should happen in America." He started making speeches against imperialist war. He was given a sabbatical and told not to come back to work. He was the professor in charge of the music department, from roughly 1911 to 1918, through World War I. My mother said, "Can't you keep your mouth shut? You're not going to be drafted, not with two children, and wearing glasses and all, and your deafness." But he said, "No, when something's wrong, you must speak up!" He came back East, where his parents had bought an old farm north of New York. He had a grand idea. He told my mother, who was an excellent violinist, "Why should we just play our good music for rich people in the cities? Why don't we take it out to people in the small towns, in the countryside?" Kind of like Chautauqua. He spent the whole year building one of America's first automobile trailers. Tongue and groove, maple, brass screws. It was meticulously made. It looked a little bit like a covered wagon. Instead of a team of horses pulling it, it was a Model

T Ford. He had a special low gear put on the Ford so he could pull the trailer up hills. They started off. . . .

I was the third of three boys of my father's first marriage. My two brothers had tiny bunks in one end of the little trailer. My cradle hung from the hoops that held up the canvas top. My father and mother slept in a big bed at the other end. It was a beautiful little trailer. There was a six-foot-square platform, which could be pulled out from underneath the trailer. My mother would stand up there playing her violin, Chopin, Bach, Beethoven, and Brahms. My father bought a folding organ, the kind the chaplains used in World War I. It had about five octaves there, and he would accompany my mother. They headed down through Virginia, into North Carolina. When I was a small child, my father told me a story of a terrible rainstorm. The roads weren't paved in those days; they were all dirt roads. The ruts got deeper and deeper. Once the rain just kept on going all day long and the puddles got deeper, until finally the road was *completely* under water. My mother was getting hysterical. She says, "Charlie, why don't you turn around?" He says, "I can't turn around, it's only a one-lane road. All we can do is go ahead. There's another town up ahead and we'll get there." The water got over the tires, then it got over the hubcaps. My mother was hysterical. She was ready to abandon things. But all my father knew was to keep on going ahead. "If it doesn't get to the carburetor, the motor will keep on going." So that little Model T Ford kept up, putt-putt-putt-putt. When I was a small child, he'd tell this story to me every night, over and over. Finally, way up ahead, they saw some trees, and sure enough it got shallower. They were on more or less solid ground. My mother said, "Charlie, this is not going to work. We're going back to New York. I can get a job teaching, you can get a job teaching." She knew Frank Damrosch, who ran the Institute of Musical Art, that later on became Juilliard. My father said, "We can't get back, the roads are too bad." Next morning they were woken up by five or six local farmers, with guns, who said, "We don't want no Gypsies around here." My father, in his New England accent, says, "We're not Gypsies, we're musicians." "You're what?" My mother brings out her fiddle and my father unfolds the organ. The farmer says, "Well, I guess you are." My father says, "Actually, we're looking for a place we can spend the winter because the roads are so bad we can't get back up north." One of the farmers said, "I got a wood lot. If you don't mind camping out there, you can stay there for the winter." So they spent the winter in a wood lot. My mother, washing my diapers in an iron pot over an open fire, and scrubbing them on a washboard, with her violinist fingers and all. One evening they took the good music, Bach and Beethoven, up to the McKenzies' farmhouse to show them what kind of music they played. The McKenzies were very polite. They said, "Oh, that's very nice. We play a little music too." They took down banjos and fiddles off the wall and fiddled up a storm. Years later, my father said, "For the first time, I realized that people had a lot of good music in them. They didn't need my good music as much as I thought." [Laughs] In Chapel Hill, about three years ago, I'm singing and two middle-aged women came up to me and said, "Are you by any chance related to the Seeger family that spent the winter with the McKenzies in Pinehurst?" I said, "Good Lord, are you from that family?" She said, "Well, I'm the great-granddaughter. My mother never stopped talking about that family from New York that spent the winter with them." Nineteen twenty. [Laughs] This was in 1995 or something. My mother finally was fed up with my father's not very businesslike way of handling the family's finances and their marriage gradually broke up.

My father, a few years later, met a talented young composer, Ruth Crawford. She was writing what they call modern music, dissonant counterpoint. She was living in Chicago, a close friend of Carl Sandburg's. She'd written the accompaniments for some of the songs in his book, *The American Songbag*. My father was teaching at the Institute of Musical Art, Juilliard. She wrote him a letter. She gets a letter back: "Dear Miss Crawford, there have never been any good women composers. I think you should turn your talents to other fields." She was outraged. She went east and the moment they met, they got along famously. I once saw my father and my stepmother sit down at a piano and with their four hands play Stravinsky's *Le Sacre du Printemps*. It's all full of notes going here, there, and everywhere at the same time. Somebody turned the pages for them, and they went right straight through that whole thing without a stop. I was amazed. My stepmother stopped composing. She says, "I'm composing babies." Michael was her first and Peggy was her second. She had two more, both girls. In 1935, '36, they go down to Washington to work in the New Deal. My father worked in the same little office that Ben Shahn, the painter, was, along with Nick Ray, who later on became a well-known Hollywood director—he directed *Rebel Without a Cause*. Nick, working with Alan Lomax, was put charge of the archive of folk song of the Library of Congress. Alan had been helping his father collect ballads and folk songs with very heavy recording equipment. About a hundred pounds of batteries and turntables and so on, they had to lift in and out of a car. Around 1933, when Alan was eighteen, he said, "Father, I want to carry on your work." With great self-confidence he went up to New York and knocked on the door of the president of Columbia Broadcasting System and said, "You've got a school of the air. Why don't you take a year to tell the American people about American folk music? I'm in charge of the Archive of American Folk Song and I plan the programs for it. And you can have the Columbia Symphony Orchestra get composers like Roy Harris, and Aaron Copland, and Ruth Seeger to make symphonic arrangements of these folk songs." So first there'd be a program, there's old sailor dad from Sailor Snug Harbor. This was 1939. The *Columbia School of the Air*. And there would be old sailor dad, singing in his cracked old voice some old sailor ballad from the nineteenth century.

Before you know it, Ruth and my father were working with Alan Lomax, and Ruth got deeply into the music that Alan had collected. Not only the old Irish American cowboy songs, but the newer African American work songs. Old John Lomax had contacts in Texas. He says, "I've got a recording machine here, and it's important that I record the folk songs of Texas." They let him right into the prison farms, and he went out with the chain gangs and recorded people singing music that might have had English words, but the tunes went right back to Africa. I remember one of the songs Alan and his father collected was "Long John." I used to sing it . . . [He sings, "He's Long John"] And the crowd says, "He's Long John . . . He's long gone . . . He's long gone." Just a solo and a repeat, a solo and a repeat, each line. Whatever they were doing. I think they were chopping. An anthropologist who came back from West Africa around 1951 had a little portable tape machine. And he recorded that exact same melody in West Africa. [He hums the tune] Ruth was fascinated with this music and she learned how to transcribe it very accurately. In a sense, she had a second career. Her first career was writing very complicated modern music. Ruth's *String Quartet* is quite famous around America now. Now she was transcribing folk songs. Just as Ruth was planning to get really into composing again—she was fifty-two years old—she got cancer and just was carried away a few months later. I was always learning new songs from Alan and from other people, Leadbelly and Woody Guthrie.

We were raised with the promise of hopefulness. But often it was misplaced hope. During the 1920s my father kept his mouth shut and kept his job. But along comes '29, the crash, and it seemed to a great many people this was the end of the free enterprise system around the entire world. It was going to take some discipline to see that people were fed and clothed. The question is, who would be in charge of this? My father was used to the idea of the symphony orchestra, and there was a dictator, with baton, who's completely in charge. Now the question is, who is in charge? You couldn't do it Mussolini's way. He got the businessmen of Italy behind him and they brought order out of chaos to Italy, and he called it fascism. Hitler was planning to do it in Germany, and the militarists were doing it in Japan. My father said, "Let's try it the way Lenin has tried it. He claims that the working people could be in charge." Well, that was the theory. When people ask me am I a communist still, I say, "I became a communist at age seven when I read about American Indians. They had no rich, no poor, and I decided that's the way people should live. But at this late age of eighty-two, I call myself a Luxemburgian communist." Rosa Luxemburg was a German socialist who spent World War I in the kaiser's prison. She was against the war. She writes a letter to Lenin in January of 1919, and said: "I hear that you have instituted press censorship and you have restricted the right of people to freely assemble, to address grievances." She said, "Don't you realize, in a few years, all the decisions in your country are going to be made by a few elite, and the masses will only be called in to dutifully applaud your decisions." Boy, wasn't that exactly what happened? If it hadn't been Stalin to take over, it would have been somebody else. Because if you don't have freedom of the press, if you don't have freedom of the airwaves, and freedom of speech, inevitably things go from bad to worse. The USA would not be here if it had not been for our Bill of Rights. Thanks to the Bill of Rights, the abolitionists could agitate and agitate until we got rid of slavery. And women could agitate and agitate until they got the right to vote. And black people could agitate and agitate and finally Lyndon Johnson signed the Voting Rights Act.

Before the New Deal even came along, in 1931 and '32, my father said, "We should be composing songs for the working people." So he started a composers' collective with Henry Cowell, another modern composer. There were about eight or ten members, among them Aaron Copland and Marc Blitzstein [composer of *The Cradle Will Rock*]. They tried to compose songs, which the proletariat would sing on the way to the barricades [laughs]. Three or four years later, my father said, "Let's face it. The workers don't seem to like our music." In 1934, my father said, "Let's learn the vernacular. If we want to create new music, let's start with the music that people already know." If you live in the city, you better know jazz. If you live in the country, you better know country music, and of course, there's different kinds of country music. The Cajun people have their own style in Louisiana. And the Latinos have their own vernacular. I remember my mother left musical instruments all around the house, not just piano and organ, but there was a marimba and a squeeze box, and a penny whistle. Then at age eight, she gives me a ukulele and I've been into fretted instruments ever since. I switched over to a tenor banjo so I could play in the school jazz band. And then in my late teens, my father helped me learn the long neck five-string banjo, and took me to this festival in North Carolina, where I heard some people who really knew how to play it.

When I dropped out of Harvard in '38, after a year and three-quarters, Alan had me help him out in the Library of Congress. He had thousands of records he was trying to listen to and evaluate. He went up with John Hammond, up to the CBS factory in Bridgeport, Connecticut. They were going to throw out old country records, what they called hillbilly records, or what they called race records. Alan just piled up all these records and said, "Don't throw them out." He went down to Washington with literally a ton of 78 rpm shellac records. He said, "Pete, now, you listen to them first. I don't have time to listen to all of them. If there's something strictly schlock, throw it out. If you come along something that sounds interesting, then make a note and I'll listen to it." So I went through thousands and thousands of records. This is how I became a great fan of Uncle Dave Macon, who played his banjo on the riverboats in the 1890s, and sang a song about the Coal Creek Rebellion of 1892. So it was a great education for me. I was working for Alan when Will Geer, the actor, writes me a note saying, "Pete, I've run into a great ballad singer in California. I'm going to try and persuade him to come to New York and you'll meet him. His name is Woody." And in February of 1940, Woody Guthrie hitchhikes to New York. There we had a midnight benefit concert on Broadway. Will Geer was playing the lead in *Tobacco Road*. The scenery on the stage had two sharecropper cabins, and one of them had a porch. I remember Leadbelly up on the porch of one of the cabins singing some songs. I was twenty-two. Can you imagine Woody in the month of February with his thumb stuck out into the February winds, and the cars going zoom? And he'd go in for a cup of coffee and there on the jukebox, Kate Smith was singing "God Bless America." Woody made up another song, of six verses. It was "This Land Is Your Land." His original last line was "God blessed America for me."

Around 1944, he changed that last line to, "This land was made for you and me." In '49 he records it for a tiny little company called Folkways. A big sale for them was a thousand records. [It was run by] Moe Asch, the son of Sholem Asch, the famous novelist, who wrote in Yiddish. Stinson was the record producer. They went bankrupt.

You know how Moe got started making records? In 1939, his father said, "Moe, you have a recording machine. We gotta drive to Princeton to record Dr. Einstein in a short message which can be played on the radio, urging American Jews to give more help to their relatives in Germany to get out of Germany." In those days the recording machine was a big heavy thing weighing fifty or a hundred pounds. And they record the little five-minute message from Dr. Einstein. Over supper, Dr. Einstein says, "Well, young Mr. Asch, what do you do for a living?" And Moe says, "I make a living installing public address systems in hotels. But I'm fascinated with this little recording machine and its possibilities. I've met a Negro folksinger in New York named Leadbelly, and nobody's recording him because they say he's not commercial. I think somebody should record him." Einstein says, "You're absolutely right. Americans don't appreciate their own culture. It'll be a Polish Jew, like you, who will do the job." So Moe recorded Leadbelly. Years later I asked Moe, "How many records did you sell?" He said, "One hundred copies in one year." Some anthropologist might come back from the far ends of the world with some tapes. He'd call up. "Mr. Asch, my students keep wanting to listen to my tapes, or make copies. But I don't have time to make copies. Would you want to bring this out?" Moe said, "I'd be glad to put out twelve-inch LPs." Now a record comes out called *Religious Music of Northern Afghanistan*. Moe says, "Oh, here's my conditions. I will pay you one hundred dollars, and that will be all the money you will ever get. The only thing I can promise you is that this record will never go out of print as long as I'm alive, and I hope after I'm dead that it will still be in print." When Moe died his family made a deal with the Smithsonian that they could not reprint any of his records unless they'd reprint the whole catalogue, all two thousand titles. Every new month he'd bring out a new record. Music from every kind of society and culture.

I don't think we can kid ourselves. Deep in our chromosomes is the ability to hate people who look different, who speak different, who use different names for God, different customs, who eat different food. Because for two million years, maybe more, our ancestors lived in little groups, ten, twenty people, and they shared everything they had. If there was food, everybody ate. If there was no food, everybody went hungry. So within that narrow group, it was tribal communism. Even if it was a big tribe—some American Indian tribes got to be several hundred or even a thousand members. Within our own family, we had big differences of opinion. My grandfather was a small businessman, an importer. His father was the abolitionist doctor. My grandfather's father died young, and his mother really had to pinch pennies to raise three boys. He went to work as a teller in the local bank, up in Springfield, Massachusetts. And he thought if he worked hard, someday he'd be president of the bank. But he thought it would take too long. So my grandfather read in the newspaper that President Porfirio Díaz was welcoming American businessmen to Mexico to help build up the economy. My grandfather studied Spanish with a friend and got a job as a reporter on the *Financial Times,* a little newsletter for the businessmen in Mexico City. Within a year, he knew where the money was and he was in business himself. Four years later he had a house and servants.

My father was born in Mexico City. My father's younger brother, Alan, was an enthusiastic young daredevil. He said, "Who wants to live a long, boring life?" And when he graduated from college—he was in the same class with Heywood Broun, Walter Lippmann, and John Reed, and putting out the *Harvard Monthly*—he tells his parents he's going to be a poet. So he went to Paris. When the Germans invaded in 1914 he only waited three or four days and joined the French Foreign Legion. My father wrote him a letter, said, "Alan, don't you realize the class of people that run Germany are really not much different than the class of people that run France? You should have stayed out of it. I don't expect to see you again." And he didn't. Alan was mowed down by a German machine gun in 1916. But a few months before he died, *The New Republic* magazine printed his poem. [Pete shuts his eyes and recites from memory the whole poem] "I have a rendezvous with death / When spring comes back with rustling shade / And apple blossoms fill the air / I have a rendezvous with death / When spring brings back blue days and fair / It may be he shall take my hand and lead me into his dark land / And close my eyes and quench my breath / It may be I shall pass him still / A rendezvous with death / . . . At midnight in some flaming town / When spring comes north again next year / And I to my pledged word am true / I shall not fail my rendezvous." It became a famous poem. I saw a picture of troops wading across the Mekong River, and all of a sudden one line came to me: "Waist deep in the Big Muddy, and the big fool says to push on." I'm not a facile songwriter. It takes me sometimes weeks to write a decent song, or it takes other people to rewrite it. That's what happened with "Where Have All the Flowers Gone?". It was a crisis, and crises make for people wanting to sing or make up songs. It happens when somebody falls in love, they start writing poems. This is what happened in 1941, when the CIO, industrial unions, were being organized. There were four of us on the road in a jalopy, different cities and towns. We were the Almanac Singers, consisting of Woody Guthrie, Big Lee Hays, young Millard Lampell, my age, and young me. We'd sing union songs in halls, soup kitchens, on picket lines. The CIO had shown the labor movement that you could organize the unskilled as well as the skilled, if you take in everybody. All of a sudden, within three years, the CIO, Congress of Industrial Organizations, signed up like seven million new members and threw the fear of God into the Big Boys. We made up an album of union songs and we sang them all across the country. . . .

Come World War II, Pete and Millard Lampell joined the armed forces. Woody Guthrie joined the merchant marine. They sang wherever they traveled. Come the Cold War. Come Joe McCarthy. Pete, his colleagues, still singing out, were cast out of respectable circles. Now Woody is dead. So are Millard Lampell and Lee Hays. Alan Lomax is dead. Pete still is at it—singing in schools, children's songs, helping clean up the Hudson River, along which he still lives with his wife, Toshi, in the house they built.

JEAN RITCHIE
1957

We hear strings of a dulcimer. In fact, the studio right at the moment is surrounded with dulcimers and a guitar. She strums and hums in the background. She has written an autobiography, Singing Family of the Cumberlands.

I'm from Viper, Kentucky, in the southeastern tip of the state, down in the Cumberland Mountains. It's part of the region known as the Southern

Appalachians. There are a lot of people still do sing and carry on with the folk music. You know what a haunt tale is? It's a ghost story. It used to scare me to death at night when they'd put us to bed, or we'd be gathered around the fireside after supper. Mostly on winter evenings when we couldn't go out and sit on the front porch. Neighbors would gather in and the old folks, and it seemed like the older they were, the more they did believe in ghosts. They were local ghosts. [Laughs] Everybody had seen them right around their house and that's what made it that much more scary—anytime you would go out on the porch, you were liable to run into one. They all had very definite personalities, all these ghosts. One of them was a panther. A panther in Kentucky is called a panter. So they were always talking about the panter that screams up in the woods. I was always afraid to go in the woods after dark because of the panter that always got loose. It was a haunt panter. Another one was about some awful thing that would jump on the horse behind anyone that was coming home late at night. Some thing would jump on and put its arms around them. It was called "the thing." Nobody ever really saw it, but everybody had felt it jump on the horse behind them. My grandmother was the one who knew the most people who had felt that thing jump on [laughs].

My mother and father had fourteen children, and of course by the time I was born, the oldest ones had married and had children of their own, so there was always a pretty good houseful of us. I was the youngest of the fourteen. There weren't enough chairs, so children always had to sit on the floors and we'd scootch in as close to the fire as we could get so the haunts wouldn't get us in the corners. I'd always dig around in the hearth—there'd be big cracks in it, an old mud hearth—and find little things down it that I could turn into actors to act out the haunt stories. The oak splinter became a horse, and the old rusted needle was the man up on the horse. [Laughs] There's one song that we liked to sing, sort of a scary song. The scariest one was the one where you scream at the end, but I don't think the microphone will take that. [Laughs] This is called "There Was an Old Woman All Skin and Bones." [She strums the dulcimer, sings, and ends suddenly with a ghostly call.] I saw your engineer jumped a mile. [Laughs]

The dulcimer was the pear-shaped instrument that everybody had hanging over their fireplaces. Local craftsmen would make these dulcimers and each community had somebody who made them. Our dulcimer maker was Uncle Will Singleton. In those days, he sort of peddled them around. He sold them for about five or six dollars apiece. If you go buy one now, probably be a lot more. [Laughs] My husband made this one. He learned how to make them from old Jethro, who still makes them in Hindman, Kentucky. I think that's the nicest one I ever played. It's a three-stringed instrument and very simple. It has one melody string and the other two strings are just drones. It's very simple to play. I learned how to play from my father, who always used this feather quill. It's made into a long, flexible pick. He only played fast tunes on it. It's a turkey wing. I use it as a pick. [She begins to strum and sing "Shady Grove."] It's a play party song. We had play parties, usually on Saturday nights. You'd call them dances now. But back home, when my mother and father were growing up, they weren't allowed to call them dances because dancing was considered a deadly sin.

The fiddle was considered a devil's instrument?

They didn't even use the dulcimer for dancing, they just played games. Everybody, all the old folks and the preachers, joined in and had a fine time. It looked like square dancing. They sang the songs and clapped their hands to keep the rhythm.

Was the dulcimer allowed?

Yes, because the dulcimer is soft. Once a crowd of boys and girls get to dancing, you couldn't hear the dulcimer unless they had a microphone. They didn't have any microphones back in those days. The dulcimer is primarily a lonesome instrument. It sings by itself usually. My father was a lonesome man playing a lonesome instrument. [She shuts her eyes as she murmurs] Summer twilight's on the front porch where I imagine myself to be the noble lady of the ballad, followed by recollections of some very early episodes in my life which begin to teach me that real life, especially childhood, is a very hard thing. I've never been able to decide which of them I like better—those winter evenings around the fireplace, or the summer twilights where the song and tale-telling moved out onto the front porch. The fireside was more of a tale-telling place. When we got out onto the front porch and you could sit in the swing and move back and forth, we'd talk over what happened during the day, and how much corn we'd got hoed and so on. And then we'd start to sing. Everybody had his favorite, and pretty soon half the night would be gone. My favorite ones were the long romantic ballads because they talked about places I thought I would never see. They talked about lords and ladies and courts and salt seas and things like that. In the Kentucky mountains, we see dirt roads, and oh, cabins and frame houses. No castles. [Laughs]

The first settlers in the Kentucky mountains were from Scotland, Ireland, and England. They brought with them their customs and their songs and their stories. The mountains were so rough, there wasn't much going in and out after they got there, so that for, I'd say a hundred and fifty or two hundred years or more, they were shut off from the rest of the world and they kept on singing these old songs. That was the way they made their own entertainment. They didn't have anything like jukeboxes, they couldn't go to city parties, they didn't have sidewalks or anything. Nor any other influences to smooth out the songs and make them get lost. Oh, a lot of local words crept in and expressions. In one original ballad it says, "He seated her down at the table's head." And in our Kentucky version, it says, "He seated her down in a rocking chair." Subtle changes like that took place in these songs, but essentially they're the same as they were in Elizabethan England—"Lord Thomas" and "Fair Eleanor and the Brown Girl." There was Lord Thomas, tall and brave, with his sword shining in his hand, and there the wedding folk around the long table. And in some easy manner, never had to be explained, *I* became Fair Eleanor. And the movement of the swing I sat in became the slow graceful walking of the white horse. And hundreds of people lined the broad highway as I rode by, thinking I was some queen as the song wound its way to the tragic ending.

There were childhood troubles that came along. My dad had his hard ways with us. There were two outstanding times he took special notice of me. My dad was stern and quiet in his ways, but he hardly ever laid a hand on us, except for a few times. A lot of people think, "Oh, I'm so sorry for you when you got that horrible whupping. Wasn't that awful? Some psychologist should have come in and talked to your father." [Laughs] That was the way all parents were in that day and age. If you didn't control your children, why then you weren't a good parent. If you let them run off and get into all kinds of meanness and if you let them talk sassy to you, then you were considered a failure as a parent. So the women were usually softhearted, and when they gave us a whupping, my mother used to just sort of give us a slap as we ran by on the behind. [Laughs] But whenever my father would have to whip us that would be a real occasion. My father had, I guess, a pretty bad temper when it was aroused. It hardly ever was aroused.

I don't remember him getting mad but once or twice in his life. And one of the times was when he whipped me, when he got the maddest I ever saw him was when I wouldn't say please at the table. He's hard of hearing, so he didn't know what was going on. It was raining that day and he was mad because he couldn't get us all out to go into the cornfield to work. You know how people get sort of nervous.

My father would get nervous when he couldn't get out and work because he could see the corn ruining up on the hillsides, the ground getting too wet and everything. He was sitting at the head of the table and all the children were ranged around the table and all of them were talking at once. He hated that because he couldn't hear what anybody was saying. And the older girls, who'd be off to settlement schools and come back with fancy manners, undertook to teach us. I asked them to pass the bread. It was way up on the other end of the table and I had to holler for it 'cause nobody could hear me. I said, "Give me the bread, I said!" My sister sitting next to me said, "You ought to say please. Don't holler like that." They all started picking on me so I began to cry. I said, "I want some bread." [Laughs] I was a very stubborn, unreasonable child. My father all of a sudden looked up and said, "What's all the fuss about? Y'all get settled right now." Somehow or other it got worse and worse. He finally got up and said, "Who's causing the trouble?" So they all pointed at me. [Laughs] "She won't say please." He said, "I'll make her say please." I was determined not to say please and my father was determined that he would make me say please. So it developed from there. I really got a bad switching with apple tree limbs, about six of them, and a little bit of a rosebush at the end. [Laughs] He ran out of the switches. In today's society it would ruin some child for life if she got a spanking like that, but it didn't make much of a dent on me. Especially since I never did say please. [Laughs] I won the battle after all. My mother lied in my favor. She said, "Didn't you hear her? She said please." She was scared to death of what was going to happen. She'd never seen him that mad. My sister predicted that he would sure half kill me, and he just about did. I was pretty sore for a few days, on my back and up and down my backsides. And couldn't go to sleep on my back. I used to have to sleep on my stomach until I got well. My mother would sneak in, in the middle of the night, sort of jiggle the bed and make it nice, sort of like a little ride. I told her I'd like for her to sing the "Darby Ram" because that was the one that she always sang to us when we got hurt or when we stubbed our toes. It always made us feel better.

Do you recall your mother's version of "Darby Ram"?

Oh, sure. [She sings "Darby Ram" softly and sweetly.] One of the many tales my father told me about his boyhood was about how he heard the fiddle played for the first time. How he himself learned to play it. Something happened with that whupping that I'm just beginning to realize. I realized after we'd had this big fight that we were pretty much alike, I guess. Both stubborn. [Laughs] I knew that he couldn't do anything worse to me, I guess, so I wasn't afraid of him as I used to be. Fathers in those days didn't communicate with their children too well. The babies they liked to sort of dandle on their knee and rock and everything, but as soon as they got big enough to talk to and to need some sort of bringing up, the mothers took over and the fathers were unapproachable sort of gods in the family. [Laughs] I found out that my father was a lot like this because his own father had been much worse than he was. The children were even afraid to speak to him and they always asked his mother. If they wanted something, Father would say to his mother, "Mammy, will you ask August to give me his knife for a minute?" August was my grandfather. Because it was thought to be impertinent for children to speak to their fathers without being spoke to first.

I began to talk to him and I found out that he knew more songs than my mother did. I found that my father was quite a gay young man, a gay blade as they say, when he was growing up, and he knew a lot of courting songs and game songs and things that my mother never heard. One day my mother heard him singing something to me and she said, "I didn't know you knew that." He said, "Well, I know a lot of things you don't know I do." [Laughs] He taught me a lot of game songs. Then I got my dad and mom to remembering their courting days. At first, they were very shy about that, but little by little we broke down their resistance. The rest of the children were interested too in how things went on in their day. I learned to know my father very well and we got to be right good friends after a while. I learned many songs and stories of the old days from him. My mother remembers the days when Daddy came to see her. He walked I don't know how many miles, maybe thirty miles, to come and see her. He had written to her first, he wrote her a letter because somebody had said that she was a nice, pretty young girl. So he wrote her this very scholarly letter. He had finished the eighth grade and taken penmanship and was going to be a teacher. So he wrote in these very curlicued letters. Mama still has the letter at home. It's very beautiful to look at and also nice reading. My father at the time lived at Dwarf, Kentucky, he was one county removed. [She reads.] "June the twenty-third, 1893. Miss Abigail Hall, Viper, Kentucky. Unknown friend." [Laughs] "A friend of yours, Miss Sally Hall, says that you said you wanted some pretty boy to write to you. I guess you was just joking if you said that to Sally. But nevertheless, I take the liberty of addressing you, asking you to pardon me for my boldness. You need not think me good-looking by me writing, for I'm not. Some of the boys has told me you are a nice, pretty girl, and of course I would love to see you for I think we could be friends, don't you? I will give you a brief description of myself so that you may judge what I look like. I'm a young man, twenty-three years of age; height five feet ten inches, weight a hundred and fifty pounds, fair complexion, black eyes, light hair, and stoop-shouldered." [Laughs] "If you accept me as a correspondent, I think we could have some real good fun writing to each other, and very likely, our correspondence would lead to something more serious. There is nothing that gives me more pleasure than receiving nice letters from the girls, except being honored with the company of the writer." He was a flatterer. [Laughs] "If you answer this favorably, I think I can interest you next time. If you should care to see my picture, I will send you one with pleasure if you will send me yours after I send mine." [Laughs] "Waiting anxiously for a favorable reply, I remain, your unknown friend, Baylies Ritchie, Dwarf, Kentucky." That was Mama's first and only love letter. She answered the letter and he came to see her. She still has it. And then I guess in about a year and a half or two years, they got married. He was studying for his teaching certificate. In those days, they just had to go through the eighth grade. They studied in the old blue-back speller and all those books where all the knowledge was condensed into one or two books. My mother felt a little self-conscious because he seemed to know so much. She thought he knew as much as the president. [Laughs] My father had to study most of the time, of course, in school or at home thirty miles away, and she didn't see him very often. But they had decided to get married. My mother was in about the fifth or sixth grade. She said she didn't learn much that winter for thinking about what her wedding would be like and what kind of dress she was going to have. You know how girls can pick up things like that and make it, "They're playing our song," that kind of thing. [Laughs] So she learned this little song and still thinks of it as her own courting song. It's called "Somebody's Tall and Handsome." I'll sing it for you. [She sings.] I remember that you were asking me how songs get changed. The end of the verse of the song, my mother deliberately changed. It's supposed to be "Somebody's hair is very bright and somebody's eyes are blue." She changed it to suit my father's coloring. "Somebody's hair is dark, somebody's eyes are too." She confessed to that.

You mention the custom of shivaree, the wild celebration kidding the bride and groom.

My granny played a big part in that. She was a character, one of these very kindhearted but sharp-tongued vinegary kind of people. [Laughs] Very skinny. My father's mother. Her name was Rachel Ritchie and everybody called her Granny Catty. She was about the oldest person around, I guess, and first charter member of the old regular Baptist church and all that. Everybody was sort of afraid of her because she had such a sharp tongue. They hadn't been married but about four or five days, I guess, and Mom and Dad were at home one night and Granny was there, too. They were staying with Granny until they could get their own house built. They heard this noise, people laughing and cowbell jingling. They were trying to keep it quiet but they heard these little sounds of people slipping up to the house. So Granny said to Mom, they were finishing up the dishes in the kitchen, "I swear, those young'uns are coming to shiver you all, and you'd think they'd be decent enough to wait for a week or two anyhow. You all get out of the house, sneak out the front door and get down there in the bottom and hide and I'll tell them you've gone." They stumbled out the front door and went down into the garden and hid in a little holler down there. And people all started ringing the cowbells, and they burst into the house, "Where are they? We know they're here!" Granny just laid them east and west, give 'em a piece of her mind. She said, "You just get out of here. I'll just get the poker and I'll beat every one of you." [Laughs] She said, "Shame on you. They've gone into hiding, they're not here." So they said, "Well, we wasn't gonna do anything to 'em." The custom is they ride the groom on a rail and they scare the bride and do all kinds of awful things to 'em. And they want a treat, a handout, a little bit of elderberry wine, or something like that, whatever was around the house, homebrew, cider. They said, "We just was going to have a little fun. We weren't going to do anything to the bride and the groom." Finally she relented. She called them and told them to come on in the house and they had a big party. Dad and Mom led the quadrilles and the dances, the play parties. She caught two or three of the men scheming out under the pear tree. She listened to 'em out the little window and she heard the talking, making up to carry on with the original shivaree idea. So she grabbed up a shovel and ran to the fireplace and grabbed up a big lot of hot coals and threw them out the window. [Laughs] It landed right in the middle of that lot of men, and you should have seen them climbing over the fence as they started getting away. [Laughs] There wasn't any more meanness that night. The things that were sung at shivarees were the play party songs. Mama said the one they led off with that night was the one about Charlie. That's from Scotland, I suppose. Refers to Bonnie Prince Charlie. It says, "Charlie's neat and Charlie's sweet, and he's a dandy. And Charlie, he's the very lad that stole my strap and candy." In some other versions I've heard that he likes girls and brandy. It goes like this . . . [She sings.] If it was a Saturday night, they would have to break up soon as it got Sunday. Otherwise, they could carry on as long as the lady of the house would let them. She's the one who would shoo 'em off finally, when she got tired or when she thought they'd had enough.

My uncle, Jason Ritchie, told the story about the Ritchies in Virginia and the Ritchies in Kentucky, who hadn't met each other for a generation or two. During the Civil War they met at the same trading store, near the border. They got talking, they seemed sort of like each other, and finally they asked each other their names and it turned out they were cousins. [Laughs] One was rebel and the other was a Union family. But they guaranteed them safe journey, so they went to visit the family in Virginia. Uncle Jason said one of the games they played at that party was Killy Kranky. [She sings] The boys and girls liked to do that 'cause it was a chance to put their arms around each other. [Laughs] Like little children, little girls in school sometimes play the same game. The end one will put his hand up against the wall and then he'll sing a song and turn in and out until the whole mess is wound up together, everybody's arm is around everybody else's neck or something. [Laughs]

My father learned to play the fiddle by accident, a real accident. He was thrown off a wild filly and broke his right wrist. The only doctor we had for miles around was away on a case. He found some old neighbor man and he said, "You have to do something because this thing is killing me." The neighbor man just reached up, took hold of the arm and pulled it back around. [Laughs] And twisted it sort of like unscrewing a bottle cap. It just about liked to kill my father, he just hollered and hollered. After that he did go to a doctor who set it for him. Even now, my father's about ninety, and his arm still bothers him there. He can't really carry a tune anymore. He hums little things to himself, but he can't really sing a song anymore. But because of this accident, he learned to play the fiddle. While his arm was healing, he couldn't hoe corn and he couldn't plow. The only way he could go, with his arm in the sling, was just to move his arm back and forth. So they went out and caught a possum, then he got some hairs out of a horse's tail, and they got a gourd, and they made him a gourd fiddle. He learned and he just kept on fiddling around with it by himself until he played his own style in his own way. He played it pretty well. He played for dances around there for a long time. But he never would have learned if he hadn't broke his arm.

What about the word hillbilly? *Is it resented by mountain people?*

Yes, it is. It's the same as saying an Okie. It's humorous and sort of pokes fun at the mountain people. You think of a hillbilly as being somebody who, like the cartoon, the mountain boys who lie around and they never do any work, they have a jug and they're barefooted. Of course we resent this because we're really not like that a-tall. [Laughs] But I've got so I can laugh at it, I think it's kind of funny. I don't get as mad as I used to. [Laughs] "Carry Me Back to Old Virginny" is partly old English style, and there's just sort of a hint of this new style that was coming in when my father was young. The latest rock and roll of 1893. [She sings] Some of the words are Old English–like. "Some dark valley." That was changed to "Some dark holler." [She reads from her book.] "The long warm evenings were somehow saddest of all. We'd get our bit of supper over and work done up. The cow milked, the horse and pigs and chickens fed, the coal and kindling in." That feeling was when I was the only one left. We weren't always sad. It's just that everybody was gone away from home but me, and I still was there just with Mom and Dad and it was quite lonesome. [She reads.] "We'd sit around the front room and I'd get my lessons, and Ma would piece quilts or mend, and Dad would maybe take down the dulcimer off the wall and make the old tunes ring proud on the still forsaken night. Have you ever heard a dulcimer played on a still, soft night by a lonesome person?"

We never called it a town. It had about three hundred people in it. I guess it's called a village. Christmas was about the happiest time of the year. There's something special about my memories of our Christmases. It seems like we had more fun. Maybe that's a sign of getting old. [Laughs] We got up at four-thirty in the morning and went to sing carols, the family and the neighbors. All fourteen were never home at the same time; some were married by the time I came along, so I have nieces and nephews that are older than I am. It's that kind of family. If we didn't have fourteen children, we made it up with the grandchildren that lived near. We'd all go singing carols on Christmas morning, very early. And it was a beautiful time of the morning. You know four-thirty? I doubt if anybody knows much about four-thirty around here. [Laughs] The Ritchies, the Breashers, and the Halls. I remember my granny's favorite carol. Whenever she'd stay with us, we'd always make her sing "Brightest and Best." She never celebrated December 25. She always held out until Old Christmas. It was when they went by the old calendar, before it was changed, and Christmas used to fall on January 6, or Twelfth Night. Granny Catty didn't hold to these newfangled things about changing calendars. [Laughs] According to her, Christmas was still on the sixth of January, and Christmas Eve was January 5. Of course, there's a sort of a new thing too, you know, giving presents and having Santy Claus and Christmas trees and things like that. Granny said that in the old days, they didn't do any of this, all this commercial selling, and all these Christmas trees and Santy Clauses. She said in the old days, it was more of a religious holiday. She told us that on January 5 at midnight, if we'd go out to the barn, we would peep in through the cracks and see that on the stroke of midnight, the horse and the cow and all the animals would kneel down. And that if we looked into the fence corner, we'd see the elderberry bushes blooming out, which they did on the stroke of midnight. Of course, they'd vanish before the morning. And we were always too sleepy to get out that late to see whether the elderberry bushes were blooming or not. [Laughs] But the way she told it, I really believe it. Then she would sit in front of the fire on Christmas Eve and sing "Brightest and Best" as an instruction to us that this was really Christmas and this is the way it should be celebrated. [She sings] It had many other verses, too. The last one is the main instruction which says, "Vainly we offer each ample oblation, vainly with gifts would his favors secure. Richer by far is the heart's adoration, dearer to God are the prayers of the poor."

You mentioned a song from the "colored children."

That was "Children, Go Where I Send Thee." In the days when I was growing up, the schools were segregated. A teacher from Hindman School used to go out into the local schools and sing with the children, and she also went to the colored school. One day she came early and she heard them singing one of their own songs. I guess it could be called a spiritual, I don't rightly know. Or maybe it's just a Negro carol. The little boys were lined up on one side of the house and the little girls on the other, and they were answering back and forth to this little cumulative song. It builds up like the "Story of Twelve" or "Green Grow the Rushes." But this was about the little bitty baby. It's one of the songs that we treasure in our family as one of our own now. The cumulative song is Old English, and before that, Old Danish and Norwegian. The Scottish, English, and Irish songs, I think, originally came from the Scandinavian countries. [Laughs] There were the Vikings and you could just keep on going. Before that, I don't know where they came from.

All my life up to then, I had dreamed and longed and schemed to leave home, to go places like the others. But when the time was coming near, I hated the thought of getting through high school and was scared to death of the time when I, too, would have to go away. [Again she reads from her book] "It was like a big something was pushing me out of the house, down the branch, and off onto the railroad trains when I didn't want to go. I wished I could start getting younger instead of older. I wished I could do something about the calendar so that December wouldn't come and bring my birthday so that I could always and forever remain sixteen. It was on such a night, late in the month of May. We were sitting like this, the dulcimer was crying and the moon was rising and a spring mist, and the lonesomeness moved down from the hills and sat with us." The Short Dog is a passenger train that went by. The seven-fifteen Short Dog moaned by, blowing for the crossing. It was a night like a hundred other nights, with us sitting there, working, talking a little, humming, thinking to ourselves. And first thing, my sister May came running in, and several of the other children came home from schools far away. They had made it up to have a reunion without telling us about it. And it was one of the happy things that happened in that year when everything was so lonesome. We all gathered out on the front porch again, like we always used to do. We had had many different experiences by then, we were all scattered out all over the United States, and yet we found when we got back together on the porch and started to sing, that we were still as close a family as we ever were. Because as soon as we started to sing the songs that we all knew, all these new experiences were sort of forgotten, and we were back again where we used to be. The lovely past was not gone—it had just been shut up inside a song.

JANIS JOPLIN
1968

Janis Joplin was perhaps the most popular of all the young white blues singers of the late sixties. At the time we spoke, I had slight reservations about her as a singer of blues, but nonetheless, seeing her on the stage, the powerful animal quality that she had obviously registered with the young came through. Our conversation took place in the very crowded dressing room of the Aragon Ballroom. Her coterie was all about her—these were former colleagues of hers, because at that time she was with a new group. It was a conversation in the middle of all sorts of back-and-forth movements in a rather shoddy dressing room as various other rock artists were passing through the corridor. The audience was hardly visible in the dim lights. It didn't matter too much; most of them were stoned. All the energy came from the performer, who was tippling from a fifth of Southern Comfort.

How'd you come to the blues in Port Arthur, Texas?

It was very strange. Somebody played a Leadbelly record for me one day—I was about fifteen, sixteen—and I just freaked, I really liked it. And I started listening to a lot of Leadbelly, and then I started reading books on the blues that I found in the Port Arthur library. They kept mentioning Bessie Smith and I said, "Wow, far out, a chick blues singer," 'cause I hadn't even heard of one before. So I ordered all of her records from some strange mail order house, you know, they didn't sell them in Port Arthur. And I just fell in love with her. You know how kids listen to radio and all. I never listened to radio, I didn't never get into that rock-and-roll trip. I just listened to blues. It seemed real. The other stuff seemed so tacky, teenagey. It didn't seem to have any truth in it or something. From the first moment I ever heard it that was my music. I always liked it.

> *People speak of how you make a song your own. A good example, I think, would be "Summertime" from your album* Cheap Thrills. *This is a wholly different "Summertime" than one we are used to hearing from* Porgy and Bess. *It's hard to explain. It's not an operetta singer doing Gershwin.*

I don't know what it is. I never sang a ballad before. It's the only one I've ever done. We did it because we needed to fill a number one night. You know, when I'd just joined the band, they started playing it and said [stage whisper], "Hey quick, 'Summertime' in D." So I sang it and I'd never sung it before and we've just been working on it ever since. I'm really anxious to get some more ballads. There's a Billie Holiday tune I want to start working on—"Gloomy Sunday." A fantastic tune, isn't it?

> *You know the story behind "Gloomy Sunday"? It's about a suicide. It's originally Hungarian.*

A Hungarian suicide song, right.

> *I imagine that Janis Joplin's "Gloomy Sunday" with Southern Comfort would be really fantastic.*

I'm just really excited to do it because I think, like, for example, that tune I think increased my, you know, chops, if you can call a singer having chops. Because I'd never done anything like it and I learned a whole lot by doing it and I'm sure I would by doing "Gloomy Sunday" too.

> *Billie has had an effect on you too?*

Not really as much as people would like to think. I listen to her a lot but I don't have any of her subtlety. The same way I don't think Aretha Franklin's had much effect on my singing. Otis Redding had a lot of effect on my singing, but Aretha Franklin is a lot more subtle. It's going to take me a few years.

> *A phrase used years ago was "blues shouter."*

Yeah, well, see, I've only been singing like really about two years, so I don't have it down yet, that's all.

Where we are now, this was the kitsch, 1920s, ersatz, Spanish-style-waltz ballroom.

Ah! They sure got lousy dressing rooms. [Laughs]

Do you occasionally get older people in your audience?

See, you don't get to see the audience too much anymore. Like when we're playing a ballroom situation the audience is all around you, it's almost like 180 degrees audience, and they're very close to you and you can see them. Now, in a situation like this, I can't hardly see people. I don't know how old they are.

I don't mean visually at this moment, but you yourself are aware of your audience, you know, aren't you?

The older people don't come back and talk to me, so I'm not really aware—I don't even know if they come to see me or not. The only older people that I know come to see me are the president and the vice president of Columbia Records.

Have you ever heard Mahalia Jackson sing "Sometimes I Feel Like a Motherless Child"? Has it occurred to you there's a similar pattern there between the spiritual "Motherless Child" and "Summertime"?

Groovy. I like Mahalia Jackson too.

You've said that Big Mama Thornton has influenced you.

Yeah, we played with her twice. She's fantastic.

You and she sang together?

I wouldn't get on the same stage with her, she'd kill me. [Laughs] No, but we've played on the same bill and I was absolutely terrified, but it was really a thrill for me. We heard her do "Ball 'n' Chain" one night. We went and saw her at a little dinky club in San Francisco, there was no audience. She's playing all over, she's like a real working entertainer—I mean she's too much. I heard that tune and I just really loved it. And I went backstage and asked her if I could do it. [Imitating Big Mama] "I don't care what you do. I don't care what you do to my tune, just let me get it recorded first." So we started doing it. She doesn't do it anymore. I kept asking her when we were playing with her to sing it. She said, "I don't do that in these small clubs." I went backstage that time and asked the guitar player for the chord changes and I only heard it once and like half the words I don't think are even hers. 'Cause like I forgot, I only heard it once. So I just sort of made up half the words, but the arrangement is hers, and the chords are hers, and the basic idea.

You said something about your always seeking nuances, looking for more and more subtleties.

You gotta do that, man, or you end up sounding—I'm not going to sing "Down on Me" for twenty years.

You're going to go for the ballads now.

Well, I'm going to work on that. I also want to work on "Road Runner" by Junior Walker. I like rock tunes, too. I don't know, I'm just going to keep on trucking.

Your shouting style also reminds me of singers of another time. The electrified instruments play a role here too. No longer the acoustic instruments with softer singers of the blues. Now you're battling electricity.

Boy, you sure are. I always sang real loud. But I never sang as driving as I did before I was with an electric band. I sang more open, like "Turtle Blues," you know, easy open, because you can sing like that. I sang with an acoustic guitar player. But when you sing in front of a drummer and amplifiers you've got to push a lot harder. I guess that's the reason I sound like that. When you're in a live performance you can get away with a lot of mistakes because the excitement is there. But when you're recording live, unless you play perfectly, it just sounds awful. That's why there's not more live records made, I'm sure you know that. We just lucked out. No one really made any mistakes on this particular cut. Ten minutes, it's pretty good. We didn't have to make a single change, a single cut in the studio, which is pretty hard.

I gotta ask the clichéd question about the blues being a black man's music. Josh White some years ago was saying no white person can sing the blues. So your reply to this is what?

I was quoted in *Time* just last week. What did I say? Even a housewife in Nebraska can sing the blues. Anybody can sing the blues. Well, I don't know whether they can sing them or not, but they can feel them. All you gotta do is have a throat, the throat's the difference. Everybody's got feelings inside of them. It's just the faculty of being able to transform it into music. I mean, everybody's got 'em. [Shouts] Everybody's got 'em, Mama got 'em, Papa got 'em, everybody's got 'em! Everybody's got those things, they've just got to know what to do with it. You either repress it or you use it. Sort of. I feel better after singing, yeah.

There's an old country blues singer, a guy named Big Bill Broonzy. About the writing of blues he says there's about five things you can do. He said you can even do a tune about a knife—a knife. You cut your nails with, shave with, kill with.

Well, I'm not really a songwriter. When I write a tune, it's just about the way I feel, so my songs sort of sound the same after a while. They're all about people's insides. I can't write a song about a knife. I can only write about the inside of Janis Joplin. I write very subjective tunes. I don't write third-person blues, I write first-person blues. I just don't know how.

You're from Port Arthur. What about fellow Texans?

I hate 'em. [Laughs] They're really not the brightest people. I don't like Texans.

Has your father heard you sing?

He said he likes Bach. He said he couldn't get into it. He said, "I'm sure that you're doing something up there that's good, Janis. The kids all seem to like it, but I couldn't really get behind it." Which is fine, that's generous. He could say it was bad. My mother says, "Why do you have to sing so loud?" She says, "You have such a pretty voice, Janis." She doesn't understand.

Prettiness. For years we think of the young girl and pretty songs.

No one's ever brought that up before. I think that's a really valid point. Like most chick singers, like any female, they're very ladylike in their conduct. That's why I think they don't think they can sing the blues, you know what I mean? I don't mean to sound trite. But, I mean, you can't sing the blues and have your hair bleached platinum blond and look like a cheerleader. I mean, you gotta have something else going. You gotta be able to act a little, feel a little, think a little, guts. And so most chicks don't do that. I don't think American girls want to be any other way than that. Like I got a sister that's just exactly like that. And she doesn't want to be any other way. Which is fine, it's fine for her. It's just not fine for me. I gotta do my own thing and that's the way I turned out.

The credo of Janis Joplin is very simple: nobody can tell you what to do.

That's right, baby. It's very strange. I had a girl arguing with me last night about it, about what do you do about the people who don't feel things. And I didn't have any answer for her. I don't know, I suppose that's what they come for because that's what our music is. Our music isn't perfection of any kind, but when it's working it makes you get outside of your head and just have a good time, and that's what I think kids are after. They're not really after a cerebral trip. I mean, I know there are wars going on and things like that. But I'd rather just get stoned and have fun. And I think that's the way they kind of see us.

We'll let it go with that. Why did you call your new album Cheap Thrills?

We were going to call it *Dope, Sex, and Cheap Thrills*, because we figured that was something that no one could argue with, right? Who can put that down?

To use an old Woody Guthrie phrase, "Take it easy, but take it."

～ Impresario (3) ～

ALAN LOMAX
1994

There is no one in America who comes close to Alan Lomax as a collector of American folk music, white and black. Even as his father, John Lomax, in collaborating with Carl Sandburg in the classic The American Songbag, *was collecting songs, Alan was there as a kid, helping in that masterwork. From then on he was on his own, traveling thoughout the Deep South and elsewhere, as well as in European countries. He collected perhaps more songs from more countries than anyone else. But he was more than a collector: it was he who recorded and preserved hundreds of these classics, whether they were songs, cries, or hymns. When we think of Lomax, we think of Leadbelly, Woody Guthrie, Big Bill Broonzy, and then you start thinking of all the others who would otherwise have been among the anonymous and forgotten. They owe him their remembrance.*

[Alan Lomax begins by singing out an old Southern folk song] My father sang it while he was clearing bottomland down in a Texas farm way back in about the time of the Civil War. He sang it sometimes when he'd get up in the morning wearing his flannel nightshirt, sort of get the fresh air of the morning into his lungs. Looking out over green hills, it would remind him of his boyhood, and he'd sing that song about Saturday night. It's a Negro song, it's a white song, it's a Southern song. Into it, the Southerners have poured that peculiar kind of joy that's Southern. That wild, tangy feeling about life that you don't have anywhere else in America but down there. Because life is so mixed up, everything is so awful, and so bad, and so tremendous. [Laughs] I don't suppose any Southerner would have given up growing up in the South. You may want to leave there, but you have something out of growing up down there that you can't have anywhere else in America.

Until about the end of the war, I'd been collecting steadily with a recording machine in America since I was seventeen—close to eighteen years. I'd been in every back alley and every little town east of the Mississippi. It got so I wasn't feeling fresh about America. It seemed to me that the big problem at that time was to make the world feel like a world of various people speaking various languages all about the same big human problems. Since we had now the tape machine and the long-playing record, we at last had a chance to put all that together in a picture so that the world could hear the world singing: vox humana. So I got up at a learned meeting of folklorists from a lot of countries, and proposed this: I said, "Let's form a committee and put all our records together and inform ourselves about what we have. I don't know what you've got in Sweden or Indonesia, and you don't know what I've got in America. Let's make a pool." They voted me down. This was at an actual meeting in Indiana, and it made me so mad. I had one man to vote with me. I said, "Doggone it, I'll do it myself if they won't do it with me." I went to New York. And Goddard Lieberson said, "Sure, if you think the stuff is there, go and get it." I got a Magnacord and got on the next boat pretty nearly. I thought that oh, it would maybe take me about a year. (Laughs.) We were going to do forty albums: one from each main country or human region, ethnically. I'm now at album eighteen, and that's about nine years ago this began.

I'm not a musicologist. I can't even read music. I'm a writer, I'm a recording engineer, I'm anything but an ethnomusicologist. I asked a New Orleans trumpet player if he could read music. He says, "Yes, I can read music, but when I'm reading music, I can't hear the music that's going on in my head. I

want to hear what's going on in my own head and those notes get in the way."
Anthropology is what I studied in college. That's it. My father, John A. Lomax, was a professor of English. He took it out on me at night. He read
me Shakespeare every single night. He fixed the cadences of the greatest
prose and poetry in English in my head. Whenever I sat down to type out my
little first beginnings, that music would rise between me and the end of the
first sentence, and I would quit. The ghost of Shakespeare would overtake
me and trip me and flatten me.

I had to figure out a way to write about blues, spirituals, black people's
music, to folk music as a whole. When I came along, Carl Sandburg was
touring with his little guitar. Much of what he learned were songs from my
father. And then later from me. I played a little guitar, and I actually lobbied
the Archive of [American] Folk Song of the Library of Congress into existence in Washington. I was the singer at all those New Deal parties and we
put on a radio series on CBS. I gathered kindred spirits around me, Burl Ives
and Woody and Pete. It was called "Back Where You Came From," and it was
on for fifty-two weeks. We actually had to do a survey of the whole country.
We put that into the Library of Congress, into that archive of folk song. We
gathered lumberjacks and lake sailors and old ladies, and the whole popula-
tion of the United States. By the time we had passed it onto others, we had a
representative picture of the whole country on record. First time in history,
in any part of the world. There had not been good enough recording ma-
chines to take out there and bring 'em back alive, all the voices. My father
and I had an aluminum disk machine weighing a ton. My father continued to
collect for the Works Progress Administration till very late in his life. Acade-
mia didn't approve of the recording machine. It got their hands dirty and they
had to lift too many things and they had to meet too many unconventional
people who were déclassé.

There were prison songs, there were work songs. Leadbelly was a work
song singer. Most people have never even heard those songs. Here's a Leadbelly song that I think is almost his supreme thing. It's a mule-skinning song
from the Louisiana levees. [Belting it out] "Honey, I'm all out and down /
Honey, I'm down in the bottom / Skinning for Johnny Ryan / Writing my initials on that mule's behind / With my line, babe / With my line, babe / With
my line, babe." It wasn't the whipping, it was also the music that inspired the
mules. They sang songs that they said would make a mule work himself to
death. Sometimes the singing would get so good the mules would join in, just

like it was lunchtime. Leadbelly was the lead man on the lead rope. He would sing, and the guys with him—gandy dancers, tapping wheels—they'd sing with him. They were putting their stamp on Southern life, on every part of it. Every tool was renamed, every job was renamed, every place was renamed, every boss was renamed. They had nicknames for everything. They reconstituted their African world in their new African Creole speech, their new African Creole music, in their habits, in their church style, in their courtship style, in their children's games.

So the South became a province of Africa, a part of the Caribbean. A typical Caribbean place, dominated by Presbyterianism and by the hard-boiled, flinty-hearted managerial style of northern Europe, which wasn't relaxed like Latin America. You couldn't marry across the race line and didn't get your bastard children sent to school like in the North. But there was occasionally a certain kind of amity between the two groups. The blacks learned the European ballad style, among other things. They learned to make a very good quatrain narrative song. Out of it came their best songs, and the very best American ballads. [He sings] "Frankie was a woman everybody know / Spent about a hundred dollar to buy her man some clothes / And he was her man, and he's doing her wrong . . ." That top ballad was much more popular than any of the cowboy songs or lumberjack songs. [Sings with more power] "When John Henry was a little baby / You could hold him in the palm of your hand / He'd point his finger at a little piece of steel / Says 'I'm gonna be a steel-driving man.'" Steel-driving was a pun for sex. For when John Henry got sick, Polly Ann, his wife, came in. [Sings] "John Henry had a little woman and her name was Polly Ann / John Henry took sick and he had to go to bed / Polly Ann drove steel like a man." Now, a chorus of laughter would go up in the sweaty confines of the tunnel where that song was being sung 'cause everybody knew what was happening. There were double entendres, all those songs.

The blacks did the tunneling work in West Virginia because the whites couldn't stand the high temperatures. They refused to do the work, but they leaned over the edge and they learned the blues, and they learned the work songs as they were sung. And they developed their own kind of bluesy songs out of the black material that they heard. [Sings] "I was born and raised in East Virginia, North Carolina I did go / There I courted a fair young lady, and her age she did not know / Well, her eyes of a dark sun color, and her cheeks of a rosy red / The way I love that brown-eyed darling sends aching pains all through my breast." Well, there's a kind of bluesy mountain song. You can hear it, right out of "John Henry," right?

The interesting thing about the blues is it's the first popular solo song style in the black culture. They normally had dancey tunes and work song tunes that a group could participate in. [Sings]: "Way up yonder, darlin' / 'Bove that sun, sugar / Girls all call me honey / Sugar plum, sure 'nuff / It's all right, honey." Now that's a typical pre-blues kind of Southern ring-game song. But the blacks had a new experience on the levees. First of all, they were not only totally déclassé and out of caste, but they'd lost their homes. These were homeless people, migratory labor. And they drifted from job to job. "You were nothing but a black face to those bosses," they tell me. There was no law. And law was the pistol on the boss's hip. Mr. Charlie would ride out in the middle of the cut, throw his hat up in the air, shoot three holes in it before it hit the ground, and tell the boys, "Hand me my hat." He said, "Now, I want to get some dirt out of here. Are there any questions?" That was the way the job would begin. That was Mr. Charlie the boss.

The Texas prison was the cruelest of all, and it produced the most magnificent songs. I've begun to understand why sorrow produces great songs. The people confronted with an odd and painful situation have to dig deeper into their cultural resources and get the most profoundly strong and ancient things to help them. That was what they faced in these prison camps and on these levee camps. So they dug back into their real primal African heritage. They produced absolutely remarkable things. Those Texas prisons, I think, are the most savage in the South, because they were manned by people who loved to kill Mexicans and coloreds, and a few poor whites, too. They were just shooters. They were Texas Rangers who were disappointed they hadn't got the job, so they gave them a shotgun and put them on as straw bosses. The blacks dug deeper into their African treasure for those songs. I think the greatest American song in many ways is the theme song of Texas prisons. [Sings]: "Go down old Hannah." That's the sun, you know. "Well, well, well . . . Don't you rise no more / Don't you rise no more / Go down old Hannah / Oh, you don't rise no more." They worked from sunup to sundown. From can to can't. The thing that hit me as I went along these long lonely roads was, first of all, I was with the most creative people of the country, constantly. They were my boon companions.

My father and I both spent time with Leadbelly and helped to get him out of the penitentiary. I recorded his songs and reflections for the Library of

Congress. That experience helped him to solidify his appreciation of his own stuff. It was just drifting around his head. It got crystallized as he listened to his own playbacks. Same thing happened to Woody. Same thing happened to Aunt Molly Jackson [a mountaineer midwife who sang songs in support of Harlan County coal miners]. I took Big Bill Broonzy, Memphis Slim, and Sunny Boy Williamson up into the Decca studio where I had access to a nice quiet place and did for them what you're doing for me. I said, "What is the blues really about? We white people really don't understand. Can you tell us?" And they turned away from me and talked to each other for two hours. I just flipped the discs. I didn't have a tape machine. I tried to keep up flipping the discs. And they told the damnedest story that was ever told. They went from disappointments in love to economic problems, to exploitation problems, to chain gang problems, and finally ended up with a story about Mr. White. They got dissolved in the irony and laughter of the whole thing. Mr. White had this place and he was bugged on white. He painted the trees white, everything white. He wanted to get rid of anything that wasn't white. All the blacks said, "We'll take everything you got that ain't white." I don't know if he was nutty. He was just a rather extreme case of Southernism. He had a sign, edge of his property, says, "Negro turn." And that meant you turned and walked down the side road and didn't cross his land. Laughter is a way of actually turning the tables on the situation by saying, "Yeah, that happens, but I know how ridiculous it is. It's perfectly absurd." They ended up with the following story: "Now, we got a place down there, Chickalah, Arkansas." "Yeah, Chickalah," laugh, laugh. "And a black man drove his wagon up to a rail and the rail was rather high. He had a white mule on the front of the wagon. And the rail got stuck and he says he looked around and there was a white man, and he says, 'Get up, Mr. Mule.' It was a white mule. He wouldn't dare call him 'mule.'" Then Bill, when he went to the store, he said, "When you go in there to buy that Prince Albert tobacco, you have to ask for 'Mr. Prince Albert tobacco.'" [Laughs] And then he laughed. And that was the end of the first recording. That was the first time that working-class blacks ever told about whatever had happened to them. When I played them back the record, they were terrified. They swore me into silence that I would never identify who they were. Now, this was in 1948! I used pseudonyms. In fact, they got on the train, went back to Chicago, would talk no further, and I saw them not at all for many, many years.

All these years that I was making recordings, I was asking them what they felt about what they sung. They've got these wonderful statements about psy-chology and about life. I began to realize that the prose was even better than the songs in many cases. I began to work up the whole idea of folk biography. I recorded Leadbelly's biography, then I recorded Aunt Molly Jackson's auto-biography, along with all of her songs. Aunt Molly was a union woman. She says [he sings], "I am a union woman just as red as I can be / And I don't like the bosses and the bosses don't like me." So I visited the Appalachian whites, the striking miners, the African Americans, the black guys who worked the plantations and the railroads. All those years, I was collecting union and protest songs. I'm the first person to ever record the great CIO song [sings], "My daddy's a miner / He's now in the air and sun / Be with him, brother workers / Until the battle's won / Which side are you on? / Which side are you on?" The song swept the CIO into victory. Made up by a little twelve-year-old miner's daughter, Florence Reese.

Down at the bottom of every society, we have creative artists, the likes of Woody and Leadbelly and Burl Ives and the Golden Gate Quartet. You real-ize that Thomas Dorsey created a whole new kind of music, an old jazzman moving into the spirituals. It's now a world music. But you can't have black art without it being group art, see. Africans don't make music in solo singers like we do. It's always a group thing. There are always people beating rhythm or doing something in the group. And what we've tried to do is let everybody into the game, that's the whole point. This history is written by the singers and the geniuses in four hundred cultures, who represent all the geniuses who've ever been. It's been buried by this conceited group of people that call themselves writers and historians for the last three hundred years—the peo-ple who wrote all these manuscripts telling what happened. It was mostly about kings and princes and left out the real events that were happening out in the fields and the pastures.

~ Part Four ~

Variations on
∾ the Theme ∾

LARRY ADLER
1976

We never regarded the harmonica as a serious classical instrument. It was something kids played on the street—nickel, dime, quarter harmonicas, and play. Until Larry Adler came along. And Larry Adler seemed to experiment with harmonicas, and they weren't fancy ones. As a result of which he did something quite outrageous and remarkable, playing Bach, Vivaldi, and Brahms on the mouth harp, as it was called in some quarters. It was a ten-cent instrument. The high moment came when he joined Paul Draper, a remarkable tap dancer. Together, the Adler-Draper act filled auditoriums with both classical and popular music fans. Their popularity was quite remarkable. And so it was that one man's ingenuity with one deceptively simple instrument was transformed into a serious instrument for classical music. Thus it was recognized, even in a perverse way, by Jimmy Petrillo, the iron-handed boss of the American Federation of Musicians. During a celebrated musicians' strike, the harmonica was not forbidden, so Larry Adler had considerable work, though he himself was pro-strikers. The harmonica became so accepted in "respectable" music circles that Petrillo was compelled to recognize the harmonica as a legitimate instrument. A side item: Larry Adler and Paul Draper took part during those Cold War and McCarthy days in political activities. They spoke at many rallies dealing with civil rights and civil liberties, as a result of which they were blacklisted. The notorious case was one involving the wife of a Time *magazine editor who accused the duo of being communists. They sued, and it ended in a hung jury. Both sides were devastated.*

Before you came along the harmonica was something kids played in the streets and there was Borrah Minevitch and his Harmonica Rascals in vaudeville.

I auditioned for Borrah. When I came to New York, my idea of heaven was to be accepted as a member of Borrah Minevitch's Harmonica Rascals. I was only fourteen years old. I came from Baltimore. I auditioned for Borrah, and all the boys in his harmonica band stood in the doorway and listened to me as I played "Poet and Peasant" [an overture by Franz von Suppé]. When I finished playing, Minevitch said, "Kid, you stink." I cried like a baby. Remember Johnny Puleo, the dwarf? He came up to me and patted me on the shoulder and said, "Don't mind Borrah, he's not feeling well today." I felt my world had collapsed. Three months before the Minevitch audition, I'd won a mouth organ contest in Baltimore. I played Beethoven's Minuet in G. I bought a mouth organ to get into the contest. I don't think I ever played one before. All the other kids were playing things like "St. Louis Blues" and "Black Bottom," and I had elected to learn the Minuet in G mainly because the notes lay next to each other and were quite easy to play. The judge was a classical musician, the conductor of the Baltimore Symphony. When I played Beethoven I was a cinch, I won.

We think of the harmonica as an instrument of pop tunes. How did you transpose Bach?

It took me years before I got to that. That same week where Minevitch rejected me, I got a job with Paramount, a forty-four-week contract which included playing in Chicago at the Oriental Theater when I was fourteen years old. I did a twelve-minute act. I did "Button Up Your Overcoat," I did "I Want to Be Loved by You" imitating Helen Kane, the Betty Boop girl, on the mouth organ, I did "St. Louis Blues." That was my act. It never occurred to me that I could play serious music. After a while, I just got a little tired of playing the pop tunes, and I started to play Vivaldi, and a bit of Bach, and a bit of Monteverdi. I tried a recital in England in 1937, which worked pretty well. The critics didn't pay any attention to it, but it worked. In 1939, in Sydney, Australia, there was a benefit for the relief of brushfire victims. I played Vivaldi's Violin Concerto in A Minor. That was my first time with a symphony. It didn't even have to be transcribed for harmonica. I played the violin part exactly as written.

I play an ordinary harmonica. It's a twelve-hole instrument, it's got three octaves on it. Within those three octaves, theoretically at least, I should be able to play anything. I can't, of course, but all the notes are there. When I was sixteen, I'd been in show business nearly three years. Paul Whiteman played at the Roxy Theater on the bill with his own film, *The King of Jazz*. I wasn't working. I stayed outside the stage door and whoever came in or out, I'd start to play the mouth organ, hoping somebody would say, "Hey, what a talented kid." Well, Frankie Trumbauer, the great jazz saxophone player, did hear me play, and he took me inside to Paul Whiteman's dressing room. I played something for him. When I finished, Whiteman said, "Can you play *Rhapsody in Blue*? I was sixteen. I couldn't play it, but neither could I admit to Paul Whiteman that there was anything I couldn't play. So I said, "I don't like *Rhapsody in Blue*." He turned to a man on his left and says, "How do you like that, Gershwin, this kid doesn't like *Rhapsody in Blue*." And it was George Gershwin. That was the first time I met him.

Today, the mouth organ is an accepted, respected member of a symphony orchestra.

It would never [have been] an instrument in a symphony orchestra. It has no projection power, it needs a microphone; it would be drowned out, even by a flute. If I were playing with a string quartet, I'd have to use a mike. Otherwise my tone, my sound will just fade against the greater projection power of the viola, the violin and the cello. The harmonica was officially recognized by the musicians' union right here in Chicago, in 1948. I was playing at the Palmer

House. The musicians' union had gone on strike against the recording companies a few years before that and refused to let their members make records. The mouth organ not being recognized by the union, all the recording companies got mouth organ groups. So Dinah Shore and Frank Sinatra recorded with mouth organs. I refused to record at that time. It just seemed like scabbing. Even though I wasn't in the union, I didn't like the idea. In 1948, the musicians' union decided if there was another strike like that, they better make sure the mouth organ players aren't around to scab it, so they recognized the mouth organ. James Petrillo [president of the American Federation of Musicians], in a very touching ceremony, touched the tip of his little finger to the tip of my little finger. Apparently he had a germ phobia, but he seemed to think there were no germs on the tip of my little finger. I was accepted into the union and became respectable.

Classical composers began to recognize the harmonica as a serious instrument because of your virtuosity.

Darius Milhaud heard me one night. I did a concert with the San Francisco Symphony playing *Rhapsody in Blue*. Milhaud was teaching composition at Mills College at Oakland. He came backstage and said he'd like to know more about the mouth organ. I explained what the mouth organ could do. He said, "It's a very interesting thing for a composer to find a new sound. One is so used to writing for the violin and the cello and the piano. I'd love to write a work for you." I gave him a diagram showing what the mouth organ could do and what it could not do, its advantages and its limitations. He wrote this three-movement work, *Suite Anglaise for Harmonica and Orchestra*. When he finished it, I found I couldn't learn it. It was a kind of modern music which at the time I was incapable of appreciating. It took me several years before I would dare to play the work in public.

I learned to read music after Milhaud wrote this work. Up until then, I learned everything by ear. I had studied the piano for about two years, between the ages of eight and ten, but I'd forgotten how to read. I was a natural by-ear man. I hated to practice, I would never practice the piano. I got expelled from the Peabody Conservatory in Baltimore—the only student ever to have been expelled. When the mouth organ came along this was absolutely perfect because there was no Jascha Heifetz of the mouth organ. You couldn't say, "Why don't you play more like this other fellow?" There was no other fellow. I was the first. So for a lazy man, there was nothing that could have been better than the mouth organ. This is one of the great sins of my life. When I look back, I always think that the omissions were more horrendous and more horrific than the actual sins I committed, the things I didn't do. Duke Ellington and I went out to the Grand Terrace Cafe where Earl Hines had his band. Earl called on Duke and me, and we got up and played a duet. Duke Ellington's manager was at our table and when we finished, he said, "How'd you like to record with the Duke, kid?" Sure, that was great. I was all of about seventeen or eighteen, it was a marvelous idea. He said that he would give me $25 a side, and I would make fifty sides with Duke Ellington. I had read that week in *Variety* that Bing Crosby got 7½ percent royalty. So I said to Ellington's manager, "I don't want $25 a set, I want 7½ percent royalty." So he told me what I could do with my 7½ percent royalty. So I never recorded with Duke. Isn't that awful? Just 'cause I was an arrogant punk of a kid.

Malcolm Arnold did a suite for you, didn't he?

A concerto. Malcolm Arnold is one of the leading English composers. The BBC commissioned this work and told him they wanted a nine-minute concerto and by golly, that's exactly what they got, precisely nine minutes. He's quite an amazing composer. He's a big Falstaffian man with an enormous belly. He weighs about four hundred pounds, he drinks much too much. But he can write for anything. He did the score for *The Bridge on the River Kwai*. That was a folk melody, but Malcolm made a fortune out of that score. If I were asked to do that movement right now, I wouldn't be able to. For that particular movement, Arnold set a metronome tempo at such a speed that I have to be in as fine shape as an Olympic athlete to be able to handle the speed of that run. If I were suddenly asked to play it tonight, I wouldn't be able to do it correctly. I've got to start practicing with a slow speed and gradually increase the speed, like an Olympic runner practicing, until finally I can get up to the speed that Malcolm Arnold required.

There are several blues harmonica players you like, like Sonny Terry. . . .

What Sonny Terry does, I couldn't do. Only Sonny can do that. I've never heard anybody else who can do it as well as Sonny. When you play like Sonny

Terry, it's because you've lived Sonny Terry's life. He's playing his guts out when he plays. I play my life, he plays his. I couldn't duplicate his. That's a very special sound he makes.

Sonny Terry, who is a blind, black harmonica player from Carolina, who remembers as a kid hearing the sound of a train and the sound of a fox being hunted. So that's his life he re-creates.

Exactly. How could I do that? I didn't live that life. Especially from the thirties up until the Second World War, there'd been the beginning of a mass movement of mouth organs all over the world. After World War II, it dropped considerably. The guitar superseded the mouth organ completely. Then, with the advent of the pop groups, with Mick Jagger playing, John Lennon, Bob Dylan, it started to come up again. Now, there is an absolute revival of the mouth organ, a tremendous revival. I know this because of the Hohner Company that makes my mouth organs—there are two models with my name on them, for which I get a royalty. I can see by the royalty statements, it's just going up and up. Also, there are classical mouth organ players all over the world. There's a very good one in Japan, for example. There are two excellent ones in England, there's one in France. John Sebastian [father of the Lovin' Spoonful rock musician] and I were contemporaries here. Anything that I could play, John could, and vice versa. We were very similar. I think that John came before me. When I won that contest in Baltimore, I have a dim memory of hearing that John Sebastian had won the Philadelphia championship before I won the Baltimore one.

Vaughan Williams. He seems to be a favorite composer of yours.

This was a giant. Maybe once every ten years you're in the presence of a man and you say, "This is a great man." Vaughan Williams was a great man. He was brought over to my house in London by Stewart Wilson, the musical director of the Arts Council of Great Britain. I played for him, and Vaughan Williams said, "Look, you exhale for X, you inhale for D." I said, "That's right." He said, "If you have to change your breath to get different notes, you can't get a smooth tone, you can't get a legato." I said, "Well, I'd never thought about it, and logically you would seem to be right. Let me play something for you. I'll play a slow movement of Bach and see if you can see where

I change my breath." I played the slow movement of the Bach A-minor concerto and Vaughan Williams said, "I couldn't tell where you changed. You do
get a legato." He then suggested that I take any work of his I liked and he
would adapt it to the mouth organ. I selected something called *The Lark Ascending*. He changed his mind and decided to write an original work for me.
I couldn't believe it. I learned it. I then went down to his house to play it for
him. I said, "Mr. Vaughan Williams, forgive my saying this, but there's about
eight bars where it isn't quite right for the mouth organ, it just doesn't fit.
Would you consider just changing those eight bars?" Vaughan Williams was
deaf, but I think it was a very editorial deafness: he heard what he wanted to
hear. He said, "What'd you say, young man?" I said it louder. He said, "Oh, so
you don't like my music, eh?" That wasn't what I meant at all. So he says, "If
you don't like the way I wrote it . . ." long pause . . . "I'll change it. If you
don't like it after that, I'm going to rescore the whole bloody thing for bass
tuba!" It was perfect when he did that revision. We played it at the Proms
with Malcolm Sargeant conducting, and Vaughan Williams was in the audience. It went over. It got such a tremendous ovation we had to do it a second
time; the first time in the history of Albert Hall that a new work had to be re-
peated. Vaughan Williams came up on the stage and he sat down in the viola
section while we did it the second time, and the crowd went mad. There's
nothing they revere more than age, and remember this, Vaughan Williams
was eighty-three years old when he wrote this work for me. To me, it is remarkable that a man will learn the new technique of an instrument at that
age. I'll never forget him for it. That was the essence of Vaughan Williams'
music. You probably know that *Fantasia on a Theme by Thomas Tallis*. Well,
that and this, I think, are Vaughan Williams' best works.

All kinds of classical composers have written works for me. Arthur Benjamin, Gordon Jacob, Villa-Lobos. I get a little embarrassed by the profusion
of works because I don't have all that much opportunity to play them. When
a symphony orchestra asks for me, they ask to see my repertoire. What they
want are the name composers. There's a French composer, Serge Lancen,
he's written a marvelous concerto. None of the symphony orchestras will play
it because they don't know his name. I don't think I ever do a performance
without Bach. It's a very peculiar thing. You play Bach on the mouth organ
and to me, it sounds as if Bach wrote for the instrument. I've also done music
for two films—*The Great Chase* and *Genevieve*. That's a British film. A producer called me up and he said, "Would you be interested in doing the score

of my film?" I said, "I've never done a film score." He said, "I know you haven't. I'm offering you the score." My agent called me up and said, "Larry, forget it. This is a two-bit company, they haven't got any money." I said, "No one's ever asked me to do a score before. I'm very flattered." Graham Greene has the same agent that I had, and Graham Greene called me and said, "Larry, you're out of your mind. This picture will never make its cost back. You're going to work eight or ten weeks for nothing. Don't do it!" I said, "I'm going to gamble on it." The picture made its costs back in four weeks. My children went to college on *Genevieve*. I've made a bloody fortune out of that film. It was a comedy about the automobile, the annual run from London to Brighton. Everyone in that film became a star. Incidentally, my music was nominated for an Academy Award. But my name wasn't on the picture. I was still in the blacklist. Ira Gershwin called: "Larry, I thought you wrote *Genevieve*. How come Muir Matheson [the conductor of the film's orchestra] has been nominated?" So I then called Charlie Brackett, who was the head of the motion picture academy, and I said, "Charlie, I wrote that score." He said, "Larry, this is the information we got. Muir Matheson wrote it." He wired me back, he said, "Yes, you wrote it, but it's too late to change the nominations." And no correction was ever made [until 1986].

How long have you lived in London?

I've lived in London since 1949, and I love it. I'll go back a bit. Hugh Gaitskill, at the time the head of the Labor Party, said to me, "Why do you live in London? With that marvelous luxury of Beverly Hills, what made you decide to live here?" I said, "I once got into political trouble in the United States. I was blacklisted. If I ever get into trouble again, I'd rather get into trouble in England than anywhere else, because you simply get a fairer deal, a squarer shake here than anywhere else." That still holds true. The kind of things that happened to me here could never happen there. On that subject, the blacklist, the horror, aside from ruined lives, mostly the waste of talent. Think of all the artists who were out of the scene for awhile. Some never came back. To me, that is the horror, the loss of beauty. I don't think any country can afford to waste talent, and America wasted a lot of talent in those days.

RICHARD DYER-BENNETT
1953

Richard Dyer-Bennett was an anomaly who sang both folk songs and art songs. Dyer-Bennett found his own audience—perhaps it was a cult audience, but it was a fervent one. When he sang a song it was hard, in fact, to tell whether it was a folk song or an art song. Thus it was when Dyer-Bennett sang Der Lindenbaum, *from the Schubert song cycle* Die Winterreise, *for example. He embraced both traditions since many people in Germany knew it as a popular song they had learned as schoolkids. This was not a kind of fusion but a connecting link, a respect for the music, whether it be by some anonymous writer or by Beethoven. It was Dyer-Bennett who wanted listeners to appreciate a folk song with the same profundity as classical music lovers appreciate a Schubert* lied. *He arranged his concerts not in the traditional form—say, chronologically—but as a mood, what he felt was the right feeling at the right moment for one song to follow or precede the other. This is what made Richard Dyer-Bennett a unique artist.*

You have been described as a twentieth-century minstrel. You are an art singer who sings folk songs as well as lieder.

I just do what the old minstrels did: sing songs that they composed themselves, or other minstrels composed, or traditional songs. Actually, my repertoire is in many ways very similar to John McCormack's. Mr. McCormack sang a great many traditional songs and folk songs, and what the Germans called *Volksturm Lieder*. He would often open a program with a Bach or a Handel aria, while I may open with an Elizabethan lute song. His programs went back and forth from straight art song to folk song. I think McCormack must have simply learned any songs which he longed to sing, whatever they were. I do the same thing. I don't learn a song unless I feel I *must* sing it, whatever kind of song it is.

Beethoven's Scottish Songs . . .

That's an interesting story. There was a Scotsman named George Thompson. He lived some time in the late seventeen hundreds, into the eighteen hundreds. He was a government official of some sort. His hobby was collecting the traditional songs of Scotland, and to some extent of the rest of the British Isles. This man had the feeling that the tunes were beautiful. He thought in many cases the words were second-rate, and he felt that the general piano accompaniments in the drawing rooms of his day were execrable. So he commissioned outstanding poets of the day to write new lyrics for these songs. Among those were Robert Burns, Sir Walter Scott, and William Smyth. Thinking that there were no musicians in the British Isles capable of setting these beautiful tunes, he went across the channel and engaged European musicians. Among them were Haydn and Beethoven. Beethoven set 168 of these songs. He took the traditional tune and set them for symphonies, as Thompson called them when he published them: symphonies for piano, violin, and cello. They're relatively little known. They're not all good. A lot of it was hackwork on Beethoven's part. He was simply paid to do it, and he obviously wasn't inspired by it all. But some of it I think was inspired, you feel the melody really invigorated him. You hear little snatches of the kind of thing that you hear in all his good chamber music. The songs are charming. But what are they? It isn't Beethoven; it certainly isn't folk song anymore. But why does one have to call it anything? They're lovely songs.

You've spoken of the influence of the old Swedish minstrel, Sven Scholander.

When I heard him in 1935, he was seventy-five years old, and he hadn't even touched his lute for several years. I told him that I had come halfway around the world to hear him and I was damned if I was going back to California without hearing him sing. So, shrugging his shoulders and pretending to be put out by this, but really secretly pleased, he went to his lute case and opened it up and found that most of the strings were broken. He called up a big music shop in Stockholm and ordered some strings. They sent them out by a motorcyclist. He strung up his lute and he sat down and he struck a chord, and with this old, somewhat quavery baritone, he just looked right at me and he sang. "There was a ship that sailed upon the lowland sea, and the name of our ship was the Golden Vanity." And from those two lines and this moment, he had me. I felt that he had been there. Everything he sang was this way. He didn't act out the songs, he suggested sometimes the characters in the songs, but he remained always the narrator who suggested the characters and suggested the scene. He looked at you and you felt this man is speaking to you out of his own life. He could do this whether the song was a thirteenth-century mini-lied, or an eighteenth-century French court song, or a nineteenth-century Swedish sailor song. You had the feeling this man is like the Flying Dutchman—he's been all over the world, through all of time, he knows everything that human beings have ever thought and felt, and he can tell it to you out of his own life.

He was a rare bird. I don't know of anyone like him since Carl Michael Bellman's time in the late 1700s in Sweden. This self-accompanied song tradition carried to a high art, began to die out when the keyboard instrument took over and music became much more complex. Because both hands were free to play the notes, you didn't have to stop strings with one hand and pluck with the other, as with the old lute. So both hands were free for making music, and therefore the music became more complex, and therefore a man began to specialize. Whereas the musicians had often been singers and instrumentalists and accompanied themselves, they now became either singers *or* instrumentalists, and the day of the self-accompanied singer, as a highly developed artist, tended to die out. There have been one or two who kept it alive: Bellman did and Scholander did. This was what touched me.

There's the subject of Stephen Foster. In school we learn some sentimental, maudlin songs of Foster, and yet you do Stephen Foster songs and they're quite moving and beautiful.

I went through all of Foster's songs—I think there are about 182 of them. Some of the ones that we still know today are among his best, such as "Jeanie with the Light Brown Hair" and "Beautiful Dreamer." But I found several in there that are not heard today at all. I think this man was potentially a Schubert. He had the great melodic gift. He had no musical training. He may have had two or three lessons from a German-born musician in his town, Pittsburgh. Incidentally, he never was in the South until he had made his name as a composer. I was interested to discover that he himself sang to his own accompaniment. He learned to play the piano, violin, flute, and banjo. Self-taught. Had he had a chance to develop his own musicality, particularly his harmonic sense, we might really have had a Schubert. He certainly had a feeling for a soaring melodic line. I think most of his best songs were settings of his own verse—he wrote the verse, too, and I believe that's so in his "Linger in Blissful Repose." I found some notes about Foster rather touching. "He died in Bellevue Hospital from the ravages of excessive drinking, possible tuberculosis, and loss of blood, having fallen during the night at his lodging house and gashed his neck on a wash basin or pitcher. His personal belongings were the threadbare clothing on his body, a warn leather purse containing thirty-eight cents, and a piece of paper on which he had penciled, 'Dear Friends and gentle hearts.' The world was singing his songs. He was thirty-seven years old."

Why do you wind up each concert with "Lonesome Valley," with its lines
"You got to cross that lonesome valley / You got to cross it by yourself"?

I'm not sure that I understand my own reasons entirely, but I've found it to be a song that has continual meaning for me beyond the fact that it is a good song musically. Of all the songs I have ever sung, this more than any other is universal in its appeal. It isn't a song which delights people, it isn't a song which charms them, it's a song which forces, almost makes everyone who listens to it accept the truth in the statement. The statement in the song is that you cross the lonesome valley by yourself. Whatever religious persuasion one has, there is an inescapable truth. Every man feels it. There are many moments during life when no one can help you. You feel entirely by yourself. Whether this lonesome valley is of life itself or whether one thinks of it as the valley, the transition from life to something else, if one has a belief in some hereafter, is beside the point. The business of the many lonely moments in life is not speculation. I can't come too closely to grips with my own feeling about it except that there's an inescapable truth in the song and every time I sing it, I feel it. I have the feeling that every person in the audience feels it also. The verse about the depth of the river and that it's cold and it's chilly, but you can't drown a good man's soul, and the wonderful verse about how whether John was a Christian or whether John was a Jew is beside the point. "He was a natural man and he was a preacher, too." But these are side statements. You are, in the last analysis, in the most difficult moment in your life, on your own. You have to cross that valley by yourself.

JULIAN LEE RAYFORD
1973

One day, the folklorist Jack Conroy introduced me to Julian Lee Rayford.
From the moment I met him till the moment we parted I was able to get
in only two or three words. Julian Lee Rayford was just bursting with the
street cries and train calls and hawker calls he heard as a kid in Alabama,
mostly from the black stevedores and the black hands who were doing all
sorts of work on the docks and in the community. He listened and he
heard the railroad songs and the sea calls that Mark Twain so often wrote
about. For Julian Lee Rayford, music was in all those calls and cries.

[Rayford begins by singing "The Boatman Song."] That song I just sang for
you was sung by Abe Lincoln when he made his trip down to New Orleans
on the flatboat on the Mississippi.

The Mississippi. When I think of the Mississippi I think of Mike Fink
[Fink (1770–1823) was king of the kneelboatmen, "the strongest, rowdi-
est bunch of fellows ever to work on the Mississippi"].

"Child of the Snapping Turtle." That's what I call him. [He lets loose] Half
horse, half alligator. [Calls out] *Half horse, half alligator / And the rest of me*
is crooked snags and red hot snapping turtle, ah . . . Here, let me do you a
Mike Fink chant and we'll get him out of the way right now.

Later. I'd like to hear about Neal Hornback, the ugliest man who ever lived.

Oh, you want Neal Hornback? [Cries out] *Neal Hornback's body it were*
enorm / Legs was long and slim / Good Lord, it would make you sore / Was you
to look on him / He went crooked back and arm-shoulder-red / And with thick
lips is blessed / And for to make him ug-ay-lee / The Lord had done his best.
[Without missing a beat] Whenever Mike Fink came into town, he used to
brag. To go upstream against the Mississippi and the Ohio, it took a keelboat
from March until October to go from Baton Rouge to Cincinnati. When
Mike Fink finally got to town some way, he'd feel pretty horrible, so he used

to stand up and chant this: *I'm a salt river roarer / I'm a ring-tailed screamer / I'm a just a little bit stronger than ten thousand goring, stomping, fighting, bellowing, stampeding bulls / I keeps a cattle herd down inside my shirt just to scratch my shoulders / I keeps a rattlesnake in my hand just to find out directions / I can take a string of latitude and lasso the moon / I can take a rope of longitude and haul in a constellation / My voice can rise the dead, can it rise the dead / My name is disaster in a land of desolation / Half horse, half alligator / And the rest of me is crooked snags and red hot snapping turtle, ah / I'm the very baby that refused its mother's milk on the day of its birth and called for a jug of Old Monongahela / I can outrun, outjump, outswim, outfight, outeat, outlove any man ever was known / I can squat lower, dive deeper, come up drier than any man alive / I can whip 'ary man on either side of the river from Pittsburgh to Wheeling / To Marietta to Cincinnati to Louisville to Caedmon Rock to Shawneetown to Fort Madsack to New Madrid to Walnut Hill to Natchez under the hill to Baton Rouge to Bayou, to New Orleans and on back upstream to St. Louis and all points east and west and north and south / Oh, I'm an avalanche, I'm hurricane, I'm a disciple of destruction / My voice is a trumpet doom of revelations / Don't look at me with the naked eye / Wear smoked glasses when you look at me or I'll burn your eyeballs to a cinder / I shine like the sun and I burn like a comet / I'm the handsomest son of E pluribus unum / My mammy is liberty's most attractive daughter / I'm a child of the snapping turtle / E pluribus unum is my daddy and my mammy is the eldest daughter of liberty / Oh, the alligator is my brother / Oh, the mustang is my sister / I was raised on the milk of a wildcat / I chawed the horns off a buffalo the day that I was born / I can bay like a hound dog / I can bellow, bellow, bellow like a bull / I can drown any planet with tobacco juice / Oh, my and for the good of the nation / Don't let me take aim at the sun or the moon / 'Cause I can drown any planet with tobacco juice / Well, I'm a child, child, child of the snap-snap-snapping turtle, ah-h-h / E pluribus unum is my daddy / I'm a hallelujah howler from away-y-y back yonder.*

Take a deep breath, Julian Lee Rayford.

Mike Fink wasn't mythical at all. There was a historic Mike Fink. He was born about 1780 and died in 1823. Mike Fink was the greatest primitive poet who ever lived in America. Everything I sang here just now was his own. But I want to do you some street cries. Street cries have been heard in the streets of the world and the cities of the world for five or six thousand years. Coming up from Sumaria, through Babylonia, through Chaldea, through Egypt, through Greece and Rome, into Europe, into Renaissance Europe and modern Europe, and coming on over to the colonies in America, and all through the streets of the colonies, these sounds. Here's one that went through the streets of my hometown, Mobile, for 125 years, and vanished about 1940. I heard it over fifty years ago when I was a child. The Negro newsboys used to sing it every Sunday morning. [Cries]: *M-o-b-i-l-e, Sunday morning, ready store / Get your Sunday morning paper / Sunday morning paper / Sunday morning paper.* My grandfather heard it, my father heard it, I heard it. It vanished. Intrusion of the machine age, the coming of radio and television. Listen to this, here's a man repairing pots and pans on the streets: *Tinware m-a-n any day / I want you to know that I'm on my way / Tinware m-a-n / Hee! (He's on his way, again.)* Here's a man collecting rags and bags: *Any r-a-g-s, any b-a-g-s, any bottles and bones today / Here please, the rag man coming your w-a-y-a-y.* Here's a hot dog man in Houston, Texas, at a prizefight: *Get 'em hot, get 'em hot, get 'em wild-sized here / Don't wait until I is gone / Get your red hots, get your red hots, get 'em now.* My friend Paul O'Neill heard this in 1916 in Hope, Arkansas: *Hot tamales f-i-n-e / Backbone and tender-l-i-n-e / Some folks eats 'em all the time, time, time / For a nickel or a dime / Buy 'em hot, red hot, red hot / I'm gonna tittle up a tot / For a nickel or a dime / Buy 'em hot.* Now here's one quite remarkable because this one goes in Mobile and in New Orleans, sung the same way in each town: *Charcoal m-a-n, charcoal man / My horse is white, my charcoal is black / I sells my charcoal two dimes a sack / I sells to the rich, I sells to the poor / I sells to the pretty girl standing in the door / Charcoal m-a-n.* Now here are three, the most beautiful I've ever heard: *I've got coal, I've got ice / The coal I've got, it's mighty nice / I's got splinters, fat lighted splinters / I's got the bestest splinters / I's the splinter m-a-n / Gallberry brooms, gallberry brooms / Sweep your yard clean as your upstairs rooms / Gallberry brooms, gallberry brooms / Pine straw, pine straw for your hen nest-es.* Here's a man going through the northern section of Mobile and he's selling oysters: *Oyster m-a-n, Oyster m-a-n / Oh man, oh man, Oyster man / Oh lady, oh lady of the land / Oyster man, oh man, oh man, oh man, oh man, oh man, a man a man a manaman, amanamanaman Oyster m-a-n.* Now, here's one from Slim Vermont. Slim Vermont was a famous black-face comedian back in 1924. He was 6 foot 6, and he'd slouch around the stage, slomp around stage singing this: *Straw-w-w-berries, steeraawberries, oh stee-rawberri-e-s-s-s / I'll be glad when grapes get 'chere.*

[Quickly] An interjection here. In Porgy and Bess, *the Strawberry Lady sang a song. Her name was Helen Dowdy. She told me that George Gershwin said to her, when she was in the original cast, he had an idea, but she should go ahead and do it her way. She remembered her mother re-creating these cries. She may well have heard Slim Vermont. The Strawberry Lady song in* Porgy and Bess *is so closely related to what you just chanted.*

Is that so? I've had many people tell me that when I sang this.

The supermarket doesn't have these cries.

Oh, the supermarket has nothing. It's got the goods, but it hasn't got the human voice. We're talking about the end of the human voice when it comes to selling.

Vox humana. I heard you do train cries once, too.

[After a hacking cough] Yeah, you'll get that in a minute. Here's from Atlanta, Georgia: *Oh, little Chilean, bigguh Childean, playing in the s-a-n-d / Oh, run and tell your mammy here's the jelly coal man / I got that easy-burnin' jelly coal, coal, coal, coal.* You speak of the supermarket. Listen to what things used to cost in the old days. Just think of this: *Watermellion, watermellion, fresh off the vine / If you wants your watermellion just pull out a dime / Vegetable man, vegetable man / Got turnip greens and mustard greens and collard greens and cabbage greens / Vegetable man / Got northern beans and Yankee beans and Boston beans and navy beans, lima beans and butter beans / Vegetable man / Oh-h-h man, out on the job today selling okree / One quart five cents, two quart ten cents, one quart five cents, two quart for a dime / Oh-h-h man, out on the job today selling okree.* Here goes your train cry from M&O Depot in Mobile on Beauregard Street. Sure, I remember it. I remember way back in 1918, 1919: *Northbound train going to St. Louis / Right train leaving at 6:45* P.M. *tonight / Train for Whistler, Oak Grove, Citronella, Yellow Pine, state line, buckets out of Waynesburg, diesel told me, Artesia, Tupelo, Corinth, Jackson, Tennessee, Cairo, Illinois, East St. Louis, Illinois, and the St. Louis, Missouri, al-l-l-l a-board.* You don't hear train callers no more, no more. Listen, my father and Casey Jones worked side by side on the M&O between Mobile and Meridian. They were fireman together in 1885, '86, and '87. My father knew Casey Jones very well. My father became the best engineer on the M&O, the Mobile & Ohio. Casey Jones was not a greater engineer than my father at all. My father pulled the first Havana Limited into Mobile. The Havana Limited came down from Chicago to St. Louis and then down the M&O into Mobile, and then people got aboard, went directly by hack over to the Mallory Line docks and got on a Mallory liner, went over to Cuba. Once a week that train came into Mobile. That was way back around 1907.

Tell me about yourself. When did you, Julian Lee Rayford, start?

I started from the time I was born. My nurse, Nanny, raised me. She was an old French woman. She was descended from the oldest French on the Gulf Coast. They came from Bienville, her people. My mother just turned me over to Nanny from the time I was born, and Nanny raised me. I slept with Nanny till I was ten years of age. We slept downstairs, the rest of the family slept upstairs. She told me about the building of the cathedral in 1857 in Mobile. She told me how the creeks were full of fish, so many fish you could see the fish tails beating the water; see the tails of cotton-mouthed moccasins, other snakes swirling in the water there when they pass along driving out into the country with her father. She told me all sorts of old stories. And so the legend began with me from the time I was a child.

So all sorts of cries—French, Creole cries, and, naturally, black people's music of the streets.

Indeed. I want to show you the banana docks. Here is a great cry of the checkers on the banana docks, when they unloaded banana boats in Mobile. Mobile, mind you, was discovered 321 years before Christopher Columbus by Madog ab Owain Gwynedd, a great Welshman, and he came here in 1171. That's 802 years ago. Long before Christopher Columbus.

There was a Welshman who—

Hell, Columbus ain't in it with us.

This guy preceded Leif Ericsson then, too?

No, he came just about a hundred years after Leif (pronounced "Layfe") Ericsson.

You pronounce it "Layfe"?

That's right. There's nothing like being proper.

So there was a Welshman . . .

Yeah. These are the banana docks, and the checkers are calling out the grades and qualities and ripeness of bananas. They're white men and they're direct- ing the whole operation. Occasionally you'll hear a song from one of the Ne- gro dock wallopers, they're toting bananas. The dock wallopers understand where to take all these bananas, and they'll call out things like "jumbo white flag," they call out things like: *Nine below, eight below, seven above, nine out- side, yellow outside, nine across, and a light nine, and a light nine, and a medium nine, and a heavy nine.* Those are all calls. This is the most exciting thing you ever heard in your life. Hold on, you'll drop dead of heart failure. At the foot of St. Francis Street, riverboat chutes tie up and you could hear a gangway man calling out to a winch man in the old days there along there. He'd say [cries]: *Tell Louise I'll see her in the morning / Oh, tell Louise I'll see her in the morning / Oh, tell Louise, I'll see her in the morning / When the day- light come / Oh, the time ain't long and work ain't hard / Ain't gonna be much longer / Just all night long / Just all night long / Tell Louise I'll see her in the morning / When the daylight come.* At the foot of St. Francis Street riverboats used to tie up. The *Helen Burke,* the *John Quill,* the *Chickasaw,* the *Demopo- lis,* the *Mary S. Blease.* Hundreds of riverboats tied up there in times gone by at the foot of Dolphin Street. At the foot of Dolphin Street, a cluster of tug- boats was tied up: the *John Faye,* the *Harry Daugherty,* the *James Lidel,* the *Nimrod,* the *Buzzard,* the *Echo.* Between the foot of Dolphin Street and the foot of Government Street, banana boats unloaded, many of them small boats, little white banana boats, the *Musa,* the *Herman Winter,* the *Mexico Trader,* the *Vera,* the *Gansgourd,* the *Liasgourd.* Hundreds of men toting ba- nanas, burdened like Atlas with monstrous stems of bananas, those working at the conveyor tables crying out: *Come over here, boy, pick it up, pick it up, pick it up, pick it up / Come on, Charlie, take 'em on down / Step along here now, step along / Red above, yellow below, green across, jumbo, white flag / Hey,*

*white flag / White below, red below to the west, Chinee on the wharf / Hey, boy,
on the wharf / Nine below, eight below, seven above / West to the west / Nine
outside, yellow outside, nine across / Ching-ching-ching of the tabulating ma-
chines / The hum and the click and the roll and the bumpity thumpity clanking
of the conveyors / The chanting of the checkers and the steady hum of the men
toting bananas, and occasionally a fragment of a song / A long time sweet daddy,
a long time sweet mama / Oh-h-h doo-da, doo-da, doodle-ah, doodle-ah, doodle-
ah, doo-da-a-a / Green flag, black flag, a light nine, and a light nine, and a
light nine, and another light nine, and a light nine, and another light nine /
Medium nine and another medium nine and another medium nine, and another medium nine / And a heavy nine, and a heavy nine, and a light nine, and
another light nine . . .* [He keeps going] *And another yellow, yellow, yellow,
yellow / Hey, boy, Chinee to the warehouse / Green flag, red flag, a black flag /
Light nine, heavy nine, black nine, yellow nine / Green flag, green, light nine,
yellow, black flag / Walk Charlie, let your green, green, green, yellow / Go above,
come above, come on in, come on in, going by, my my my my my my / Come and
get your lovin' daddy / Oh, I am so sad and so blue and I think about you more
and more every day / Ah, lord, more and more every day /* [Softly] *Green flag, another green, another green, yellow, yellow, yellow / Get 'em green there, Johnny,
get 'em green' / Come on in, come on in, going by, going by, Chinee to the warehouse / Hey, boy, Chinee / Come on Charlie /* [loud] *Walk, Charlie, walk.*

> *Wow. What you've done here is vocally paint a picture. . . . It's a huge
> tapestry of everything going on: sad songs, blues, fragments, cries, calls,
> guys pushing each other, foremen, the dock wallopers, all one.*

Max Perkins read this poem. Max Perkins was the greatest editor of the
twentieth century.

> *You're referring to Maxwell Perkins who discovered Thomas Wolfe and F.
> Scott Fitzgerald and Ring Lardner?*

And he discovered me, too. [Laughs] He read this poem, he says, "Write me
a book around this." I wrote him my book *Cottonmouth* after that. You want
to hear another one? Here's my own poem on a piece of absolute direct history out of the state of Alabama. These are the Muskogee Indians coming up
from Mexico, around Mexico City, where they become the Creek Indians.

Just listen to this: *We were the Muskogees, we were the Muskogees / We were happy until Cortés came and claimed our lands with guns and torture / Our people looked around at the destruction wrought by Cortés and they said / If we do not leave this place, they're going to kill all of us / We rose up and we walked out of Mexico / Walked out of Mexico, walked out of Mexico / And we rose and we walked out of Mexico / We walked irresistibly to the north / We defeated every tribe that faced us / We crossed the Rio Grande / We walked on up to Texas / We defeated every nation that opposed us / We defeated every people that opposed us / We fought our way into Arkansas and walked east / We crossed the river of all rivers / We crossed the old man of all rivers / We crossed the father of waters / And when we saw the golden hills of Alabama / And when we saw the Golden Rivers of Alabama / The Muskogees became the Creeks of Alabama / And we said Alibamo, Alibamo, Alibamo / For Alabama is our land / Alibamo here we rest / For Alabama is our home / Alibamo here we rest / And we rose up and walked out of Mexico / Walked out of Mexico, we walked out of Mexico / And we rose up and we walked out of Mexico / We walked irresistibly to the north / We defeated every tribe that faced us / We defeated every nation that opposed us / We defeated every people that opposed us / And when we saw the golden hills of Alabama / And when we saw the golden rivers of Alabama / The Muskogees became the Creeks of Alabama / And we said, Alibamo, Alibamo, Alibamo / For Alabama is our land / Alibamo here we rest / For Alabama is our home / Alibamo here we rest / Alibamo.*

Where did you first hear that?

That story? I got that in a very ancient book on Alabama published way back in the early part of the nineteenth century. You want another one? *Mobile, down by the riverside, looking out over the bay / Early explorers called it Esperito Santo, Bay of the Holy Spirit / Indians felt the mystery here, they had the temple on Dolphin Island / They had a sacred fire burning in the temples century after century / From all the Western Hemisphere Indians came to gather fire from the temple on Dolphin Island / To carry fire to their people / Regardless of distance or hardship / Mobile Bay may be the first body of North America to have been colonized by Europeans / Madog Gwynedd brought 120 settlers from Wales and placed them somewhere on the shores of Mobile Bay / Madog Gwynedd was here 321 years before Christopher Columbus discovered John Watling's Island in the Caribbean / Madog Gwynedd / Madog Gwynedd was*

*here 800 years ago in 1171 / Mobile, down by the riverside / For two and a half
centuries Mobile has taken its name from the biggest Indian city in North America, Mobila / Mobile, Mobila, the name is the same / Mobila behind its walls
stood eighty longhouses / Each one capable of accommodating one thousand
people / A city of eighty thousand people in the Alabama wilderness in the year
of 1540 / To Mobila in that year of 1540 DeSoto brought his expedition /
Tuscaloosa, the Mobila chief was so big his feet dragged the ground when he sat
on any Spanish horse / DeSoto beat the Mobilas / Some say he killed seven thousand / Some say he killed eleven thousand / Some say he killed eighteen thousand Mobilas that day / But Tuscaloosa's people broke DeSoto's heart / They
wrecked his expedition / He never made his rendezvous with Maldonado in Mobile Bay / He wandered brokenhearted through the wilderness / He discovered
the Mississippi River / But he was defeated by the people of a town named Mobila / Mobile, child of legend, city of mythology, bay full of mystery /
Tuscaloosa, DeSoto, Madog Gwynedd, Dolphin Island / Mobile down by the
riverside.*

They should have made that Gwynedd Day instead of Columbus Day.

Surely. Eleven seventy-one! He came out west from Wales and he fell to the
south and sailed to the west and fell to the south and sailed to the west and
was blown to the south till he rounded the horn of Florida and came up
through the gulf and found land on Mobile Bay.

*I remember one I heard you sing about twenty-five years ago. It was some-
thing involving biblical connotations and ancient cities and cultures.*

I can't recall what that was, but I can give you something that'll go back just
about as far. Here's one on Paul Bunyan: *Why sure / Paul Bunyan was the most
powerful, wonderful, grandest, marvelous, colossal, important, originating, in-
venting, engineering, laboring, logging, pile-driving, farming, wheat-farming,
bean-farming, potato-farming, tomato-farming, pea-farming, split-pea-soup-
farming, every kind of farming, and block-and-tackle, knock-down-and-drag-
out, hell-and-high-water, wind-speed, and the most ramstuginous magnificent
man ever was knowed / Walking from Atlantic to Pacific from Pacific to Atlantic
all before sundown.* Why sure, if'n you don't know that every word truth, then
you ain't a genuine 100 percent honest-to-God proud-as-a-peacock real

American, on account of Paul Bunyan, he invented America, Paul Bunyan, he led America out from the woods, out from the mud, m-u-d spells mud, out from the sticks, away from the cocklebuzzin, rattlesnakes and coyotes, on account of Paul Bunyan, he is a high 'un, he is a mighty 'un, he is a supreme bull of the woods. Wheeeee. He did everything and he went everywhere in America. The greatest story I ever heard about Paul Bunyan comes out of Arkansas for that matter. That's "Buttermilk Pipeline."

[Timorously] Would you like some water or something stronger?

I'll sing you one on a hero here that will surprise you in a minute. Let me do you this first one, the buffalo: *Did ya ever see a buffalo / He was a martyr to this land / He was persecuted out of this land / Like a herd of thunder he rolled on feet that shook the earth / The buffalo was grave and solemn and dignified / He had a head like a head that a god would have borne on shoulders big as a mountainside / Poor buffalo, poor buffalo, he was annihilated, exterminated, the greed of America crucified him / May his soul live on within our land / For the buffalo people were mother and father to the courage of this nation.*

You said a certain hero was going to surprise me.

Here, here he is. I won't even tell you his name, I'll just let you hear it: *Oh, more than a fighting man entered the ring when Jack Dempsey came down ready to fight / He was fierce as a cougar, fierce as a panther, savage as a catamount / Oh, his fist was like a buzzsaw, like sledgehammer / Oh, his fist was like a shotgun, slashing, tearing, smashing, slam, bam, bang / In him was the fire of eagles that lay in the eyes of pioneers / Through him the energy of old Mike Fink surged and surged like an avalanche / In him the irresistible coordination of Billy the Kid, and in him the unflickering fury of Davy Crockett / Oh, more than a fighting man entered the ring when Jack Dempsey came down ready to fight / For he was compounded of all the mauling and terrible brawling of the early frontier / All of old-time America stood there flailing away and Jack Dempsey's furious, furious, furious, furious, furious arms.* And you don't know the half of it. When I first wrote that back in 1939—

You wrote that one?

Sure, these are all mine. I went to Dempsey's restaurant on Eighth Avenue and I found him and I said, "Mr. Dempsey, I just wrote this change on you and I came to sing it for you, this poem." He said, "No, kid, my God, not that, not that," and he stumbled back, knocked a chair over, stumbled against a table and said, "See my press agent, see my press agent." His press agent came out in a minute and he sat down and talked to me, we had a cup of coffee. All these men, larger than life or imaginary, whether it be Paul Bunyan or Mike Fink or Pecos Bill or John Henry. None of them licked boots. They never accepted authority as the last word. Listen to this: *Abraham Lincoln, Abraham Lincoln, he come from the wilderness / A man of the prairies, a man of the woods / Oh, he come from the piney woods / Oh, long, tall, gaunt, thin, strong and lank and lean / He could see about the people around him / He had a vision like an eagle in the sky / He freed himself of the love of one section / He took the nation into his heart / He loved every state in the Union as much as he loved Ill, Illinois / He saw his nation as one unified land / Oh, he knew his people, he knew the heart of his people / He loved his people, he loved them as they were / Abraham Lincoln, Abraham Lincoln, he come from the wilderness / A man of the prairies, a man of the woods / He come from the piney woods.* Now here's a poem—I've written a great deal of poetry concerned with American cities, with American life. Listen to this. This is appropriately enough on Chicago. I wrote this when I was an art student at the Art Students League when they kicked me out of there. I was at the Art Institute in Chicago, that was in 1932. I lived here that winter and I left here in June and went to New York. I was so damn poor I went to the Lodge at Grand and Union, three thousand in one building. The Depression was at its last gasp and I lived there for eight months.

So you were in this big flophouse. There's a poem you have about Chicago.

Is there ever a poem on Chicago: *A cathedral of systemized confusion is Chicago / Ended up a stairway of decades of century in expanse / Things are done in Chicago with a boom / With a boom bang, with a boom bang shout bigger, efficiently, instantly / Like an alluring woman is Chicago in the night / Wearing strings of diamonds and sapphires / Reaching up forty stories high / Wearing ruby necklaces that are three hundred feet long.* Carl Sandburg was crazy about this. He made me sing it for him time after time. I met Vachel

Lindsay at the American Poetry Society in 1930, 1929, one or the other. And he got up and recited that one about General Bramwell Booth. He preached it. "Take that damn microphone out of here, I don't want it." [Laughs] This old lady sat beside me and she said, "Listen to him, damn fool, listen to him, damn fool." But he stood there and recited his poetry. Bang!

I know that your stuff is limitless, you have a half a century of collecting and writing and remembering and howling and raving. What's one to end the hour with?

I'm the most wildly unknown poet in America. I'll do you a poem. I have got poems in the Library of Congress, but they're straight poems. This is called "A Certain Seclusion." This was published in the old *Scribner's Magazine* back in 1937. [He starts in a normal tone, and gets louder and louder] *A certain seclusionary, a certain seclusion in the noise and confusion / Noise and confusion of Chicago / For passing along Wabash Avenue under the elevated trains / And walking along with the street cars that roar and roar explosively by / You may chant a poem at the top of your voice and no one will know you have spoken.*

You are truly splendiferous and stupifracturous.

And ramstuginous.

∾ Postlude ∾

A Graceful Goodbye

LOTTE LEHMANN
1960, 1964, 1967

"I like to feel that my singing is not a finite thing in itself, but rather the means of communicating my personal convictions." She has been regarded as the most celebrated lieder singer of the century. For a number of years she taught master courses for young singers at Northwestern University's School of Music. We were listening to a tape of her announcement at the end of her concert, at Town Hall in New York, February 16, 1951. Her devoted audience was unaware of what she was about to say.

"Tonight is my farewell recital in New York." [A stunned "No! No!" from the crowd] "Thank you. I hoped you would protest. But please don't argue with me. You see, I started to sing in public in 1910, and after forty-one years of hard work, inner tension, and nervous strain, I think I deserve to take it easy and to relax.

"I think you know that the Marschallin in *Der Rosenkavalier* has always been one of my favorite parts. The Marschallin is a very wise woman. She looks in the mirror and sees it is time. So I, as a singer, look into the mirror and I see it is time." [More protest] "Oh, yes." [A low roar] "I have made up my mind. These have been very, very happy years, which I have sung for you. And Town Hall has always been a kind of a home—a home which, now, reluctantly and sadly, I have to abandon.

"Perfection has always been a goal for me and never attained. So, sometimes I failed. But you, as a public, have been perfect. You were kind and understanding. You gave me enthusiasm and you gave me your heart. So when I say goodbye to you, I say goodbye to a very beloved person. And I will cherish the memory as long as I live. You have given me much inspiration. You were the winds on which I soared. And if sometimes, it was possible for me to take you with me on my flight into beauty and into a better world, then perhaps I have achieved a fraction of what I wanted to give you." [The house goes wild.]

Madame Lehmann, Ernest Newman [the English music critic], in seeing you as the Marschallin, said you are "an exquisite singer, an actress whose quiet ease is the perfection of the art that conceals art."

[Laughs softly] Quiet ease. Mr. Newman exaggerates, because I remember the performance very vividly. I was for the first time in Covent Garden. I got this offer some weeks before. The contract depended on my singing the Marschallin. At the time, I sang Octavian, the young lover. I hadn't learned the Marschallin at all. But when I read that Bruno Walter was the conductor, I signed very boldly. I have never regretted it. I came to London with great misgivings because the Marschallin is one of those parts that one has to grow into. One cannot conquer this kind of role very quickly. I knew it musically, but that was really all. Bruno Walter helped me tremendously. I trembled slightly that night and almost died from stage fright. I have sung in *Der Rosenkavalier,* all three roles. First, as a young beginner, Sophie under Sir Thomas Beecham. I replaced Claire Dux, who crafted the role. Beecham heard me later as the Marschallin and he said, "Is that the same person who sang Sophie and almost died on the stage from fright?" I think that the greatest singer on earth, if she is not an actress, can never be a good Marschallin. She is a many-faceted, sparkling human being, a bewitching lover, and a conversationalist of the highest order. What is it about the Marschallin that makes her so wise? She's on the threshold of that age where resignation waits around the corner, and has a last fling with her young Octavian. I don't think she really has taken this affair very seriously. She is enchanted by him, but she is much too wise not to know that this will have a very, very sudden ending. The ending is earlier than she likes, perhaps, but she is great enough to say goodbye with a smile. Personally I have learned very much from this role. When I stopped singing concerts, it would have made me terribly unhappy, but thanks to her, I have learned that one has to obey the command of time. Without flinching. Without repulsing this idea. And therefore, I really *could* say goodbye with a smile. When I was a young singer I had already decided when the time comes, I think I should stop. And I will. If one always remembers me in that role, it does a grave injustice to those who come later. I think the greater a personality, the less one should compare. A Marschallin entirely different from mine may also be quite wonderful. Nowadays, there are very good Marschallins: Elisabeth Schwarzkopf and Régine Crespin, I think of immediately. But they are a little bit too sentimental. I don't agree that the Marschallin weeps in the presence of Octavian. And I don't agree that she goes to pieces on the end of the first act. The key to her whole character lies not in the words, but in the how. She takes the mirror and is stunned a moment when she sees the ravages in her face, but she immediately catches herself: "I have promised I will end with a smile," so that's how the act ends.

Art is a many-splendored thing, has many facets. If somebody *honestly* feels sentiment, it would be wrong to try to destroy that because that's her personality. One cannot, should not, make over a person. That's what's so interesting about different artists. Elisabeth Schumann was Sophie, who just came out of the convent. She had this aura of the convent about her, pure, virginal. Anneliese Rothenberger was a much more vivacious Viennese girl. Both were excellent in their own way. It would be wrong to say to Miss Rothenberger, "Don't be so vivacious. You just came out of a convent. There you have lived a very restricted life and you would not be allowed to flit around as you do." No, no, it's her personality and let her do it. The moment she has made it her *own,* and she really becomes an artist.

When I think back to lieder singing, for instance, I have the feeling that if I could have my voice back and sing again, I would have been so much better. I have really much more understanding now than I had in my time because I was already an artist who sang out of intuition. Today, this intuition has become knowledge. But now it is too late. I talked about this with Bruno Walter. He said, "That is the tragedy of growing old. Now you *know* how you would like to do it. Don't you think I feel the same?" I talked with Toscanini about it and he said absolutely the same thing. I had sung in Hamburg when I had not the faintest idea what a lied really is. I had a nice voice and people applauded me and I thought I was a great lieder singer. I have learned that very late after I finished opera singing. It was in my opera experience that I found my way to the *knowing* feeling. The truth is I felt that lieder singing was a substitute for the opera. Because I really belonged to the stage from head to toe, through my whole life. Lieder singing was a new world, quite wonderful, but it could never be what opera was to me. If I am reborn again—I don't believe it, but I hope—I will be an actress. The lied is a small framework of the opera. To make a lied, one has also to forget one's own person and become the person whom one portrays. A different role for each lied.

Let me tell you about *Meistersinger*. I was always scared to death of it. I always trembled and never sang Eva very well. Bruno Walter took away my fear. He said, "Where Hans Sachs says, 'Now, you make a speech,' you think as Lotte Lehmann—'Oh my God, have I enough breath, will it be all right?'—you are lost. But think as Eva: 'I have never done this in my life, but I really shouldn't be frightened because I am among friends—Hans Sachs, whom I adore, and here is Walther, my great love. Why should I be unhappy? This is such a happy day.' The music starts and you have forgotten all about Lotte. You are Eva." And he was so right. This is something that went through my whole career. When I was in *Die Frau ohne Schatten* and I asked Richard Strauss, "What shall I do here?" he said, "What shall you do? Nothing. Stand there. Have the courage to stand there. If you really think you're that woman, it will go over to the audience." I strongly believe in a magnetism which goes from the artist and jumps over the footlights. Even if one stands with one's back to the audience, if one is *in* the role, one will feel that.

Toscanini saw me in *Tannhäuser*. He said afterwards that he watched me very closely all the time and I appeared to be standing and not doing anything, no acting. He said, "You acted so *inside* that it made me very happy." The moment you step out of the other, the role you're playing, you are lost. I remember *Die tote Stadt,* a terribly tiring role. The stage director said to me, "Now, here, you can relax." I said, "No, I can't. I can't. If I relax, I'm Lotte Lehmann." The secret is really of interpretation. Let's say in a concert program. Some artist has sung it beautifully. If everybody took this one singer as a model and does it the same way, wouldn't that be boring? It *should* be different. It should fit through the personality. I always strive to do this in my teaching. I don't want my students to imitate me. Imitation is always a sign of weakness. I only want to arouse their imagination and to develop their personalities. I can only open a door.

In America, one has heard me mostly in Wagner. I have always disliked being called a Wagnerian soprano. I really had a tremendous repertoire and I sang all the Italian and French roles. I have developed slowly. For quite a while I sang small roles. And I think that is good. Nowadays, the girls turn into stars overnight and that is not so good. They are in danger of being swallowed by the commercialism of today. In my time, let's say in Vienna, we loved the house—it was our musical home. We were very proud to be part of a wonderful ensemble. Today singers flit from one city to another, from one country to another. It is a jet age. Perhaps, if I were young, I would do the same. It is always very tempting, not only to make money, but also to conquer new audiences. But I don't think I would sing as long as I did, forty-one years. I doubt that singers nowadays will be able to perform so long. They sing sometimes five times a week because it's so easy to fly. When one comes from Europe to America, the sudden time difference is something terrible to the body and the spirit. I went by boat. One had a marvelous rest.

When I said goodbye in 1951, all my friends were horrified. Everybody said, "That's ridiculous. You could certainly sing some more years." That may have been possible, but I didn't *want* to. I was always an artist who gave everything, the fullness of my emotion. I couldn't do that anymore, because when I made up the program, I had to leave out songs which were too strenuous for me, too dramatic, were not any more in my reach. Through the last years of my concert career, I suffered terribly. I was not fooled by the applause and by the loyalty of my audience. Very often, when I came home from a concert which had been tremendously successful, I was weeping the whole night, because I had the feeling that I had betrayed my audience. Your own standard is more important than the standard which others set for the artist. My accompanist, Paul Ulanowsky, would come to me during intermission. I said, "Oh, I was terrible." He said, "Lotte, don't be so foolish. Didn't you hear that wild applause?" I said, "They applaud because they like me and pity me." [Laughs softly] A very strange thing happened. Very soon after that last concert, my voice disappeared entirely. This may be my imagination, but it's too strange. I listen now to the recording, it's not too bad. But that was it. The voice has absolutely left me forever. It's as though my voice said, *That was very good, my dear, now I go away*. My friends said, "Oh my God, if you retire what will you do?" I said, "What will I not do?" There are so many things with which one can fill one's life. I paint, I write memoirs. When I see a new craft, I immediately try it. I cannot sit there in a rocking chair and let life pass by. That's not my way. And, of course, I teach. I don't teach vocal technique. I have no interest in it whatsoever. I have only interest in developing a character, developing understanding and the background of a song. It is always my goal to bring the drama of life which lives in every song, every aria, every role. The voice itself is an instrument, but what one does with the voice, one's only personality, is the main thing. The understanding makes the artist. Nothing makes me more nervous than if somebody sings slowly and has nothing behind the slowness. You can express great passion in a slow tempo. It has nothing to do with forte or piano, it has to do with your feeling. The audience is really very sensitive. They may be fooled by for a time, but in the long run only the sincere artist will hold their love. It must always be give and take with the audience. There are two kind of singers: those who stand on a pedestal and sing above the heads of the audience; and those who feel one with the audience. To me, the audience is one person to whom I can speak. I know this person understands me and enjoys the moment as I enjoy it.

The first year I officially started singing was 1910. I was sitting on a cloud. I remember all my relatives had warned me, "Oh, it's so immoral and you have to be very careful. The director and the conductor and everybody want to seduce you." Professor Schultz, who taught me at the Berlin Hochschule and who looked like Santa Claus, said to my father, "I hope you will never allow your daughter to become an opera singer. She's much too good a girl." [Laughs] I was armed to the teeth when I came there. I visited our general manager. He was a tiny man, very old and in a bad humor. I came in and I thought, "If that man is fresh with me I'll hit him." He said, "What do you want?" I said, "I want to say hello." He said, "Hello. Get out." [Laughs] So my virtue was safe. I remember in Hamburg, they had a questionnaire: What is the most important thing in art, in a character? My answer was: humor. Humor overcomes everything.

Toward the end of her 1951 farewell speech, she paid tribute to her long-time accompanist, Paul Ulanowsky. "He has been an ideal accompanist for me. We understood each other musically, and when I sang with him, it was as if the hands of an angel have supported me. He has a very keen sense of humor, and that is a great asset on concert tours when many things happen, where one gets upset. But he smoothes everything out and he has always made me laugh, turning every tragedy into a joke. I hope that my successors will be as happy as I have been with him, musically and personally." Thunderous applause. As an encore, she sang Schubert's "An Die Musik," her hallmark lied. She couldn't finish it.

~ **Biographical Notes** ~

∞

LARRY ADLER (1914–2001), born in Baltimore, was the world's greatest harmonica virtuoso, whose career spanned seven decades. Self-taught and playing a simple pocket harmonica, he is credited with elevating the instrument to concert status in the classical musical world. He performed on film soundtracks and was a soloist with many of the world's major orchestras; composers such as Ralph Vaughan Williams and Darius Milhaud wrote pieces especially for him. After being blacklisted in the 1950s, he moved to London, where he lived for the remainder of his life.

MARIAN ANDERSON (1897–1993), the American contralto who sang opera, Negro spirituals, and lieder—her voice in fact ranged from low baritone to high soprano notes—was born in Philadelphia, the daughter of an ice and coal salesman and a laundress. She showed precocious vocal talent at the age of ten, and when she afterward tried to apply for admission to a local music school, the admissions clerk's racist comments later drew forth the singer's reflection: "I don't think I said a word. I just looked at this girl and was shocked that such words could come from one so young. . . . I could not conceive of a person surrounded as she was with the joy that is music without having some sense of its beauty and understanding rub off on her. I did not argue with her or ask to see her superior. It was as if a cold, horrifying hand had been laid on me. . . . I turned and walked out." She thereafter found two voice teachers and later went to study in London, visited Finland, where Jean Sibelius dedicated the song "Solitude" to her, and, while touring Europe, elicited Arturo Toscanini's comment, "Yours is a voice one hears once in a hundred years." Returning to the United States in 1935, she became, under the management of Sol Hurok, one of the world's most popular and successful artists. In 1939, when the Daughters of the American Revolution refused to allow her to perform in Constitution Hall because she was African American, Eleanor Roosevelt, who withdrew her membership in the DAR forthwith, scheduled the concert on the steps of the Lincoln Memorial, drawing a crowd of seventy-five thousand and a radio audience of millions. She had to wait until she was fifty-eight, in 1955, to make her debut at the Metropolitan Opera—the first African American to sing a leading role there—in the role of Ulrica, the Gypsy fortune-teller, in Verdi's *A Masked Ball,* receiving ovation after ovation. She was named to the U.S. delegation to the United Nations in 1958. Anderson made a farewell tour throughout America and Europe in 1964–65 and retired from singing in 1965. Singers such as Jessye Norman, Leontyne Price, and Kathleen Battle, among others, have all spoken of Marian Anderson as their inspiration in their quest to begin their own professional careers.

LILLIAN "LIL" HARDIN ARMSTRONG (1898–1971), called "Hot Miss Lil" and the "First Lady of Jazz," was, along with Jelly Roll Morton and James P. Johnson, one of the most influential early jazz pianists. She was born in Memphis, Tennessee, and played piano and organ in her school and church; her upbeat, livened-up rendition of "Onward Christian Soldiers" at one Sunday service brought her the opprobrium of both the minister and her mother, who detested the blues and popular music. "I was just born to swing, that's all," Lil Armstrong once said. "Call it what you want, blues, swing, jazz, it caught hold of me way back in Memphis and it looks like it won't ever let go." In 1917 she moved to Chicago and played in Freddie Keppard's Creole Jazz Orchestra and then in 1920 with King Oliver's Creole Jazz Band, where she met Louis Armstrong, who had joined the band in 1922. They married in 1924. She launched and managed his career, arranged his recording sessions, published his music, accompanied him on piano, and promoted his history-making Hot Five and Hot Seven records. After they separated in 1931—though she continued her professional relationship with him—she made for herself a successful career as a pianist, singer, songwriter, and bandleader, and later performed for four years in Europe in the 1950s. Performing at the televised 1971 memorial tribute for Louis Armstrong, she died onstage after suffering a massive heart attack.

LOUIS ARMSTRONG (1901–1971), indubitably the greatest jazz trumpet player—and some would say the greatest of all jazz musicians—of the twentieth century, once said: "What we play is life." Writing about Armstrong's early recordings, the critic Martin

Williams compendiously sums up his all-encompassing influence on our musical life: "By the time [his] ideas had spread to other musicians, to jazzmen in general, to swing bands by the hundreds, yes, also to country-and-western singers and groups, by the time they had filtered through hundreds of pop songs and Broadway and Hollywood show tunes—by the time Armstrong's vibrato had (unconsciously) entered the vocabulary of at least every other brassman in our symphony orchestras, and by the time his reassessment of the technical resources of the trumpet and even of its very function as a carrier of melody—by that time, this black man from New Orleans, La., U.S.A., who had by then also touched the feelings, and the thinking, too, of millions, had altered the musical culture and the musical sensibilities of the world."

LEONARD BERNSTEIN (1918–1990) was one of the great American conductors, composers, pianists, and teachers of the twentieth century and has been called "music's most exuberant hero" and its "most adventurous spirit." Born in Lawrence, Massachusetts, he was the first American to be appointed music director of a major American orchestra (the New York Philharmonic) and made more than five hundred recordings during a lifetime that was dedicated to the notion that music was as necessary to children's and adults' personal and spiritual beings as food, clothing, and shelter, manifesting a "total embrace" of life's possibilities.

ALFRED BRENDEL, born in 1931, is the distinguished Austrian pianist, highly praised for his performances and recordings of, among others, Mozart, Beethoven, Schubert, and Arnold Schoenberg. He is also a formidable writer and the author of *One Finger Too Many* and *Alfred Brendel on Music: Collected Essays*. His musical credo: "If I belong to a tradition, it is a tradition that makes the masterpiece tell the performer what he should do and not the performer telling the piece what it should be like or the composer what he ought to have composed."

BIG BILL BROONZY (1893–1958), perhaps the greatest of our country blues singers, was born William Lee Conley Broonzy in Scott County, Mississippi, one of seventeen children of Frank Broonzy and Mittie Belcher, an ex-slave who lived until the age of 102. (His twin sister claimed he was born in 1898.) Before the family moved to Arkansas, the ten-year-old boy learned how to play a handmade fiddle from his uncle Jerry Belcher and began performing at country dances, picnics, and at church, eight years later becoming a preacher. After serving in World War I he moved to Chicago in 1924, where he learned how to play the guitar from Papa Charlie Jackson, and in the 1930s he became one of the outstanding performers on the Chicago blues scene, working with other great Chicago musicians such as Tampa Red, Lonnie Johnson, and John Lee "Sonny Boy" Williamson. In 1938 he made his New York City debut at Carnegie Hall—the first time he had ever played in front of a white audience—for John Hammond's legendary "Spirituals to Swing" concert, and in the following year he appeared with Benny Goodman and Louis Armstrong in the film *Swingin' the Dream*. In 1951 and 1952 he toured Europe to enormous acclaim, and in 1980 he was inducted into the Blues Foundation's Hall of Fame. Broonzy recorded more than 250 songs, the best-known of which include "Keys to the Highway," "Make My Getaway," "Feeling Low Down," and "When Do I Get to Be Called a Man." In a most unlikely appreciation, Elvis Presley once told an interviewer: "[As a child] I'd play guitar along with the radio or phonograph, and taught myself the chord positions. We were a religious family, going round together to sing at camp meetings and revivals, and I'd take my guitar with us when I could. I also dug the real low-down Mississippi singers, mostly Big Bill Broonzy and Big Boy Crudup, although they would scold me at home for listening to them. 'Sinful music,' the townsfolk in Memphis said it was. Which never bothered me, I guess."

BETTY CARTER (1930–1998)—born Lillie Mae Jones—was one of the bewitching jazz vocalists of the twentieth century, known for what has been called her "scat-singing, fast-tempo genre of bebop." She was born in Flint, Michigan, grew up in Detroit, and at sixteen sang with Charlie Parker and later with Dizzy Gillespie, Miles Davis, and, for many years, with Lionel Hampton, who somewhat disparagingly called her "Bebop Betty." In the 1950s she toured with Muddy Waters and Ray Charles, with whom in 1961 she recorded a much-praised album of duets. In the 1970s and 1980s she performed mostly in clubs in New York City and London with her trio, occasionally working with large orchestras, and set up her own record label, Bet-Car. Near the end of her life she told Art Taylor, "I'm not doing what everybody else is doing . . . [and] it's a crime that no little singer is socking it back to me in my own field. To keep it going, to keep it alive." In 1997 she received the National Medal of the Arts from President Bill Clinton, who said, "Hearing her sing 'Baby, It's Cold Outside' makes you want to curl up in front of the fire, even in summertime."

AARON COPLAND (1900–1990), one of the major and quintessentially American composers of the twentieth century, was born in Brooklyn, New York. He wrote his first composition at the age of nine (a song now lost) but began composing seriously at the age of seventeen. When he was twenty-one he left for France, where he received his formative musical training in composition from Nadia Boulanger, the influential teacher of many American composers such as Elliot Carter, Marc Blitzstein, Virgil Thomson, and Philip Glass. Copland returned to the United States in 1924, and while working as a pianist in a hotel trio in Pennsylvania composed his first major work, the *Symphony for Organ and Orchestra*. In 1925, judging his compositions to be "too European in derivation," he began to introduce jazz elements into them in an attempt to "Americanize" his music, resulting in vivacious works such as *Music for the Theatre* and his *Piano Concerto*. After 1930—as he would do in the twelve-tone-derived compositions of his later life—he produced more experimental and technically complex masterpieces such as the *Piano Variations, Short Symphony,* and *Statements for Orchestra.* But then, drawing on New England hymnody and North and Latin American folk music, he simplified his style and wrote his most popular works—*Billy the Kid, Rodeo, Appalachian Spring, Fanfare for the Common Man,* and *El Salón México.* He also wrote music for films, plays, ballets, and the opera *The Tender Land.* His music career truly encompassed and greatly influenced all the developments of twentieth-century American music. But as Igor Stravinsky said of him: "Why call Copland a great American composer? He's a great composer."

THOMAS A. DORSEY (1899–1993), known as the "Father of Gospel," was born in Villa Rica, Georgia, where as a child he heard not only spirituals and Baptist revival hymns but also vaudeville tunes, circus songs, hillbilly ballads, and blues and taught himself to read music before moving to Chicago in 1916. In 1920 he wrote his first blues composition, "If You Don't Believe I'm Leaving, You Can Count the Days I'm Gone," and in 1924 he became piano player and director of Ma Rainey's Wild Cat Jazz Band. A few years later he and the great blues guitarist and songwriter Tampa Red joined forces (Dorsey now adopted the name "Georgia Tom") and together they wrote their hit "It's Tight Like That," the quintessential double-entendre blues whose "bawdy, witty lyrics," writes Tony Heilbut, "were to gospel as brothel is to tabernacle." After suffering from incapacitating depression and then losing his wife in childbirth in 1932, he was "saved" and composed his greatest song "Take My Hand, Precious Lord," which became part of history when Dr. Martin Luther King Jr. requested its performance a few moments before his assassination. (Mahalia Jackson calls it her favorite "love song.") "Precious Lord" was rivaled only in popularity by his "Peace in the Valley," first popularized by hillbilly singers and later turned into a hit by Elvis Presley. His gospel—"good news, good music, a good heart"—lifted the spirits of poor blacks during the Depression, and his enormous musical influence is attested to by the innumerable versions of his songs performed by everyone from Mahalia Jackson, R.H. Harris, and the Dixie Hummingbirds to Sister Rosetta Tharpe, Bessie Griffin, and Marion Williams. Thomas Dorsey once said: "I'm going to live the life I sing about in my song; I'm not much of a singer but I thank God for my songs."

EMANUEL DUNN was born in 1924 near Liberty, Mississippi, the seventh child of parents who abandoned him and his siblings shortly after his birth. As Dunn once laconically stated, "I was laid by the buzzard and hatched by the sun." At the age of seven, after five days at school, he went to work in the fields for thirty-five cents a day for twelve years, after which he lived for a short time in Kentwood, Louisiana—and later in Baton Rouge—where, as he sang in one of his songs, "I worked at a sawmill / Them saws were ringin', oh, ringin' in my ear / Until I almost went deaf." Dunn was known for his talking blues and particularly his inventive storytelling—someone once called him "an early 'rapper.'" Most of what we know about him comes from the folklorist Dr. Harry Oster, who recorded three of Dunn's songs—"Working on the Levee, Parts 1 and 2" and "My Mule 'Grey'"—for Arhoolie Records.

RICHARD DYER-BENNETT (1913–1991), who called himself "a minstrel or trouba-dour," was born in Leicester, England, but as a child emigrated to British Columbia and then, in 1923, to Berkeley, California. At thirteen, influenced by recordings of Caruso and John McCormick, he began singing in a children's choir, taught himself guitar, and developed a distinctively high tenor voice. Although he was known for his perfor-mances of Schubert lieder, he began specializing in Anglo-American ballads, sea chanteys, country and folk songs, and African American spirituals after returning from a trip to South Wales, where he performed for out-of-work area miners. During World War II he traveled to the Philippines to sing for wounded soldiers in field hospitals. Re-turning to New York, he joined a concert tour, organized by the impresario Sol Hurok, that also included Marian Anderson and Andrés Segovia. Relocating to Aspen, Col-orado, in 1947, he founded an experimental school devoted to keeping alive the tradi-tions of minstrelsy. Suffering a cerebral hemorrhage in 1972, he was obliged to give up playing the guitar. He died of lymphoma nineteen years later.

BOB DYLAN—singer/songwriter, performer, memoirist, actor, filmmaker—is one of the most influential and heralded musicians and poets of our time.

GERAINT EVANS (1922–1992), the bass-baritone, was born in the small Welsh town of Cilfynydd ("Edge-of-the-Mountain"). A boy soprano in his local church choir con-ducted by his father, he developed into a baritone, and at seventeen appeared as a soloist in a performance of Mendelssohn's Elijah, where he was discovered by an opera singer who persuaded him to undertake serious vocal training. Highly praised for his characterizations of Papageno in The Magic Flute, Leporello in Don Giovanni, Sixtus Beckmesser in Die Meistersinger, and Wozzeck in Alban Berg's Wozzeck, Evans was also acclaimed as a foremost interpreter of Sir John Falstaff in Verdi's Falstaff, and made his Metropolitan Opera debut in that role in 1964. He was awarded an honorary doctorate of music by the University of Wales and, at the end of his life, became high sheriff of Cardiganshire, a ceremonial role complete with costume worthy of his opera career. He once said: "There are audiences for opera at any age from nine to ninety, and if one can but open a door for them to enter the world of infinite delight that it's been for me, then I will know that its all been worthwhile."

DIZZY GILLESPIE (1917–1993), the legendary, innovative jazz trumpeter—known for his identifying goatee, beret, and bop glasses—was born John Birks Gillespie in

Cheraw, South Carolina, one of nine children. His father, a bricklayer who played piano in a local band, encouraged his son's musical proclivities: at five years of age John was playing the piano, and by the age of twelve he had taught himself the trombone and trumpet. After working in the cotton fields during the Depression, he moved to Philadelphia in 1935 and joined the Frankie Fairfax Band, where his stage shenanigans one day provoked the drummer to ask, "Where's Dizzy?" (The name is history.) Moving to New York City in the late 1930s, Dizzy performed, at various times, with popular bands like the Savoy Sultans, Chick Webb's orchestra, the Billy Eckstine Band, and eventually with the Cab Calloway Orchestra. His greatest musical collaboration, however, occurred in the 1940s when, with Charlie Parker, Bud Powell, and Kenny Clarke, he was instrumental in creating the musical revolution known as bebop, from which emerged his signature song "A Night in Tunisia," about which Gillespie once announced, "I'd like to play for you one of my compositions, my only composition." (His classic tunes "Groovin' High" and "Manteca" belie this pronouncement.) According to his biographer Alyn Shipton, it was Gillespie who "organized the principal ideas of the beboppers into an intellectual framework [that enabled the public] to progress beyond a small and restricted circle of after-hours enthusiasts." Later, Gillespie simplified his musical palette by absorbing and adopting the melodies, rhythms, and style of Afro-Cuban jazz and the bossa nova and using elements of these in his performances and in the compositions he wrote during the later part of his life.

TITO GOBBI (1913–1984), one of the most distinguished Italian baritones of the twentieth century—known for his bel canto voice and talent for *verismo* (the operatic portrayal of everyday characters)—was born in Bassano del Grappa. He originally studied law before pursuing voice lessons in Rome. He made his operatic debut in 1935 as Count Rodolfo in Bellini's *La Sonnambula* and then his debut at La Scala as Belcore in Donizetti's *L'Elisir d'Amore*. The role that first made him famous was as Wozzeck in the first Italian performance of Alban Berg's opera in Rome in 1942. He played Scarpia in Puccini's *Tosca* in his Metropolitan Opera debut in 1956. In the 1960s he began producing operas, and he retired from the stage in 1979. He appeared in twenty-three films and wrote an autobiography, *Tito Gobbi: My Life* (1979),

WOODY GUTHRIE (1912–1967), the most important and influential folksinger and songwriter of the twentieth century, was born in Okemah, Oklahoma. A product of the Great Depression and the Great Dust Storm, which devastated the Great Plains in 1935, Guthrie took to wandering throughout the United States, riding freight trains and even walking to California in 1937, then making his way east in 1939 to New York City, where, after years on the road, he returned in 1946 to settle in Coney Island, where he died of Huntington's disease. "This land is your land, this land is my land," he sang, "from California to the New York Island / From the redwood forest to the Gulf

Stream waters." Speaking radical truth to entrenched power, Guthrie was a recusant social critic, reflected in his antifascist songs and working-class anthems. His love songs and children's sing-alongs are also nonpareil. His musical heirs, from Leadbelly to Bob Dylan, were legion, and his influence has never waned. "So long," he sang, "it's been good to know you." And as someone paying homage to him once remarked, "It was good to have known him."

JOHN HAMMOND SR. (1910–1987) was the record producer, talent scout, and writer responsible for helping to discover and record musicians such as Robert Johnson, Billie Holiday, Count Basie, Benny Goodman, Charlie Christian, Aretha Franklin, Bob Dylan, and Bruce Springsteen. The scion of a wealthy New York family (his mother was a Vanderbilt), he frequented music clubs, theaters, and gospel churches in Harlem as a rebellious teenager; attending a Bessie Smith performance at the Alhambra Theater in 1927, he once said, was one of the highlights of his life. He traveled to Tuskegee to write articles about the Scottsboro Boys trial, was an investor in the first integrated nightclub (Cafe Society), was a board member of the NAACP, and is credited as a major force in integrating the music business. He wrote an autobiography, *John Hammond on Record* (1977).

EARL "FATHA" HINES (1903–1983), considered, along with Art Tatum, the most influential jazz pianist of the twentieth-century, was born in Duquesne, Pennsylvania. As a child he studied trumpet with his father and then piano with his mother. He first played piano professionally in 1918, developing what has come to be known as his distinctive "trumpet-style" technique. In 1928, Hines and Armstrong recorded jazz classics such as "West End Blues," and the incomparable trumpet-piano duet "Weather Bird." In that same year, Hines formed his own band, which performed at Chicago's Grand Terrace Ballroom for more than ten years—achieving nationwide fame through its coast-to-coast radio broadcasts—and at times the musicians he called up included Charlie Parker, Dizzy Gillespie, Billy Eckstine, and Sarah Vaughn. Although he was considered mainstream, Hines was open to the new post–World War II style, bebop. Between 1948 and 1951 he reunited with Armstrong and played with the Louis Armstrong All-Stars, then, mostly out of the spotlight, led his own small groups until he was rediscovered as a soloist in the 1960s. Of his first meeting with Louis Armstrong in a Chicago union hall, Hines recalls the two of them playing pool. Then Louis heard some music in the next room, and he and Hines went over to investigate. "So we went up there and sat down and started playing and foolin' . . . and it caught me off guard."

SOL HUROK (1888–1974), the world's foremost and most flamboyant impresario, was born in the Ukrainian village of Pogar, where, as he later recounted, people sang in the streets and around campfires, and where he learned to play the balalaika. In 1906 he emigrated to the United States, settling first in Philadelphia and then in Brooklyn, where at various times he worked as a peddler, bottle washer, newspaper wrapper, streetcar conductor, and hardware salesman. Keeping his day jobs, he began organizing Sunday concerts in Brooklyn called Music for the Masses—he had at that time joined the Socialist Party. (On the day he died he collapsed of a heart attack on his way to meet with David Rockefeller.) Soon he was managing the dancer Anna Pavlova and, through her, met the revolutionary dancer Isadora Duncan, whose recitals he presented in small American towns that had never previously seen a dancer. (Duncan's onstage pronouncements about free love and socialism led to the cancellation of many of her performances.) In his heyday, Hurok presented thousands of artists and companies such as Marian Anderson, Van Cliburn, Artur Rubinstein, Sviatoslav Richter, Isaac Stern, the Old Vic Company, the Comédie Française, and, at the height of the Cold War, the Bolshoi, Kirov, and Moiseyev ballet companies—a who's who of the music and dance world. Of his idiosyncratic artists he stated: "If they're not temperamental, I don't want them. It's in the nature of a great artist to be that way." And of his business acumen he once said: "If I would be in this business for business, I wouldn't be in this business."

MAHALIA JACKSON (1911–1972), the Queen of Gospel, who spread the "good news" of sanctified gospel music throughout the world, was born and raised in a shack on Water Street in New Orleans. She made her debut at the age of four in the children's choir of the Plymouth Rock Baptist Church and several years later joined the Mount Moriah Baptist Church's junior choir. As a teenager she was deeply influenced not only by Bessie Smith and Ma Rainey but also by Enrico Caruso. In 1927 she moved to Chicago, where she worked as a domestic while at the same time joining her pastor's three sons in their group, the Johnson Brothers. After the group broke up, she commenced a solo career, singing at funerals and churches, traveling to cities such as New Orleans, Birmingham, and her birthplace New Orleans. For five years she toured with Thomas A. Dorsey at gospel tents and churches, then in 1947 released a single, W. Herbert Brewster Jr.'s "Move On Up a Little Higher," which became the best-selling gospel record of all time. In the early 1950s she was a regular guest on a Chicago television series hosted by Studs Terkel, and in 1954 she became host of her own nation-wide radio series on CBS. A close friend of Martin Luther King Jr., she sang at rallies he organized and at his funeral, and she also performed at John F. Kennedy's 1960 in-augural ball. In his classic book *The Gospel Sound*, Tony Heilbut percipiently and wit-tily describes Mahalia Jackson: "If America knows no other gospel singer, she has conferred a blessed status on Mahalia Jackson. All by herself, Mahalia is the vocal, physical, spiritual symbol of gospel music. . . . In a Herbert Gold story, a cynic says to a disheartened writer, 'Trust in the Lord,' and gets as reply, 'You sound like Mahalia Jackson.'"

KEITH JARRETT, one of the great improvisatory pianists of our time, was born in Allentown, Pennsylvania in 1945. A child prodigy, he was playing piano at the age of three, gave his first recital at seven, and was a professional while still in grade school. As a teenager he also mastered the vibraphone, saxophone, flute, and percussion. In 1962 he studied at the Berklee College of Music in Boston but was thrown out for strumming the strings inside the piano (something that composers such as Henry Cowell and John Cage had done previously in their compositions), after which he worked as a cocktail pianist in Boston. He moved to New York City in 1965 and began performing with Art Blakey, Charles Lloyd, and Miles Davis' fusion band, playing organ and electric keyboard. His 1975 *The Köln Concert* was the best-selling solo piano recording of all time (more than a million copies sold), and he went on in 1976 to release thirteen sides of improvised music recorded in Japan (*Sun Bear Concerts*). He also extended his recorded repetoire to include albums devoted to the music of G.I. Gurdjieff (*Sacred Hymns*), masterly renditions of the keyboard pieces of J.S. Bach, and performances of his own music for piano and string orchestra. As the the critic Yasir Aqhar summed up the pianist's musical influences: "You will hear down-home blues right next to the European Classical tradition as stated by Delius, Debussy, and Satie, sedate lines of plainsong can crop up alongside hot gospel; explorations of some ancient Moorish scale can suddenly give way to some raunchy rock & roll. Jarrett's music is primeval and futuristic at the same time."

JANIS JOPLIN (1943–1970) was the most popular female white blues singer of the sixties, whose tempestuous, flamboyant life and untimely death made her a legend during a turbulent time. Her recordings include *Cheap Thrills; I Got Dem Ol' Kozmic Blues Again Mama!* and *Pearl*. Among her most celebrated work is her version of the Kris Kristofferson song "Me and Bobby McGee."

JOSEF KRIPS (1902–1974), the last representative of the great Austrian conducting tradition, was born in Vienna and studied at the Vienna Academy with the renowned conductor Felix Weingartner and became his assistant at the Vienna Volksoper from 1921 to 1924. In 1933 he was appointed resident conductor at the Vienna State Opera, but after Hitler's rise to power he was forced to leave Vienna and emigrated to Yugoslavia, where he conducted the Belgrade Philharmonic and later worked as a factory worker. Returning to Vienna in 1945, he began conducting the Vienna Philharmonic and orchestras in Europe and America. He had in his repertory some 130 operas ranging from Pergolesi to Richard Strauss, but he was most respected for his performances of the operas of Mozart, which he considered the most difficult to conduct. "And I can tell you why," he once explained. "Two bars, and you are suddenly transported to heaven. It's very hard to keep your bearings when you are up there."

LOTTE LEHMANN (1888–1976), soprano, was often called "the Eleonora Duse of opera." Her most famous role was that of the Marschallin in Richard Strauss' *Der Rosenkavalier*—he considered her the finest Marschallin he had ever heard—but her performance as Leonore in Beethoven's *Fidelio* at Salzburg was the high point of her career. She had close working relationships with Arturo Toscanini, Bruno Walter, and Strauss, who wrote the part of the Empress in *Die Frau ohne Schatten* especially for her. From 1916 until 1938 and the Nazi Anschluss, she was a top star in Vienna. With the coming of Nazism, she soon departed for America. After a remarkable career in opera as well as on the opera stage, she settled in Santa Barbara, California, and continued to sing lieder recitals until 1951, when she was sixty-three. Richard Strauss said of her, "When she sang she moved the stars."

ALAN LOMAX (1915–2002) was the preeminent curator and collector of such American folk music traditions as Delta blues, field hollers, and Appalachian songs. The son of noted folklorist John A. Lomax, himself a noted collector of country songs, he visited as a young man the honkytonks, levee camps, and prisons of the Deep South, where he discovered singers such as Leadbelly and Mississippi Fred McDowell. Using a five-hundred-pound portable recording machine, he recorded church services, children's games, work songs, and rural storytellers, and made the first recordings of Leadbelly and Woody Guthrie as well as traditional music from Haiti, Scotland, Spain, and Italy. In 1960 he published his groundbreaking collection *The Folk Songs of North America in the English Language* and in 1993 his memoir *The Land Where the Blues Began*. Rounder Records has reissued a one-hundred-CD series featuring Lomax's legendary field records. His recorded archives were acquired by the Library of Congress in 2004.

CATHERINE MALFITANO, the contemporary soprano known for her commanding acting abilities, was born and raised in New York City. The daughter of a ballet dancer mother and a violinist father, she originally intended to be an actress or a dancer, but soon chose singing as her career. "My mother," she once remarked, "strongly influenced my way of moving and acting. Later my father taught me to study singing in a disciplined way. He broadened my technique." After studying at the Manhattan School of Music she won the *Daily News* contest for new singers in 1966 and made her singing debut in 1972 at the Central City Opera in Colorado, performing Nannetta in Verdi's *Falstaff*. Her wide-ranging repetoire of more than sixty roles covers the history of opera from Monteverdi, Mozart, and Puccini to Shostakovich, Kurt Weill, and William Bolcom. She has also often appeared on the cabaret stage, singing songs like "Blues in the Night," "Moonlight in Vermont," and "Boulevard of Broken Dreams." As she has explained: "I have always been fascinated by different styles of music. My father played modern, classical, and baroque music, so I follow in that line. My way of dealing with them is that I see each as [its] own language. I do not change my tools or my way of approaching them—as well as you don't change your voice-mechanism if you speak one language first and then the other. Of course every language has different sounds that require specific lip-movement . . . but in the end you don't change anything fundamental."

EDITH MASON (1893–1973), one of America's most popular divas, was born in St. Louis and studied in Cincinnati and Paris. She appeared for the first time at the Metropolitan Opera as Sophie in Richard Strauss' *Der Rosenkavalier* in 1915 and was a a principal member of the Chicago Opera from 1921 to 1929, where she gave her farewell performance as Mimi in Puccini's *La Bohème* in 1941. Her voice, in the words of the magazine *Opera Now,* was that of "a light, lucid, sparkly soprano . . . poised like an angel in flight."

JOHN JACOB NILES (1892–1980), often called the dean of American balladeers, was born in Louisville, Kentucky, and raised on a farm in rural Jefferson County, where he began collecting folk music, which he would continue to do for seven decades, making it his goal to preserve and popularize American musical folklore. He also composed now-famous songs such as "Go 'Way from My Window," "I Wonder as I Wander," and "Black Is the Color of My True Love's Hair." Accompanying himself on a dulcimer or a lute, he sang in a haunting voice resembling that of a Southern banshee. About him Bob Dylan has written: "A Mephistophelean character out of Carolina, he hammered away at some harplike instrument and sang in a bone chilling soprano voice. Niles was eerie and illogical, terrifically intense and gave you goosebumps. Definitely a switched-on character, almost like a sorcerer. Niles was otherworldly and his voice raged with strange incantations."

BIRGIT NILSSON, the Swedish dramatic soprano whose potent voice was once described as an "expressive laser beam," was born in 1918 in the town of Västra Karup in southern Sweden. As a child she sang in a church choir, and after completing her studies at the Royal Academy in Stockholm she made her operatic debut in 1946 as Agathe in Carl Maria von Weber's *Der Freischütz* on three days' notice. Her breakthrough performance was as Lady Macbeth in Verdi's *Macbeth* at the Royal Opera House in Stockholm in 1947. Nilsson was considered the greatest Wagnerian soprano of her time. Her portrayals of Isolde and Brünnhilde are legendary. As one critic remarked: "Just hearing her Battle Cry in *Die Walküre* makes you want to hear it again just to make sure you've heard right." She also gave astonishing performances in the title roles in Richard Strauss' *Electra* and Puccini's *Turandot*. She retired from the stage in 1984.

GARRICK OHLSSON, born in Bronxville, New York, in 1948, is one of the major American pianists of his generation. He won first prize at both the 1966 Busoni Competition in Italy and the 1968 Montreal Piano Competition, but it was his victory in the Chopin Competition in Warsaw in 1970—the first American to have done so—that launched his career; he is one of the few pianists to have performed and recorded Chopin's complete piano works. But his repertory extends from Haydn, Mozart, Schubert, and Liszt to extraordinary presentations of the compositions of twentieth- and twenty-first-century composers such as Ferruccio Busoni, Anton Webern, Alexander Scriabin, Elliot Carter, and John Adams.

ROSA RAISA (1893–1963) was the beloved Polish soprano diva who was born Raisa Burchstein in the Jewish ghetto of Bialystok, Poland, emigrated to Italy at the age of fourteen, and made her debut at the age of twenty in Parma as Leonora in Verdi's *Oberto*. She thereafter sang in major opera houses throughout the world, often working with Arturo Toscanini, with whom she introduced two world premieres—Boito's *Nerone* and Puccini's *Turandot,* whose title role was written especially for her. She died in Los Angeles, California.

JULIAN LEE RAYFORD (1908–1980), novelist and folklore aficionado, was born and raised in Mobile, Alabama, and was part of the Southern literary renaissance that had its beginnings in the 1920s. He was the author of many novels, including *Cottonmouth* (1941), *Child of the Snapping Turtle* (1951), and *Whistlin' Woman* and *Crowin' Hen* (1956). In addition to his writing career, he collected folk- and supernatural tales and performed and made astonishing recordings of Mobile street cries. He is buried in Mobile's Church Street Cemetery.

JEAN RITCHIE—the legendary folksinger, songwriter, and folk music collector—was born in 1922 in the Cumberland mountain town of Viper, Kentucky, the youngest of fourteen children. As a child she worked on the family farm and engaged in a continual family songfest singing mountain and children's game songs, hymns, English ballads, and Stephen Foster melodies. Graduating from the University of Kentucky Phi Beta Kappa with a degree in social work, she moved to New York City and got a job at the Henry Street Settlement, singing her ballads and mountain songs to entertain the children. Although she lacked formal musical training, she had learned as a child to play the dulcimer—an hourglass-shaped, fretted, three-string instrument that she plucked with a turkey quill—and began, in 1948, to perform in public and popularize songs such as "Shady Grove," "The Cuckoo She's a Pretty Bird," "Fair and Tender Ladies," "When Sorrows Encompass Me Round," and "Blue Diamond Mines," which describes the deleterious working conditions in the Appalachian coal mines. Her work has influenced many folk and country musicians, from the Judds and Tommy Makem to Johnny Cash and Bob Dylan. She has recorded more than thirty albums and is the author of ten books, including the classic *Singing Family of the Cumberlands* and the prize-winning *Celebration of Life.*

ELISABETH SCHWARZKOPF, the renowned soprano, was born in 1915 in Jarotschin, Germany, and in 1928 performed in her first opera in Magdeburg, Germany, as Eurydice in a school production of Gluck's *Orfeo ed Euridice.* In 1938 she became a member of Berlin's Städtische Oper and made her professional stage debut as the Second Flower Maiden in Wagner's *Parsifal;* during this time she performed only once outside of Germany, in 1941, at the Paris Opéra as Adele in *Die Fledermaus.* In 1946 she joined the Theater an der Wien in Vienna. In 1947 she made her debut at London's Royal Opera House and in 1949 at La Scala. In later years she performed almost exclusively, and incomparably, in five roles: the Countess in *The Marriage of Figaro,* Fiordiligi in *Cosi Fan Tutte,* Donna Elvira in *Don Giovanni,* Countess Madeleine in Richard Strauss' *Capriccio,* and, most notably, as the Marschallin in *Der Rosenkavalier,* the role with which she ended her operatic career in 1971 in Brussels. She spent the next six years concentrating on lieder recitals around the world. In 1992 she was created Dame Commander of the Most Excellent Order of the British Empire.

IRMGARD SEEFRIED (1919–1988), one of the most admired lyric sopranos of the twentieth century, was born in Köngetried, Germany. She began studying voice with her musician father before enrolling at Augsburg Conservatory. In 1940 she made her stage debut at the Aachen Stadttheater performing the role of the Priestess in *Aïda,* and was engaged at that opera house by Herbert von Karajan. In 1943 she moved to Vienna, where she made her debut at the Vienna State Opera as Eva in *Die Meistersinger* with Karl Böhm conducting and then made her reputation as a leading Mozartian, singing the roles of Pamina in *The Magic Flute* and Susanna in *The Marriage of Figaro,* the latter role with which she made her Metropolitan Opera debut in 1953. She also made many cherished appearances at Chicago's Lyric Opera beginning in 1961. A nonpareil lieder singer, she single-handedly rediscovered Mozart's much-maligned lieder and featured them in her recitals around the world. Elisabeth Schwarzkopf, among others of her peers, regarded Irmgard Seefried highly, saying: "Singing just came so easily to her."

PETE SEEGER, born in 1919, is the renowned folk singer, songwriter, social activist, environmentalist, and one of the founders of the folk groups the Almanac Singers and the Weavers. In 1935, when he was sixteen years-old—expressing no interest in the classical music his parents taught at the Juilliard School of Music—he began playing tenor banjo in his school jazz band. That same summer he attended a square dance festival in Asheville, North Carolina, and fell in love with the old-fashioned five-string banjo. As he later stated, "I liked the rhythms, the melodies, time-tested by generations of singers. Above all, I liked the words." For more than six decades he has been the most influential proselytizer of American folk music.

ANDRÉS SEGOVIA (1893–1987), the father of the modern classical guitar, was born in the Andalusian city of Linares, Spain, and raised in Granada. He is supposed to have fallen in love with the guitar at the age of four, when his uncle used to sing songs to him while strumming on an imaginary guitar. His parents wanted him to play a "real" instrument, but Andrés persisted in his desire to study the "unreal" guitar, and, unable to find a teacher, taught himself the instrument. He gave his first concert in Granada at the age of sixteen, and his professional debut took place in Madrid when he was twenty, a concert that included his own transcriptions from Bach, which would become a staple of his later recitals. He gave his first concert in New York City in 1928, about which Olin Downes of the *New York Times* wrote: "He belongs to the very small group of musicians who by transcendent power, by imagination and intuition, create an art of their own that sometimes seems to transform the very nature of their medium." Segovia brought the instrument to Europe and South America, and composers such as Heitor Villa-Lobos and Manuel de Falla wrote pieces especially for him. In 1987, the year of his death, he was informed that more than two million Japanese students had been inspired by him to take up the classical guitar. "Lean your body forward slightly to support the guitar against your chest," he once said, "for the poetry of the music should resound in your heart."

RAVI SHANKAR, the Indian master of the sitar, was born in 1920 in Varanasi, India. George Harrison, who was his student, called him "the godfather of world music," and his legendary and electrifying performances at the Monterey Pop Festival, Woodstock, and the Concert for Bangladesh inspired an entire generation of younger people to explore the full spectrum of Indian music, dance, and culture, as well as its spiritual traditions. He has collaborated musically not only with George Harrison but also with violinist Yehudi Menuhin, the flutist Jean-Pierre Rampal, the Japanese shakuhachi master Hozan Yamamoto, and the composer Philip Glass. He is also the composer of two concertos for sitar and orchestra and has written many scores for films and ballet. About him Yehudi Menuhin once said, "Ravi Shankar has brought me a precious gift, and through him I have added a new dimension to my experience of music."

NICOLAS SLONIMSKY (1894–1995)—the legendary Russian American conductor, composer, pianist, teacher, writer, musicologist, and lexicographer—was born in St. Petersburg. A self-described "failed wunderkind," he once wrote of his childhood: "Possessed by inordinate ambition, aggravated by the endemic intellectuality of his family of both maternal and paternal branches (novelists, revolutionary poets, literary critics, university professors, translators, chessmasters, economists, mathematicians, inventors of useless artificial languages, Hebrew scholars, speculative philosophers), he became determined to excel beyond common decency in all these doctrines; as an adolescent, wrote out his future biography accordingly, setting down his death date in 1967, but survived." (In fact, Slonimsky was active until the age of one hundred.) In 1923 he emigrated to the United States and conducted first performances of compositions by Charles Ives, Edgard Varèse, and Henry Cowell. The composer John Adams called Slonimsky "a character of mind-boggling abilities . . . who had a completely eidetic memory and could recall with absolute precision the smallest detail of something he'd read 40 years before." He was best known as the editor of the 1,600-page *Baker's Biographical Dictionary of Musicians* and the author of scores of influential books including *Thesaurus of Scales and Melodic Patterns* (1947), an inventory of "all conceivable and inconceivable tonal combinations"; *Perfect Pitch,* an autobiography (1988); and the witty *Lexicon of Musical Invective* (1952), a collection of pejorative reviews of musical masterpieces. In his obituary for Slonimsky, the composer Charles Amirkhanian wrote: "When he passed into orbit on December 25, 1995 at the age of 101⅔, it suddenly became apparent that . . . Nicholas Slonimsky now had passed into Sainthood, musicologically, chronologically, and orthodoxically . . . his parting Christmas present to future writers on 20th-century music of the avant-garde."

RICHARD TUCKER (1913–1975) was probably America's best-loved tenor. He sang roles in more than thirty operas and, as a cantor, continued throughout his career to conduct services in many synagogues throughout the world. (It is said that Elvis Presley enjoyed listening to Tucker's cantorial recordings.) His funeral service was held at the Metropolitan Opera; at its conclusion only his coffin remained on the bare stage.

JON VICKERS, the acclaimed heldentenor of his time, was born in 1926 in Prince Albert, Saskatchewan, the sixth in a family of eight children. As a teenager he sang in church choirs and amateur theatricals, but planned on becoming a doctor. His career as a singer commenced with his winning a fellowship to study opera at Toronto's Royal Conservatory of Music. He joined London's Covent Garden Opera in 1957, making his debut as King Gustavus in Verdi's *A Masked Ball.* He joined the Metropolitan Opera in 1960. The most highly acclaimed Peter Grimes of his time, he was also won great praise for his portrayals of Tristan, Parsifal, Otello, and Aeneas in Berlioz's *Les Troyens,* among other roles. A "committed Christian," he stunned the opera world when he refused to perform the role of Tannhäuser because he found Wagner's knight "blasphemous." He once said: "Nature has equipped me with a certain talent, and it is my responsibility to use it for something that is uplifting, that will enhance and embellish the lives of people."